WHAT'S NORMAL?

WHAT'S NORMAL?

Reconciling Biology and Culture

Allan V. Horwitz

OXFORD
UNIVERSITY PRESS

UNIVERSITY PRESS

Oxford University Press is a department of the University of Oxford. It furthers
the University's objective of excellence in research, scholarship, and education
by publishing worldwide. Oxford is a registered trade mark of Oxford University
Press in the UK and certain other countries.

Published in the United States of America by Oxford University Press
198 Madison Avenue, New York, NY 10016, United States of America.

CIP data is on file at the Library of Congress
ISBN 978-0-19-060324-3 (hbk.); 978-0-19-060325-0 (pbk.)

To the memory of Gerry Grob

CONTENTS

ACKNOWLEDGMENTS

For the past four decades most of my work has focused on issues of mental health and illness. During this period I observed a steadily increasing transformation of what had been considered problems of living into specific psychiatric diseases that often blurred the lines between normal social stresses and mental disorders. My book, *Creating Mental Illness*, critiqued this disease model that had come to dominate the psychiatric profession. I then collaborated with Jerome Wakefield in focusing on, first, depression in *The Loss of Sadness* and, next, on anxiety in *All We have to Fear* to show the ways that psychiatry converted normal sadness and natural fears into depressive and anxiety disorders, respectively. At the same time, I began pursuing the idea that the complex relationships between normality and abnormality found in the area of mental illness also applied more broadly to a variety of topics. This book is the result of my attempt to generalize the various ways that culture and biology influence what is socially evaluated as normal or abnormal and as evolutionarily natural or unnatural.

A work of this sort, which crosses so many different lines of inquiry that are outside of my own areas of expertise, is unusually dependent on the writings of scholars who specialize in a wide variety of fields. I am especially indebted to the works of Leda Cosmides, David Kessler, Stanley Lieberson, William Ian Miller, Andrew Solomon, John Tooby, Jerome Wakefield, and Arthur Wolf for their many insights on how culture and biology shape the various topics I examine here.

I am also grateful for the institutional and personal support I received while writing this work. I began the book in the ideal scholarly environment of the Center for Advanced Study in the Behavioral Science at Stanford University. I am grateful to Steve Kosslyn and Iris Litt, who served as directors of the Center during the period of my residence there and to the fellows of the class of 2012-2013 who provided many invaluable suggestions for the book. Once again, I am indebted to David Mechanic, the founding director of the Institute for Health, Health Care Policy, and Aging Research at Rutgers University, for creating the kind of interdisciplinary environment that allows non-traditional scholarship to thrive. Conversations with a number of friends and colleagues, including Michael Anderson, Deborah Carr, Peter Conrad, Melissa Lane, Jane Miller, Helene Pott, and Eviatar Zerubavel have also immensely improved the book. James Cook, my editor at Oxford University Press, has unfailingly supported the development of this volume. I especially appreciate his wisdom in selecting two anonymous reviewers who provided extraordinarily insightful suggestions for revising the draft of the manuscript that they read. Finally, this book is dedicated to the memory of my friend and colleague Gerry Grob, who profoundly influenced my work but who died shortly before the manuscript was completed.

WHAT'S NORMAL?

HERODOTUS AND DARWIN

For if anyone, no matter who, were given the opportunity of choosing from amongst all the nations of the world the set of beliefs which he thought best, he would inevitably, after careful consideration of their relative merits, choose those of his own country.

—HERODOTUS, *1996, Book 3:38*

The same state of mind is expressed throughout the world with remarkable uniformity; and this fact is in itself interesting as evidence of the close similarity in bodily structure and mental disposition of all the races, of mankind.

—CHARLES DARWIN, *1877/1971, pp. 22–23*

Twenty-five hundred years ago, the Greek historian Herodotus, often called "the father of history," traveled widely through the ancient world, visiting Egypt, Phoenicia, Mesopotamia, and the Crimea, as well as the entire Greek world. His writings provide a foundational account of how culture shapes conceptions of normality:

> Everyone without exception believes his own native customs, and the religion he was brought up in, to be the best; and that being so, it is unlikely that anyone but a madman would mock at such things. There is abundant evidence that this is the universal feeling about the ancient customs of one's country. One might recall, for example, an anecdote of Darius. When he was king of Persia, he summoned the Greeks who happened to be present at his court, and asked them what they would take to eat the dead bodies of their fathers. They replied that they would not do it for any money in the world. Later, in the presence of the Greeks, and through an interpreter, so that they could understand what was said, he asked some Indians of the tribe called Callatiae, who do in fact eat their parents' dead bodies, what they would take to burn them. They uttered a cry of horror

and forbade him to mention such a dreadful thing. One can see by this what custom can do and Pindar, in my opinion, was right when he called it "king of all."

The Greeks burned dead bodies but were repelled at the notion of eating them. Yet, the Callatiae ate their dead and were horrified at the thought of burning the deceased. Other groups had their own idiosyncratic burial customs: Issedones mixed dead bodies with sheep and then ate them; male Persians could not be buried until their bodies were torn by birds or dogs; Egyptian customs forbade dead bodies to be eaten by animals but mandated that they be embalmed instead; and Babylonians buried their dead in honey. Herodotus' descriptions of the widely varying practices about handling the dead in the ancient world at the same time illustrate the seeming naturalness and thoroughgoing arbitrariness of definitions of what is normal or abnormal.[1]

Twenty-four centuries later, Charles Darwin also voyaged around the world, trekking from South America to the remote Galapagos Islands, followed by Tahiti, New Zealand, and Australia, and finishing with a trip to the Cape of Good Hope before returning to his native England. His observations provide a very different account of responses to death from those of Herodotus: "The expression of grief due to the contraction of the grief-muscles is by no means confined to Europeans, but appears to be common to all the races of mankind." Darwin went on to describe the similarities between grief displays among Australian aborigines and nineteenth-century Europeans:

> After prolonged suffering the eyes become dull and lack expression, and are often slightly suffused with tears. The eyebrows not rarely are rendered oblique, which is due to their inner ends being raised. This produces peculiarly-formed wrinkles on the forehead which are very different from those of a simple frown; though in some cases a frown alone may be present. The corners of the mouth are drawn downwards, which is so universally recognized as a sign of being out of spirits, that it is almost proverbial.

For Darwin, these universally shared facial expressions indicated that an inherited biological substrate underpins the diverse cultural displays of grief. Moreover, he posited a mechanism that explained the reasons for this commonality: People (and other animals) who communicate emotions that convey their need for support after losses are more likely to survive and reproduce than those who react in other ways. Herodotus' and Darwin's works exemplify the two major lenses of culture and biology that have shaped views about normality and abnormality.[2]

Contesting Normality

The roots of both the natural and cultural approaches are found in debates among the Classical Greeks during the fourth-century BCE when Western philosophy and science emerged. On one side, Socratic philosophers, particularly Plato, derived ethics from common principles that any reasonable person could agree were good. They strove to uncover the eternal constants that lay beneath the transitory appearance of customary expressions and that provided a universal and objective foundation for the distinction between what is natural and unnatural. The Socratics focused on innate aspects of human nature that allowed people to deduce which actions were right and which were wrong. These proponents of the natural tradition stressed how the laws underlying human behavior were not transient but were impervious to change over time. The object of philosophical and scientific inquiry should be these unchanging foundational laws as opposed to fleeting surface manifestations. Natural or unnatural behaviors were not arbitrary but stemmed from standards that all rational human beings can recognize are right or wrong. These rules do not vary from culture to culture but hold in all places and times.

On the other side of this controversy, members of the Sophist school, including Herodotus, asserted that what was normal or abnormal had little in common with the universal principles of natural law. The Sophists contrasted subjective and changeable customs (*nomos*) with objective and necessary properties of nature (*physis*). This school rejected the Socratic conception that rooted norms in deeper qualities of human nature. Their core contention was that normality and abnormality were arbitrary social conventions that lacked any objective basis. Culture—"shared blood, shared language, shared religion, and shared customs"—was "king of all." Normality referred to whatever taken-for-granted customs, emotions, and judgments a particular group valued. Conversely, abnormal behaviors were ones that violated these standards. Different groups had different ranges of expected behaviors so that a trait that was normal in one culture might be deviant in another and vice versa. In contrast to innate Socratic principles, cultural norms shaping how people ought to act, feel, and behave were not inborn but had to be learned. Because these norms had no objective grounding, they were always at risk of being considered capricious and, therefore, not deserving of respect. Thus, customs, despite perceptions of their inherent desirability, were not permanent but were capable of rapid transformation.[3]

Although norms rested on fragile foundations, each group nevertheless believed that its own ways of life were the best. Customs had a *normative* quality that led people to want to behave in certain ways:

> For if anyone, no matter who, were given the opportunity of choosing from amongst all the nations of the world the set of beliefs which he thought best, he would inevitably, after careful consideration of their relative merits, choose those of his own country.

Yet, Herodotus, in particular, did not condemn the differences among the institutions and ethos of the various peoples he observed but, rather, embraced an open and tolerant view of their ways of life and morals. Standards of morality in one culture were neither inferior nor superior to those in other cultures but were simply different from them. Each culture should be accepted and understood on its own terms, not judged by any worldwide system of morality. The Sophists' appreciation of the rich diversity of human customs made them the world's first multiculturalists.[4]

The contested issues about the nature of normality and abnormality that the Classical Greeks raised have echoed throughout the centuries. The two positions that they developed—one concentrating on universal, innate, and stable aspects and the other on diverse, learned, and changeable qualities—remain the major frameworks for studying what is normal and what is not. The prominence of the natural and cultural views of normality has waxed and waned during the course of history.

From Herodotus to Heteronormatively

Herodotus' works contain the seeds of cultural views that emphasize how conceptions of normality and abnormality are inherently tied to the practices and beliefs of specific communities, which vary widely across groups and over time. Discussions about the culturally relative underpinnings of normality and abnormality faded in the West during the long Christian era that lasted roughly from the fourth to the fifteenth century CE, as theologians emphasized the universal aspects of religiously based natural laws. The cultural view did not begin to reawaken until the fifteenth-century Era of Exploration when European voyagers and missionaries returned from expeditions and reported unprecedented levels of human diversity that indicated normal and abnormal behaviors were far more varied than religious scriptures taught. Subsequently, prominent thinkers during the seventeenth and eighteenth centuries revived Herodotus' notion of comparing and contrasting various groups rather than regarding them as superior or inferior. Social philosophers such as Baron Charles-Louis Montesquieu (1689–1755) stressed how social organization, not divine mandates, shaped the norms and customs of each society. Echoing Herodotus, Montesquieu emphasized how geography and history produced distinctive patterns of social interaction, beliefs, and laws. Each collectivity had a general spirit that consisted of particular ways of living, thinking, and feeling that were different from those of the spirits in other nations. That is, all human behavior is inseparable from the social context in which it arises.[5]

The philosophical tradition of empiricism that arose at the time built on this notion, initiating a long battle in Western thought against the idea that humans possess intrinsic, hard-wired proclivities. This view, best exemplified in the work of English philosopher John Locke (1632–1704), attacked the notion of an innate human nature. Instead, empiricists asserted that all of our knowledge about the world comes from experience. Locke viewed presocialized children as "blank slates" at birth who only became fully human through processes of social learning:

> Let us then suppose the mind to be, as we say, white paper, void of all characters, without any ideas; how comes it to be furnished? Whence comes it by that vast store, which the busy and boundless fancy of man has painted on it with an almost endless variety? When has it all the materials of reason and knowledge? To this I answer, in one word, from EXPERIENCE; in that all our knowledge is founded, and from that it ultimately derives itself.[6]

In the late eighteenth century, Locke's work helped pave the way for the transformative French and American Revolutions that constructed new norms unimpeded by traditional notions of religious dogma and the divine rights of royalty. Instead, governments, communities, parents, and teachers could mold human behavior into "an almost endless variety" of forms.

The French Revolution, in particular, overturned previous conceptions about normality and abnormality. It rejected any divine basis of social life and morality. The revolutionaries attempted to change such taken-for-granted aspects of the ordinary world as units of time, the 7-day week, and the celebration of holidays, which they believed were arbitrary and could easily be changed. One of their major legacies was that political action could transform capricious and flexible conceptions of what was normal and abnormal.[7]

Perhaps the major result of the French Revolution was to push individual choice and welfare to the forefront of value systems. The rights of individuals to select their own political, religious, and social beliefs contrasted with the emphasis on traditional social ties and values found in the tightly knit groups that had persisted through most of human history. Social relationships increasingly were temporary, serial, and chosen rather than stable, lasting, and compulsory. Connections to the past, to a particular place, and to one's family of origin weakened. Cultural norms in Western individualist societies came to value autonomy more than authority, uniqueness more than conformity, and newness more than continuity. Rules limiting personal freedom became less justifiable. English philosopher John Stuart Mill (1806–1873) provided perhaps the best summary of legitimate restraint over individual behavior: "The only purpose for which power can be rightfully exercised over any member of a civilized community, against his will, is to prevent harm to others."[8]

Another by-product of the French Revolution was the emergence of the scientific study of normality and abnormality. The revolutionaries' egalitarian ethos propelled the common person to the forefront of interest. This historically unique exultation of the ordinary individual resulted in a new way of thinking about what was normal. Most prominently, Belgian statistician Adolphe Quetelet (1796–1874) developed a social physics that was based on statistical indices of the average man (*l'homme moyen*), who represented the mean value of numerous observations of some variable within a particular group. Quetelet's view was radically democratic because each individual, from the most noble to the most downtrodden, had equivalent weight to every other one. Quetelet compiled aggregate statistics on factors such as height, weight, birth, and death, as well as moral qualities ranging from drunkenness and insanity to suicide and crime, to determine how each was related to characteristics such as age, sex, and marital status. He emphasized how these associations were not universal but varied across different regions, countries, and historical eras. In this sense, statistical views of normality were grounded in cultural conceptions that emphasize how normality and abnormality are derived from whatever traits are common in particular times and places.[9]

Quetelet came to view the average man not simply as embodying statistical frequency but as illustrating a moral quality. "If an individual at any given epoch of society possessed all the qualities of the average man," he asserted, "he would represent all that is great, good, or beautiful." As Herodotus had emphasized, what most people did was not just common but positively esteemed: Norms not only described behavior but also actively *shaped* standards for moral evaluation in each group.[10]

The heritage of cultural relativism that sprang from early social scientists, empiricist philosophers such as Locke, and the outcomes of the French Revolution became foundational for the anthropological view that dominated thinking about the nature of human behavior for most of the twentieth century. Based on the works of Franz Boas (1858–1942), a German immigrant to the United States, and his students Ruth Benedict (1887–1948) and Margaret Mead (1901–1978), anthropologists insisted that human behavior was not innate but varied enormously across cultures. History, circumstance, and environment were the primary forces that shaped lifestyles, human relations, and moral codes in each culture. These forces were powerful enough to override whatever inherited traits humans shared with members of other groups.[11]

Anthropologists strove to develop a new discipline freed of biological influences. Benedict's immensely popular *Patterns of Culture* (1934/1959) posited that learned, culturally specific values defined all forms of human behavior. She proclaimed, "Not one item of his tribal social organization, of his language, of his local religion is carried in his germ cell." Benedict used examples of Ancient Greek definitions of homosexuality, the catatonic trances of native healers, and paranoid character traits among the Dobuan Islanders of New Guinea to assert that virtually all behaviors that our society views as abnormal other cultures consider as normal. "All our local conventions of moral behavior are without absolute validity," Benedict concluded. From the 1940s through the 1960s, Benedict's younger colleague, Margaret Mead, was the major spokesperson for the anthropological view. Like Benedict, she was a thoughgoing cultural determinist who insisted that biology was irrelevant for explaining human behavior. "We are forced to conclude," Mead wrote, "that human nature is almost unbelievably malleable, responding accurately and contrastingly to contrasting cultural conditions."[12]

For decades, anthropologists continued to divorce notions of normal and abnormal behaviors from any biological grounding. One of the discipline's leading midcentury spokespersons, Ashley Montagu (1905–1999), summarized: "Man has no instincts, because everything he is and has become he has learned, acquired, from his culture, from the manmade part of the environment, from other human beings." Moreover, unlike genes, cultures could undergo massive changes in a single generation. "Concepts and terms like 'heredity,' 'biological influences,' and 'instinct,' dropped below the horizon in social science," historian Carl Degler observes about this era.[13]

Sociologists, too, following the lead of the discipline's central founders, Emile Durkheim and Max Weber, strove to establish a field of study that was thoroughly divorced from any biological influences. Many embraced the immensely popular works of French philosopher Michel Foucault, who insisted that social practices, institutions, and values constitute what groups conceive as pathological or desirable. Constantly transforming social definitions of who is considered mad, deviant, or defective reflect the dominant modes of thinking and power structures in different time periods. Distinctions between normality and abnormality stem from value-laden constructions that vary from group to group and lack any objective natural foundation.[14]

For most of the twentieth century, psychologists also embraced a thoroughly environmentalist view of human behavior. Perhaps the most influential psychologist of the twentieth century, John Watson (1878–1958), was intensely concerned with debates about the relative influence of nature and nurture in human development. He famously declared,

> Give me a dozen healthy infants, well-formed, and my own specified
> world to bring them up in and I'll guarantee to take any one at random
> and train him to become any type of specialist I might select—doctor,
> lawyer, artist, merchant—chief and, yes, even beggar-man and thief,
> regardless of his talents, penchants, tendencies, abilities, vocations, and
> race of his ancestors.

Although Watson initially granted that a small number of emotional states, limited to fear, rage, and love, were innate, he later denied the influence of even those instincts, focusing instead on the conditioned nature of all human behavior. People displayed the behaviors that their environments reinforced; when reinforcement ceased, so did the reinforced behaviors. Abnormal behaviors, too, did not require distinct explanations but arose from external reinforcements, not innate drives or preferences. Watson's disciple, B. F. Skinner (1904–1990), took this view to its logical extreme, believing that behaviorists had the power to fundamentally change all human behavior by deliberately and rationally modifying environments.[15]

More recently, the arbitrary aspect of social norms has become a rallying cry for social movements that promote the rights of disabled persons. Advocates for groups spanning from the autistic to the deaf to the obese and the mentally ill contend that social definitions, not biology, account for their disadvantages. They value difference and reject conformity. "I am different," proclaims iconic activist for people with autism, Temple Grandin, "not less." For example, mental illnesses are not disorders but illustrate "neurodiversity." Or, deafness is a valued difference to be celebrated rather than an impairment to be corrected. Sexual identification, too, stems from "heteronormativity" that gives unwarranted hegemony to binary categories of male and female. People without disabilities are merely "neurotypical," not normal. "You are never to use the word *normal*," Andrew Solomon notes in regard to these groups, "and you are certainly never to use the word *abnormal*."[16]

Like Herodotus, empiricist philosophers, behavioral psychologists, anthropologists, sociologists, and disability advocates assert that the possible varieties of human behavior and moral codes are virtually unlimited and unconstrained by biology. Nurture, not nature, shapes what we regard as normal or abnormal.

From Plato to Biology

There is a fairly straightforward continuity between Herodotus' focus on cultural diversity and the moral relativity that emerged in seventeenth- and eighteenth-century Europe and later became a dominant theme among anthropologists, sociologists, behavioral psychologists, and disability advocates. In contrast, the Platonic natural law tradition that used innate reason as the basis for distinguishing natural from unnatural behaviors was radically transformed during the nineteenth century.

In the mid-1800s, Charles Darwin (1809–1882) produced a new biological view of what is natural or unnatural, which came to dominate social thought through the remainder of that century. Whereas Socratics divorced the functions of the mind from the physiology of the body, Darwin grounded mental phenomena in organic processes. Despite the vast divergences in Socratic and Darwinian views, however, both sought a universal, innate, and constant basis for judging what traits are appropriate or pathological. Darwin argued that every form of life evolved according to the principle of natural selection. All organisms confront basic challenges of obtaining nutrition, defending themselves against predators, and transmitting their genes to future generations. These processes lead different traits to have different survival values in given environments; forms of life that can best adjust to their circumstances are more likely to survive and spread their genes than those that make less adaptive responses.[17]

When Darwin developed his pathbreaking theory, humans were not viewed as subject to the laws of evolution. Religious opposition to evolution stemmed from beliefs that each species arose from separate acts of divine creation. Prevalent scientific views also exempted humans from natural selection, primarily because language created an insurmountable barrier between people and other animals. In stark contrast, perhaps Darwin's most radical insight was that human beings were as much a part of nature as any other form of life. He emphasized a basic continuity across species: "There is no fundamental difference between man and the higher mammals in their mental faculties." Both mental and physical traits among humans derived from evolutionary descendants and differed in degree, not in kind, from other animals:

> We have seen that the senses and intuitions, the various emotions and faculties, such as love, memory, attention, curiosity, imitation, reason etc., of which man boasts, may be found in an incipient, or even sometimes in a well-developed condition, in the lower animals.[18]

Darwin especially focused on similarities between humans and other primates, noting "that there is a much wider interval in mental power between one of the lowest fishes . . . and one of the higher apes, than between an ape and man." Even faculties such as language, reasoning, morality, and religion, which seem to be uniquely human, are found in rudimentary forms among other animals. All forms of evidence "point in the plainest manner to the conclusion that man is the co-descendant with other mammals of a common progenitor," Darwin concluded.[19]

Darwin emphasized not just the link of humans with other species but also the link of humans with each other. He rejected prevailing beliefs that focused on the distinctiveness of various cultures. All peoples were joined by a core set of characteristics with deep physiological roots. He used evidence taken from an array of sources, including observations from other animals, infants, blind people, and informants from different cultures, to show that human emotions such as grief, fear, joy, anger, disgust, shame, and pride are inherited through a common ancestry. "It follows," he asserted, "that the same state of mind is expressed throughout the world with remarkable uniformity; and this fact is in itself interesting as evidence of the close similarity in bodily structure and mental disposition of all the races, of mankind." Because they were "the same throughout the world," they provide "a new argument in favour of the several races being descended from a single parent-stock." Darwin's own observations confirmed his theory about the resemblances among various cultures:

The American aborigines, Negroes, and Europeans are as different from each other in mind as any three races that can be named; yet I was incessantly struck, while living with the Fuegians on board the "Beagle," with the many little traits of character, shewing how similar their minds were to ours.[20]

Darwin's encounter with a native of Tierra del Fuego exemplified his complicated thoughts about how overt cultural differences reflect more universal themes:

The term "disgust," in its simplest sense, means something offensive to the taste. It is curious how readily this feeling is excited by anything unusual in the appearance, odour, or nature of our food. In Tierra del Fuego a native touched with his finger some cold preserved meat which I was eating at our bivouac, and plainly showed utter disgust at its softness; whilst I felt utter disgust at my food being touched by a naked savage, though his hands did not appear dirty.

Darwin's description contains echoes of Herodotus' account of the Greeks and the Callatiae. He is disgusted when a "naked savage" touches his food but gives equal weight to the "utter disgust" the native felt when he handled Darwin's meat. Universal predispositions to be disgusted when humans confront "anything unusual in the appearance, odour, or nature of our food" underlie the culturally variable expressions of food preferences, among many others.[21]

To Darwin, the many points of similarity across species and human races indicated that emotional expressions are inherited rather than acquired through experience. Despite the fact that he was unaware of the genetic mechanisms that transmit inherited traits, he emphasized how human behaviors are not learned through experience but are inborn responses that had been adaptive in earlier stages of evolution:

That the chief expressive actions, exhibited by man and by the lower animals, are now innate or inherited—that is, have not been learnt by the individual—is admitted by every one. So little has learning or imitation to do with several of them that they are from the earliest days and throughout life quite beyond our control.

Races as diverse as Australian aborigines and modern Europeans present their feelings in similar ways. Even the congenitally blind who could not have observed other people's emotional displays show their feelings through the same expressions as the sighted. Perhaps most remarkably, human emotional presentations show distinct resemblances to those found among other species. Human behaviors, feelings, and emotions are inborn, genetically programmed, and universally shared.[22]

Finally, Darwin highlighted the fundamental constancy of human functioning across time. He emphasized how a relatively fixed underlying psychology designed to optimally respond to ancient circumstances still profoundly influences human behavior, even though it is often ill-suited for modern life:

> The chief part of the organization of every living creature is due to inheritance; and consequently, though each being assuredly is well fitted for its place in nature, many structures have now no very close and direct relations to present habits of life.

Biological qualities of humans that were adaptive when they initially developed are often poorly suited to cope with new environmental circumstances. Nevertheless, they persist to the present.[23]

In the late nineteenth and early twentieth centuries, Darwin's theories became associated with the influential movement of social Darwinism. Darwin himself, although he shared many common Victorian notions of Western superiority, generally emphasized the similarities more than the divergences among human groups. The social Darwinists, however, viewed normality and abnormality as rooted in biological differences among individuals, social classes, and races. Applying the concept of natural selection to human societies, they unabashedly proclaimed the preeminence of White, Western, especially northern European, cultures and the inferiority of non-White, non-Western groups. Normality and abnormality became ideological tools to justify, first, Western colonialism and, later, Nazi atrocities. Although Darwin's own approach had little similarity with the racist philosophy of social Darwinism, the cultural view that dominated during most of the twentieth century discredited all biological theories, which largely dropped out of the intellectual landscape during the first half of the century.[24]

After a steep decline during the reign of the cultural and behavioral views, the biological outlook that dominated nineteenth-century thought reemerged in the mid-twentieth century. Originally, studies of nonhuman animals returned this view to public prominence. Zoologist Konrad Lorentz won the Noble Prize for his research showing how geese innately bonded with their mothers. Primatologist Jane Goodall's studies indicated a natural basis for the social behavior she observed among chimpanzees in the wild. Bestselling books such as Desmond Morris' *Naked Ape* brought the emergent ethological perspective to a broad lay audience. Cracks in the dominance of behaviorist psychology emerged as Harry Harlow's experiments found that infant monkeys had inborn preferences for nurturing mothers or mother substitutes. In addition, contradicting Watson's belief that virtually any reinforced behavior could become common, psychologist Martin Seligman's work showed that many emotions were biologically pre-prepared and defied the principles of learned conditioning.[25]

Biologists also made tremendous scientific advances during the 1950s and 1960s. In particular, Crick and Watson's discovery of DNA propelled research on the structures and functions of genes. Psychiatrists uncovered the neuronal and neurochemical structures and functions of the brain as well as developed drugs that targeted specific receptor sites. By the 1970s, imaging techniques such as computerized axial tomography (CAT) scans and magnetic resonance imaging (MRI) allowed neuroscientists previously unthinkable opportunities to view the operation of living brains. Federal research funding and policymaking turned sharply away from psychosocial to biological approaches.[26]

From the 1970s onward, evolutionary perspectives also returned to the consciousness of the general culture. E. O. Wilson's tome, *Sociobiology*, was one landmark in the re-emergence of the biological view, heralding a new stage in the debate between the cultural and biological traditions. This influential volume synthesized scholarship on how genes influenced most animal behaviors and concluded with a controversial chapter suggesting that human values also might have universal, natural underpinnings. In later works, Wilson expanded on this view, attempting to demonstrate how "all tangible phenomena, from the birth of stars to the workings of social institutions, are based on material processes that are ultimately reducible, however long and tortuous the chains, to the laws of physics."[27]

During the 1990s, a new approach to human thought and action, evolutionary psychology, emerged that focused on the aspect of Darwin's work that emphasized how the natural qualities of organisms are often mismatched with the settings in which they must function. Evolutionary psychologists emphasize how conditions in the Pleistocene Era, which roughly spanned the period when the human genome developed from 2 million to 10,000 years ago, set the baseline for natural and unnatural functioning. During this long period, faster, stronger, and larger predators posed genuine threats to humans, no adequate protections against harsh climates existed, infant mortality was common, life spans were short, diseases were impossible to defend against, and food supplies were often scarce. Humans lived in hunter–gatherer societies in which almost all interactions occurred among a small number of group members. Rare encounters with strangers usually signaled the presence of danger. Natural selection favored genes that transmitted those traits that best promoted survival and reproduction within small tightly linked groups that confronted unforgiving settings.[28]

Most activities, relationships, and tempos in the modern developed world starkly contrast with the environments humans were shaped to deal with. Nonhuman predators rarely pose dangers, most diseases are preventable and curable during childbearing years, infant mortality is rare, contraception is plentiful, and few people consciously desire to have many children. Food supplies are generally abundant, and life spans are long. Heating, air conditioning, and electric lights protect people from harsh climates. People interact with far more different and unrelated individuals. The Internet, cell phones, and other current forms of communication establish worldwide connectivity that extends far beyond the several hundred contacts people had during prehistory.

Humans now confront social structures and technologies that are often at odds with their Stone Age mentalities. Yet, human biology makes people prone to act in many respects as if we live in Pleistocene times. Men still desire numerous sexual partners, although the widespread use of contraception does not translate copulation with more women into greater numbers of offspring. People respond to ancestral cues—ranging from images of naked women on computer screens to artificial sweeteners—that resemble signals of enhanced fitness in the distant past. "Humans are not fitness-maximizers," evolutionary psychologists John Tooby and Lida Cosmides explain, "They are ancestral environment fitness-cue maximizers, a profoundly different thing." The stability of inherited predispositions is a common source of impairment, suffering, and distress in a world that bears scant resemblance to the ancient circumstances in which the human brain developed.[29]

By the end of the twentieth century, changes in both general and scientific cultures led biological views to once again gain preeminence in explaining normality and abnormality. The sequencing of the human genome, the flourishing of neuroscience, the development of new technologies for viewing the brain, and the growing popularity of evolutionary psychology restored the credibility of biologically based approaches to human behavior. Psychologists turned dramatically away from behaviorist views toward neuroscientific views. Likewise, psychiatry radically transformed itself from a psychosocially oriented discipline to a field centered on the brain. In contrast to the cultural view that dominated most of the twentieth century, Darwin's nature came to prevail over Herodotus' nurture. Turning the cultural view on its head, modern Darwinians emphasize how human behavior is more innate than learned, more uniform than variable, and more grounded in laws of nature than in arbitrary social norms. Even morality itself is an outgrowth of inborn traits as opposed to acquired human ethics.[30]

Reconciling Genes and the Environment

For most of the past century, genes and the environment were viewed as two distinct processes. Although Darwin had been intensely concerned with the interaction between environments and internal characteristics of organisms, interest in the relationship between innate traits and social circumstances waned during the course of the nineteenth and twentieth centuries. Subsequent schools emphasized either nature (social Darwinism, sociobiology, and neuroscience) or nurture (anthropology, sociology, and behavioral psychology).[31] Some signs, however, indicate that the culture wars of the past few decades are starting to wane.

Toward the end of the twentieth century, recognition began to grow that one-sided views focusing on either biology or society were inherently incomplete. For many, the issue became a question not of whether nature or nurture influences human behavior but of the interplay between heredity and culture. The notion that nature and nurture, biology and culture, are inseparable forces shaping normal and abnormal behavior became more widely acknowledged. As sociologist Ullica Segerstrale observed, " 'Genetics' and 'behavior,' were no longer seen as incompatible when it came to humans." Similarly, an editorial in *Nature* proclaimed, "It is time for sociologists and biologists to bury the hatchet." Although relatively few sociologists study biologically related topics and many instinctively continue to deny the importance of biological influences on human behavior, a number of the field's leaders have called for more assimilation of social and biological processes.[32]

One spur to the integration of the environment and genetic effects, which renewed the importance that Darwin had placed on external circumstances, has been research showing how genetic influences depend on the social contexts in which they are expressed. For example, the genes that make people prone to depression become manifest only in certain kinds of social environments. One well-known study found that genes regulating serotonin levels have no direct effect on rates of depression. However, people who both possess the short allele of the 5-HTT gene and experience especially high levels of social stress are more likely to be depressed. Conversely, favorable environmental circumstances such as high levels of family support can suppress genetic liabilities to alcoholism or delinquency. That is, social and cultural factors can trigger genetic propensities or mitigate genetic defects.[33]

The rise of the field of epigenetics has been another source for the mutual study of biological and social influences. Epigenetic studies show how traumatic social environments, especially those occurring during the first few years of life, can impact synaptic structures and neural pathways throughout a lifetime. Likewise, exposure to environmental toxins—which vary greatly according to socially patterned positions—such as inadequate nutrition or chemical pollutants can produce changes in genetic material. One study, for example, showed that individuals with prenatal exposure to famine conditions during World War II had hypomethylated genes for insulin growth factors six decades later. Although it is unlikely that these changes are transmitted to future generations, they indicate that genetic expressions are not invariant but can change dynamically over an individual's life course in response to interactional and environmental factors. Brains are highly social organs.[34]

A third factor reconciling biological and social forces has been the recognition that biological forces are neither deterministic nor unchangeable. Until recently, most observers had viewed natural influences as more impermeable than cultural ones. For example, the influential opponent of sociobiology, Steven J. Gould, criticized biological views because connecting some phenomenon with "human nature" meant that it could not be modified. In fact, technological developments have made it increasingly impossible to link biology with determinism. Indeed, improvements in normalization technologies such as drugs and surgeries as well as new procedures such as in vitro fertilization mean that in many cases it is far easier to alter biological material than cultural norms. Psychoactive drugs can alleviate the distress of people who inherit dispositions to become depressed or anxious, surgeries can reduce obesity or make biological sex conform to gender identity, and same-sex partners or infertile parents can have genetically related children. Growing understanding of the interactions between genes and environments, of epigenetic processes, and of how to modify biological processes has diminished, but far from erased, the historical disconnect between cultural and biological approaches.[35]

Connecting Herodotus with Darwin: Harmful Dysfunctions

Despite the traditionally sharp distinctions between the biological and cultural views, new interpretations incorporate the idea that concepts of normality and abnormality both have some natural basis and reflect cultural evaluations. The emerging understanding is that both Herodotus and Darwin were correct: Culture and biology mutually shape definitions of what is natural or unnatural. "Insights of social constructionism," philosopher Paul Griffiths contends, "are perfectly compatible with what is known about the evolutionary basis of emotion." The philosopher Jerome Wakefield's development of the concept of disorder as a "harmful dysfunction" (HD) is the most sophisticated effort to date that combines Darwin's focus on biological universality with Herodotus' emphasis on cultural variability. In the HD view, disorders involve both a dysfunction of some biological, psychological, or behavioral mechanism and a cultural judgment that the dysfunction is harmful. Neither a failure of natural functioning nor a negative appraisal alone is sufficient evidence for a disorder, which requires the presence of each component. Adequate definitions of normality and abnormality must contain elements of both the biological and the cultural traditions.[36]

Wakefield begins with the Darwinian notion that natural selection designed psychological and behavioral, as well as physiological, systems to perform certain functions. For example, just as the eyes are designed to convey accurate visual information or the ears to hear sounds that are present in the environment, fear emerges in response to danger, sadness to loss, jealousy to relational threats, and so forth. Conversely, a dysfunction exists when some mechanism is unable to accomplish the function that evolution designed it to perform. A dysfunction either arises in contexts it is not designed for (e.g., fear in the absence of danger, sadness without loss, and jealousy with no relational risk) or fails to emerge in contexts when it is meant to arise (e.g., serious danger, loss, or threat). Although dysfunctions are related to brain processes, they cannot be reduced to them because psychological and behavioral mechanisms are biologically shaped to respond to situational features of their environment but not to emerge outside of that range. As Darwin emphasized, evolution shaped emotions and behaviors to take into account the circumstances in which they arise.[37]

Dysfunctions must go beyond poor decision-making, bad character traits, or personal inadequacies to involve failures of some mechanism to perform as nature designed it to perform. There is far less consensus, as well as far less knowledge, about what constitutes appropriate functioning of cognitions, emotions, motivations, reasoning, and the like as opposed to physiological mechanisms. Nevertheless, no less than defective bodily organs, dysfunctions of mental and behavioral processes including eating, sexual performance, risk-taking, or language can involve incapacities to perform biologically appropriate functions. For example, reading disabilities that result from lack of educational opportunities, knowledge of the relevant language, or lack of motivation are not dysfunctions, unlike those that stem from the inability of a relevant learning mechanism to function appropriately. Or, both aphasics and monks who have taken vows of silence do not speak. Aphasics, however, are unable to talk because of a damaged brain, whereas mute monks are able to speak but choose not to do so. Aphasics, but not monks, have dysfunctional speech mechanisms. Not the absence of speech but, instead, the fact that a dysfunction has caused the failure to speak indicates a disorder.[38]

A disorder combines the failure of some biological or psychological trait to perform its naturally designed function (dysfunction) with the cultural judgment that this failure is harmful (harm). That is, disorders are not only biologically unnatural but also culturally regarded as abnormal. They involve the inability of some mechanism to execute its biological function in a way that social values also define as detrimental. The same symptoms that are normal in one context can thus be abnormal in another; the normality or abnormality distinction requires knowledge of the cultural context in which the condition develops. Fears of devils, witches, and ghosts that were appropriate in sixteenth-century England or in many current African societies with meaning systems defining these phenomena as real can indicate dysfunctions in cultures that regard such beliefs as unreasonable. This means that identical conditions such as demonic possessions can be dysfunctions in one group but not in another. Although determinations of appropriate or inappropriate functioning must take into account cultural judgments, these evaluations do not constitute this distinction, which also requires that something has gone wrong within the individual. The HD analysis thus rejects the view that distinctions between normality and abnormality are purely culturally relative while at the same time taking into account the vast amount of cultural variability in definitions of these phenomena.

From the HD standpoint, there are four ideal typical relationships between biological dysfunctions and cultural values (Table 1.1). One axis incorporates the biological distinction of whether some trait is natural or unnatural; the other axis encompasses whether cultures view the relevant trait as normal or abnormal. Biology and culture diverge when unnatural behaviors are culturally valued, on the one hand, and when natural traits are culturally disvalued, on the other hand. Conversely, biological and cultural qualities can be aligned: Harmful dysfunctions are qualities that are both unnatural and culturally disvalued, whereas behaviors that are both natural and evaluated as normal are biologically and culturally harmonious.[39]

Table 1.1 Examples of Relationships Between Biological Functioning and Cultural Evaluations

		Biology	
		Unnatural	Natural
Culture	Abnormal	I. e.g. Incest	III. e.g. Cowardice
	Normal	II. e.g. Courage	IV. e.g. Grief

Biological and cultural factors are often compatible. For example, most cultures respond to dysfunctions of mental processes such as schizophrenia or serious depression with considerable amounts of stigma, so these conditions are both dysfunctions and undesirable. Likewise, biologically natural processes that advantage beautiful women or tall, muscular men are commonly aligned with cultural values and so are neither dysfunctional nor disvalued.

Many conditions, however, are unnatural but desirable or natural but culturally disapproved. For example, from a Darwinian perspective, the inability to have children can be a serious dysfunction. Yet, cultural evaluations of infertility need not be negative. Contemporary Western values do not mandate having children; indeed, population growth in many developed countries is below replacement rates. People who are unable to conceive but who do not desire to have children and who live in cultures in which childlessness poses no handicaps have dysfunctions that are not abnormal. In contrast, infertile people who want to bear children and whose groups have values that obligate childbearing would have harmful dysfunctions. Because cultural evaluations differ so widely, infertility would be a disorder in some cultures but not in others.

Some natural conditions are nevertheless defined as abnormal. Consider social norms about handedness. For centuries, left-handed people were viewed as having a deficiency in need of correction. They were subject to regimes, often drastic ones, that tried to modify their behavior to conform to the supposed superiority of the right-handed majority. These norms about the relative worth of right and left hands, however, were thoroughly arbitrary and disguised the fact that both hands are equally valuable variants of human functioning. The requirement that a biologically unnatural condition is a necessary component of a disorder places a much-needed check on cultural (and medical) tendencies to pathologize a wide array of atypical conditions.[40]

The chief strength of the HD analysis is to combine a relatively objective, biological component with an evaluative cultural component. However, it also raises a number of issues. One is that judgments about whether psychological and social mechanisms are operating in a dysfunctional or adaptive manner commonly also involve value judgments. Assessments of what are natural or unnatural targets of sexual arousal, appropriate or pathological jealousy, or expectable or dysfunctional levels of aggressiveness inherently go beyond objective standards of functioning to include evaluative criteria. Thus, values enter into the natural as well as the cultural constituent of disorders. Nevertheless, although the dysfunctional component of the HD analysis often involves an evaluative aspect, it is not solely evaluative and ensures that concepts of naturalness and unnaturalness have some objective properties.

Another difficult issue in making judgments about dysfunctions arises from the fact that nature designed humans to respond to the ancestral, not the contemporary, world. Despite the fact that human brains are flexible and can often adapt to rapidly changing situations, they are often ill-suited, sometimes spectacularly so, to the conditions of modern life. Male desires to have sex with many females no longer lead to a greater number of descendants but instead to high levels of aggression toward women. Also, fears of strangers that were rational in circumstances in which strangers were likely sources of danger currently result in unreasonable social anxieties and intergroup conflicts. Yet, men who crave promiscuous sex or people who become nervous in unfamiliar company act in ways that are compatible with human nature. Mismatches between biologically designed qualities that optimized survival and reproduction in the ancient work and current environmental circumstances can create pathologies that do not easily fit distinctions between disordered and nondisordered conditions.

Finally, clear divisions between natural and unnatural behaviors are rarely found so that few cases fit neatly into one or the other of these categories. As Ruth Benedict emphasized, divisions between ritualistic invocation of spirits or hallucinations, justified suspicions or paranoia, and unnaturally prolonged or appropriate periods of grief are often blurry, tied to context, and subject to value judgments. Nevertheless, the fact that no sharp boundary between natural functions and dysfunctions exists does not mean that the distinction between them is arbitrary. The HD concept distinguishes clear poles of disordered and nondisordered conditions (e.g., aphasics and monks who take vows of silence) but at the same time is compatible with vague and ambiguous boundaries between each extreme. However, the requirement that disorders must involve some dysfunction of a natural mechanism usefully separates clear cases of dysfunction from cultural judgments, limits illegitimate applications of labels of "abnormality" to true natural defects, and maximizes normal human variation.

The HD view has the advantage of a biological foundation that provides the grounds for reasonably objective judgments of what is potentially natural or unnatural and normal or abnormal. Yet, it also has the flexibility to take cultural variation into account. It thus incorporates into definitions of normality and abnormality both Darwin's emphasis on natural design and Herodotus' focus on cultural variability. To date, the HD analysis has been applied only to the study of mental illness. The examples presented in this book indicate its potential for a much wider use.[41]

The Roadmap

This work shares the growing agreement that both biological and cultural factors shape definitions of what conditions are disordered or not. On the one hand, biological dysfunctions can be culturally devalued or valued; on the other hand, biologically natural states can be culturally normative or stigmatized. Its central theme, however, is that the importance and types of interactions between the biological and cultural aspects of the normal and the pathological vary tremendously depending on the subject in question. Each of the following chapters explores various ways that biology and culture influence normalcy.

Chapter 2 examines incest, which provides perhaps the best example of a behavior that is both biologically dysfunctional and culturally repugnant. Despite the widespread contention that norms regulating incest stem from the need to repress intense erotic desires toward intimates, ample evidence indicates that incest taboos reflect human nature. Incest aversion is shared with other species, need not be learned, and is difficult or impossible to overcome. Moreover, the biological reason for the taboo—the avoidance of inbreeding—as well as the mechanism through which sexual indifference is transmitted—intimate living conditions at early ages—are well understood. The result is that bans on intercourse between genetic intimates are worldwide characteristics of societies that barely vary from group to group. Biology and culture align in their intense distaste of incest.

Chapter 3 uses patterns of naming children as an example of how cultural influences on normality operate when they have no biological restraints.

Names are sounds that reflect cultural influences; they cannot be biologically unnatural. They echo dominant patterns of social relations, are highly variable across cultures, and are subject to rapid change across generations. In the past, they reinforced tradition and continuity, whereas at present they display individualism, strivings for uniqueness, and fashionable trends. If incest aversion provides one pole for how biological factors influence views of normality and abnormality, names illustrate the opposite end where purely cultural factors shape what is normal and what is not.

Chapter 4 turns to phenomena—courage and cowardice—that are in a different way from names the diametric opposite of incest aversion. Here, cultural definitions of valued and disvalued behaviors *invert* natural and unnatural tendencies. Nature created strong innate dispositions toward self-preservation so that courageously sacrificing oneself for the benefit of genetically unrelated people is unnatural. In contrast to natural tendencies, cultural norms celebrate and reward courageous behavior, especially during combat. Courage is a biologically unnatural, yet culturally revered, behavior. Conversely, cowardice is a natural response to danger because humans, like all organisms, are instinctively prone to flee from situations that threaten their well-being. Yet, for men cowardice is among the most culturally stigmatized behaviors. Esteem for the courageous and scorn for the cowardly illustrate how cultural factors can be powerful enough to override even basic biological instincts.

Chapters 5 and 6 on obesity and phobias, respectively, illustrate cases in which conditions that were naturally shaped to cope with ancestral conditions are mismatched with contemporary environments. Natural selection led humans to have voracious appetites, which were adaptive responses to the circumstances of chronic caloric shortages and fluctuations that prevailed in prehistory and remained common through the nineteenth century. At that time, mechanized food production, transportation, and storage and, later, the development of synthetic foods led calories to become both abundant and cheap. Obesity and consequent diseases result from the confrontation of normal appetites with copious and ever-present amounts of food. Moreover, normal food cravings are mismatched not only with calorie-filled milieu but also with cultural norms that value thin female bodies. Obesity at the same time results from natural tendencies and is associated with an array of biological, psychological, and social impairments.

Specific and social phobias provide another example of how innate biological tendencies are mismatched with current environments. Like our prehistoric urges to eat as many calories as possible even after this trait has become seriously maladaptive, humans commonly fear objects and situations such as small crawling animals, heights, and strangers that were genuinely threatening in ancestral times but that are not reasonable sources of fear at present. Nevertheless, these anachronistic fears are products of natural genes that are out of step with present-day dangers.

Chapter 7 uses grief after the death of an intimate to exemplify how natural emotions and cultural norms can be mutually reinforcing. Grief is biologically designed to arise after close relations die. However, unlike ravenous appetites and ancient fears, which are mismatched to modern circumstances, natural tendencies to grieve retain their designed function of attracting social support. Moreover, grief is aligned with cultural values: People who *do not* grieve after their intimates die are generally viewed as abnormal. Grief illustrates how some ancient, if distressing, biological emotions retain their natural functions at present.

The book next turns to the puzzle of what are natural or unnatural sexual behaviors. The biological and cultural approaches sharply diverge in their answers to this question. Although biological approaches regard heterosexuality as the driving force of evolution, desirable and undesirable sexual behaviors show extraordinary variability across cultures and over time. Chapter 8 focuses on the views of Alfred Kinsey, who believed that virtually all forms of sexuality were natural so that unnatural sexual proclivities, except perhaps celibacy, do not exist. Moreover, Kinsey held that people were naturally pansexual and in the absence of repressive cultural norms would enjoy all forms of sexuality. The chapter surveys sexual behavior subsequent to Kinsey to examine what sorts of sexual activities actually emerge when cultural norms permit individuals to choose a wide variety of sexual orientations.

Chapter 9 concludes the book by elaborating on how the HD account can help separate normal differences from biological defects. It examines trends that increasingly view many sorts of behaviors that have traditionally been seen as deficiencies in need of correction as instead valuable forms of human functioning. It concludes by speculating about how new technologies might increasingly prevent dysfunctional conditions from arising as well as minimize the harm that they can create. The result might be a normalization of unusual behaviors that goes far beyond anything that was possible in past eras, although it might also lead many previously normal behaviors to be redefined as abnormal. Although the views of Herodotus and Darwin maintain their relevance, they encounter conditions that neither pioneer remotely imagined. Despite their anchors in the past, future definitions of normality and abnormality are increasingly unlikely to resemble anything like either what nature designed or what any previous culture envisioned.

2 INCEST AVERSION

Margaret Mead, the best-known anthropologist of the twentieth century, became famous through her studies of sexuality in the South Pacific. Her work emphasized the highly permissive and guilt-free attitudes toward sexual activities that prevailed in the region. There was one major exception, however, to the general sexual freedom she observed among the groups who lived there. When Mead questioned members of the Arapesh culture in New Guinea about their attitudes toward incest, they were incredulous. No one could think of any such cases that had ever occurred within the group. Indeed, they could not even imagine such behaviors: "No, we don't do that. What would the old man say to a young man who wished to take his sister to wife? They didn't know. No one knew. The old men never discussed the matter." Yet, no one had taught the Arapesh any explicit rules against incest—incestuous behavior was simply incomprehensible to them.[1]

The Arapesh would understand the responses my undergraduate students make to a hypothetical case developed by psychologist Jonathan Haidt:

> Julie and Mark are brother and sister. They are traveling together in France on summer vacation from college. One night they are staying alone in a cabin near the beach. They

decide that it would be interesting and fun if they tried making love. At the very least, it would be a new experience for each of them. Julie was already taking birth control pills, but Mark uses a condom too, just to be safe. They both enjoy making love, but they decide never to do it again. They keep that night as a special secret, which makes them feel even closer to each other. What do you think about that? Was it OK for them to make love?

Many students are visibly disgusted when I ask them whether sexual intimacy among siblings is acceptable. They tend to echo the explanation of one of Haidt's students: "Um ... well ... oh, gosh. This is hard. I really—um, I mean, there's just no way I could change my mind but I just don't know how to—how to show what I'm feeling, what I feel about it. It's crazy!" Like Mead's respondents, modern American college students find it difficult to give rational reasons for their abhorrence of incest.[2]

I also ask my students whether they had ever been taught to refrain from incestuous behavior. Not a single one has said that their parents discussed incest with them. Likewise, although most of them have taken courses in sex education, nobody said their instructors discussed incestuous desires. Nor do public service announcements or any other media campaigns urge people to refrain from having sex with relatives. Unlike, for example, encouraging safe sexual practices or refraining from drug use, no one had ever told these students that they should not have sex with genetic intimates. Nevertheless, virtually everyone finds incestuous behavior to be repugnant. Perhaps this is because humans do not need to learn not to have sex with genetic intimates: Perhaps they have an innate aversion to incest.

No physiological barriers prevent people from having intercourse with genetic intimates. Nevertheless, social scientists, psychologists, and biologists display an unusual unanimity about the universality of the taboo that defines incest as, in the words of anthropologist Lucien Levy-Bruhl, "abnormal, unprecedented, against nature, something that brings disaster." All societies prohibit sexual intercourse between parents and children, and bans against brother–sister incest are nearly as universal. Even Herodotus, who was generally tolerant of almost all sorts of human behavior, was repelled by incest among genetic intimates. He left no doubt about his feelings toward Cambyses, a Persian king who married his sister, describing him as having a "serious physical malady [that] affected his brain," "a lunatic," "unbalanced," "mad," and "completely out of his mind." Moreover, Herodotus explicitly dissociated Cambyses' behavior from Persian customs: "The woman was his sister by both parents, and also his wife, though it had never before been a Persian custom for brothers and sisters to marry."[3]

Although no one disputes that (aside from extremely unusual circumstances) incest is universally defined as abnormal, intense disagreements exist regarding whether repugnance to having sex with a close relative stems from cultural norms or from a natural aversion. Most social scientists follow a long tradition that asserts the incest taboo arises because of social, not biological, necessity. The Greek Stoic philosopher Chrysippus of Soli spelled out the view that avoidance of incest was a social convention that did not reflect anything about human nature. He is said to have held that "sexual intercourse with mothers or daughters or sisters" has been "discredited without reason." The qualifier "without reason" indicates that incest prohibitions do not reflect biological instincts but, instead, arbitrary social customs. Two millennia later, eighteenth-century Dutch philosopher Bernard Mandeville claimed that "incestuous alliances are abominable but it is certain that, whatever Horror we conceive at the thought of them, there is nothing in Nature repugnant against them, but what is built upon Mode and Custom."[4]

The Elizabethan dramatist John Ford's play 'Tis Pity She's a Whore' illustrates this view in its passionate portrayal of a sexual affair between two siblings:

> Shall a peevish sound
> A customary form, from man to man,
> Of brother and sister, be a bar
> 'Twixt my perpetual happiness and me?
> Say that we had one father; say one womb—
> Curse to my joys!—gave both us life and birth;
> Are we not therefore each to other bound
> So much the more by nature?

Psychoanalyst Sigmund Freud pushed this view to its furthest extreme, positing that children universally have strong erotic attractions to opposite sex parents and, sometimes, siblings. Such conceptions assume not only that humans lack any natural aversion to intercourse with genetic intimates but also that strong cultural prohibitions must restrain their natural proclivities *toward* incest. Indeed, the very reason such intense sanctions against incest arise is to repress intense sexual desires among close family members. Anthropologist Robin Fox concludes, "Left to ourselves we will organize our sex relatively promiscuously."[5]

This chapter presents a starkly different view of the incest taboo: Strong social sanctions against incest do not repress but instead *reflect* natural sexual instincts. Incest aversion has all the characteristics of a pure Darwinian disposition: It is shared with other species, is found universally with few cultural differences, is rarely communicated through explicit social learning, and is very difficult or impossible to change. Moreover, a known mechanism transmits this antipathy: intimate living conditions during the earliest years of infancy and childhood. Humans (and many other species) do not develop sexual desires for those with whom they closely associate with during early childhood. This naturally selected trait is also congruent with cultural norms that, aside from a very small number of exceptions, define incestuous relationships as abnormal, immoral, unnatural, and repugnant. The biological strength of the incest taboo is so strong that it is extremely difficult to alter: Even if cultural norms did not forbid incest, few people would want to have sex with genetic intimates.

While incest taboos among close relations reproduce biological predispositions, social influences channel natural aversions to incest. First, living conditions during early periods of life, which vary considerably across different groups, provide the conditions that activate natural repugnance to intercourse with close relatives. Second, social proximity often creates incest taboos among people who are not genetically related at all. Finally, although all societies forbid intercourse between people who share half of their genes, and almost all societies forbid intercourse between those who share a quarter of their genes, cultural norms set the boundaries that define permissible sexual relationships among those who share more limited genetic overlap. Nevertheless, the incest taboo provides a good example of how cultural rules can reproduce a biologically unnatural condition.

What Is Incest?

Incest refers to sexual relations that occur between genetically related people. At one extreme (setting aside identical twins) are relationships among what I call "genetic intimates." These are people who share half of their genes—fathers and daughters, mothers and sons, and brothers and sisters. Sexual practices among these relations evoke the strongest natural repulsion. Most groups also preclude sex between uncles and nieces and aunts and nephews, who share 25 percent of genes. However, Herodotus, who sharply condemned father–daughter incest, described the devotion of the Spartan king Anaxandrides to his wife who was also his sister's daughter. Far more cultural diversity exists in the degree of approval for incest between first cousins, who share 12.5 percent of genes. For example, in Pakistan, such unions account for approximately half of all marriages.[6]

In addition, cultural and genetic categories of kin relationships often do not neatly overlap: Most cultures apply incest taboos to kinlike relationships that lack any genetic component. Examples in our society include adoptive or stepparents and their children, blended families in which children have different parents, or families with more than one adopted child. Many groups also forbid sex among genetically unrelated members of the same clan or other socially defined unit. Thus, although genetic intimates are naturally likely to acquire an aversion of incest, cultural definitions can lead to the same result among people who do not share genes.

The direction of incestuous desires can flow from children to parents or vice versa. Freud, who put incestuous desires near the core of his influential theories, believed that young children naturally have erotic feelings toward opposite-sex parents. He also believed that they normally age out of these urges by the time they enter puberty. In contrast, he viewed parental desires to have sex with their children as unnatural. Others, however, such as feminist Judith Herman, believe that incestuous desires typically run from fathers to daughters. Sex is the second channel through which incestuous desires run: Males might want to mate with female relatives or females with male ones. In fact, however, almost all cases of parent–child incest involve fathers and daughters; mother–son incest is extraordinarily rare.[7]

The Universality of Incest Taboos

Cultures display a remarkable uniformity in prohibiting sexual relationships among genetic intimates. Indeed, this taboo is one of the few universal social rules. In an authoritative study, anthropologist George Murdock concluded the following:

> The data from our 250 societies reveal not a single instance in which sexual intercourse or marriage is generally permissible between mother and son, father and daughter, or brother and sister. Aside from a few rare and highly restricted exceptions, there is complete universality in this respect.

Moreover, most of these groups view incest as one of the most horrendous possible actions.[8]

Consider, for example, the reputedly permissive and guilt-free sexual lives of the groups in the South Pacific that Mead and other anthropologists studied during the first half of the twentieth century. Incest, on the contrary, was extremely rare, but when uncovered, it was subject to the most severe possible sanctions. Among the Trobriand Islanders of the South Pacific, brothers and sisters who were found to have had incestuous relations committed very painful joint suicides in order to avoid even more excruciating punishments that the tribe would have inflicted on them. Indeed, their ethnographer, Bronislaw Malinowski, described the ban on brother–sister sexual congress as "the supreme taboo of the Trobriander." Anthropologist Raymond Firth's classic study of the Tikopia, who inhabit a small island in the Pacific Ocean, concluded, "In Tikopia incest between brother and sister is abhorred, and often stated to be impossible; its occurrence is denied point-blank by most people." Not only did incest not occur among this group, which otherwise promoted a high degree of sexual freedom, but also even discussing its possibility was "regarded as somewhat absurd." If such a violation were to occur, the offenders would be put out to sea where they would die.[9]

In other areas of the world as well, many groups execute those violators of the incest taboo who have not already committed suicide because of the shame of anticipated discovery. For example, the Apaches of the American Southwest consider brothers and sisters who are found to have committed incest to be witches and burn them to death. Other cultures believe that the harmful consequences of incest spread to relatives who did not participate in the banned sexual activity. For example, the Nuer group of East Africa asserts that incest can lead uninvolved family members to develop a number of serious illnesses.[10]

Evidence for incest aversion in Western societies stretches back for thousands of years. An example is Socrates' statement that repugnance of incest was so strong that "among the many there isn't the slightest desire for this sort of intercourse." The natural law tradition, which originated among the Classical Greeks, viewed the taboo against incest as stemming from "that which nature has taught all animals." Relatively recently, many societies have lifted many bans on sexual relationships between people of the same gender or of different races. No sentiment exists, however, for ending prohibitions on sex among genetic intimates. Indeed, even in the twenty-first century, societies severely sanction such relationships, which usually arise without knowledge of a genetic tie. An instance stems from an English case in which the revelation that twins who were separated at birth and married each other without realizing they were brother and sister led to a national uproar and calls for stricter regulation of genetic information on birth certificates. In another relatively recent case, a German court gave a prison sentence to a man who was adopted as a young child and only met his natural sister when he was 23 years old and she was 16 years old, with whom he had four children together (two of whom were disabled).[11]

Virtually no one disputes the existence of universal taboos against incest among genetic intimates. Nevertheless, there are a few cultures that permit and, occasionally, even mandate incest in particular circumstances. What accounts for the rare exceptions to the ban on incest?

Exceptions to the Incest Taboo

Strong cultural norms often override natural imperatives (e.g., see Chapter 4 on courage). What is surprising, however, is how rarely they overcome the incest taboo. No cases of culturally approved incest among parents and children have been documented. Among siblings, the best-known exception to the incest taboo involved royal families in ancient Egypt, where pharaohs commonly married their sisters and queens married their brothers. Sibling incest within noble and other very high-status families also appears in a small number of other societies, including royalty in Incan, native Hawaiian, and some African societies.[12]

Sibling marriages among royalty, however, were not products of sexual desire among spouses. Instead, such royal unions arose in situations in which incest had a number of contextual advantages. Cultural mandates that dictated sibling marriages consolidated royal bloodlines and eliminated the need to find appropriate marriage partners outside of the nuclear household. Brother–sister marriages among royalty also reinforced the sharp separation of divine rulers from the plebian masses. In each case, the families were powerful enough to claim that social rules such as the incest taboo that applied to common people were not applicable to them. The only documented case of culturally normative sibling marriages among common people stems from the Egyptians during the Roman period. Such unions might have accounted for up to 30 percent of all marriages during this era. Even here, however, only a dozen of 113 studied cases are reliably full siblings who were reared together. This exception reinforces sociologist Edvard Westermarck's claim that

> the horror of incest is an almost universal characteristic of mankind, the cases which seem to indicate a perfect absence of this feeling being so exceedingly rare that they must be regarded merely as anomalous aberrations from a general rule.[13]

Biblical Incest

Advocates of the cultural relativity of incest aversion also commonly cite the numerous instances of Biblical incest. It is therefore instructive to examine these parables. The best-known story involves the seduction of Lot by his two daughters, who each gave birth to sons engendered by their father. The fictional circumstances of Lot's family were extremely unusual. They had fled from Sodom and Gomorrah and lived in a cave isolated from all other humans. Neither Lot nor his daughters had incestuous desires for each other. Before having sex with their father, the daughters made him drink so much wine that "he perceived not neither when his daughter lay down, nor when she rose up." Lot, in other words, had neither incestuous intention nor even any memory of intercourse with his daughters. Like their father, the daughters did not desire sexual relations but had no other alternative for transmitting their genes to future generations. "There is," they asserted, "no man left on the earth, to come in unto us after the manner of the whole earth." In this sense, Lot's daughters were in a position similar to the relationship of Cain and his wife, who must have been his sister. Like Lot's daughters, the children of Adam and Eve had no possible sexual partners aside from each other (Noah's children would have been in the same situation). Such cases arise when incest is the only possible way to reproduce and so illustrate a rare situation in which genetic sexual intimacy makes evolutionary sense.[14]

Other cases of Biblical incest involve parties who did not share any genes. For example, Jacob married his deceased first wife's sister (a common arrangement at the time). Because no genetic relationship existed between Jacob and his second (or first) wife, their relationship was not biologically incestuous. Other cases of Biblical incest were clearly viewed as abnormal and were harshly sanctioned. For example, Amnon, King David's eldest son and heir, raped his half-sister, Tamar. When her brother, Absalom, learned of the incident, he ordered his servants to have Amnon killed.[15]

Biblical incest also illustrates the cultural variability about where to draw lines around the normality or abnormality of incestuous relationships. Whereas nature creates aversion for sex among parents and children and brothers and sisters, culture establishes where boundaries are set between approved or forbidden sexual activities among less closely related relatives. Among the ancient Israelites, sexual relationships among parties who shared less than half their genes were often normative. For example, the Bible does not condemn Abraham, who married his half-sister Sara, with whom he shared 25 percent of genes. Most commonly, Biblical incest involves first cousins, who were not forbidden to marry. For example, Abraham's son Isaac married Rebeka, his first cousin once removed. Abraham's brother Nahor married his niece Milcah, the daughter of his other brother Haran. Moses' mother was also his great-aunt.

As the Israelites show, cultural rules regarding sex among cousins are highly variable. Murdock's survey of 250 societies concludes that "significant differences between societies in the extension of incest taboos to consanguineal relatives begin, therefore, with first cousins." This comprehensive study shows that more than 97 percent of societies prohibited intercourse among aunts and nephews and uncles and nieces, but only 75 percent forbade them among first cousins.[16]

Although some cultural variability in permitted sexual relationships among people who share less than half their genes exists, sex between parents and children and between siblings is nearly universally considered to be abnormal. Cases of sex among genetic intimates are so rare that they are anomalous aberrations from a general rule. People not only do not engage in much incest but also do not *want* to act incestuously. What accounts for the lack of desire to have sex with closely related relatives?

Evidence for a Natural Aversion to Incest

The universality of some human trait does not, in itself, indicate biological innateness. All societies, for example, have developed the ability to use fire in controlled ways, but this behavior is not biologically grounded. However, when traits that are universally found among humans are also found among other species, there is good reason to think that some naturally selected biological mechanism underlies them. Incest aversion among nonhuman species cannot stem from cultural norms and thus would suggest a natural basis for the incest taboo. Good evidence shows no sharp discontinuity in incestuous practices between humans and other species.

The Pervasiveness of Incest Avoidance in Nonhuman Species

Before the 1960s, most commentators assumed that incest avoidance was uniquely human. They agreed with the Ancient Greek Stoic philosopher Chrysippus, who stated in regard to incest that "we should look to the beasts and infer from their behaviour that nothing of this kind is out of place or unnatural." Considerable evidence, however, indicates that humans share their aversion to incest with other creatures. Where rates can be detected in natural settings, species including mammals, moths, birds, amphibians, and, often, even insects have low rates of inbreeding. For example, the genetic lines of birds that are mated with their siblings quickly die out over several generations. Also, consider Canada geese: "The luckless breeder who takes a male and female from the same brood to raise geese is doomed to disappointment: The pair will not mate even if no other partners are available."[17]

During the mid-twentieth century, ethologists began to study sexual behavior among nonhuman primates in natural settings. In most species, either males or females migrate out of the group in which they were born before or at the time they become sexually mature so that opportunities for inbreeding between parents and offspring or between brothers and sisters are usually unavailable. Primates including monkeys, lemurs, baboons, gorillas, and chimpanzees all practice such forms of exogamy: Either young males or young females leave the group in which they were born at or before puberty. When genetically related primates do live together after puberty, sexual relations between siblings of the same mother are rare (it is usually impossible for primates to be aware of whether they share the same father). For example, when female chimps are in heat, they are promiscuous and allow a number of males to mount them, but they always resist their brothers.[18]

Famed primatologist Jane Goodall observed that among the chimpanzees she studied, "No male has ever been observed to try to take his mother or sister on a consortship." Popular naturalist Dian Fossey likewise concluded from her studies of mountain gorillas that restrictions against mother–son incest are "innate." In the whole animal world, with very few exceptions, no species is known in which inbreeding occurs to any considerable degree under natural conditions. Even the legendarily licentious bonobos refrain from sexual activity with genetically related others.[19]

Human resistance to incestuous sex thus demonstrates a natural continuity, rather than a sharp distinction, with other animals. We share our hardwired lack of sexual desire for genetic intimates with other species. Ethologist Anne Pusey's review of the evidence concludes that "nonhuman primates provide abundant evidence for an inhibition of sexual behavior among closely related adults. This finding is consistent with the idea that inbreeding avoidance behavior is a naturally selected behavior that was already present before humans evolved."[20] There is also abundant evidence for the reason behind the natural aversion for sex among genetic intimates.

The High Costs of Inbreeding

Humans have long intuited the genetic costs of inbreeding. Ancient Greek and Roman myths and philosophy often portray the highly negative consequences of incest for humans. Socrates, for example, noted how incestuous sexual relationships produced defective offspring. The mythology of most tribal societies also explicitly recognizes detrimental impacts of inbreeding. In one case, anthropologist William Durham indicates that informants from the Eastern Toradja group that resides in the South Pacific give the following reason for the incest taboo:

> It can happen that a man and a woman have physical characteristics . . . that come into conflict with each other when they marry. The harmful influence of this will manifest itself in the children born from such a marriage: They will be weak, sickly, idiotic and quickly die. Therefore a marriage with a person too closely related is considered unsuitable . . . their children are then not healthy and do not live long.

One of anthropologist Raymond Firth's Tikopian informants asserts, "The children of true brother and sister are not good; they are diseased and weakly."[21]

Charles Darwin (who married his first cousin) suggested in *The Descent of Man* that the deleterious consequences of inbreeding among animals led natural selection to make mating between close relatives rare. This tendency was then passed on to humans. When Darwin wrote *The Descent of Man*, however, the genetic basis for this aversion was not yet known. At the end of the nineteenth century, Austrian monk Gregor Mendel's experiments uncovered the reasons why inbreeding is harmful. Each gene has two alleles, which can be dominant or recessive. The combination of two recessive genes often poses risks, sometimes major risks, for many disabling and even fatal conditions. When two mating organisms share the same recessive gene, they have a 25 percent probability that the recessive trait will become a dominant one in their offspring. Genetic intimates are far more likely than others to share recessive genes that rarely appear together among unrelated organisms. Dangerous recessive genes that are harmless when they are paired with unlike genes often become deadly when they pair with a like gene and become dominant. People who share half their genes, therefore, are far more likely than genetically unrelated individuals to pass lethal or disabling recessive traits to their offspring. Because inbreeding inhibits reproductive capacity, often to a considerable extent, natural selection would have developed mechanisms to prevent genetic intimates from mating with each other. This powerful natural force seems to underlie the universally shared aversion to incest.[22]

It is difficult to gather data on the harmful effects of inbreeding among animals in natural settings because it so rarely occurs. Extant research shows that inbreeding among species as varied as land snails, mice, baboons, and golden lion tamarins has serious negative consequences. For example, all 7 inbred animals in a natural population of olive and yellow baboons died within 1 month of birth compared to 33 of 172 outbred animals. Laboratory studies also indicate far lower survival rates of inbred compared to outbred species. Inbred animals that do survive have harmful consequences, including less mating, sperm deformities, and sterility. Among mammals kept in captivity, rare cases of inbreeding lead to a decline in juvenile survival rates of approximately 30 percent. Although nonhuman species do not have cultural norms forbidding incest, the harmful natural consequences of inbreeding lead them to develop mechanisms that make them refrain from having sex with those they know are relatives.[23]

Inbreeding among humans, although rarely found, also entails dramatic disadvantages. Children born from sibling and parent–child unions have approximately double the chance of early mortality as outbred children and approximately 10 times the rate of genetic defects including severe mental impairments, deafness, dwarfism, heart deformities, cystic fibrosis, and other severe conditions. A Czech study of the consequences of inbreeding among 161 children of women and their fathers, brothers, or sons found that 17 percent died within their first year and an additional 25 percent had severe abnormalities. A control group of 95 children born to the same mothers found a mortality rate of 5 percent and approximately a 2 percent rate of severe disabilities during the first year. Overall, studies of children whose parents share half their genes indicate that rates of child mortality and severe disability exceed 40 percent.[24]

Inbreeding is demonstrably harmful for survival and reproduction. The only reproductive advantage from mating with intimates occurs when, as with the story of Lot and his daughters, other mates are unavailable. The consequences of inbreeding are serious enough that natural selection must have devised ways to prevent it from happening. What biological mechanisms create an aversion to incest among genetic intimates?[25]

The Westermarck Hypothesis

Near the end of the nineteenth century, a Finnish sociology professor at the University of London, Edvard Westermarck, sought to explain the universality of the incest taboo. In contrast to the dominant anthropological and sociological opinion at the time, Westermarck specifically rejected the view that social norms accounted for the rarity of incest: He wrote, "The home is kept pure from incestuous defilement neither by laws, nor by customs, nor by education but by an *instinct* which under normal circumstances makes sexual love between the nearest kin a psychical impossibility." He proposed a brilliant explanation of *how* genetic intimates developed an aversion to incest: "There is a remarkable absence of erotic feelings between people living closely together from childhood." That is, people who live in close proximity from an early age become sexually indifferent to each other (later work demonstrates that early association must begin before age 10 years and is especially productive of sexual aversion when it starts before age 3 years). Propinquity during childhood, not kinship per se, provides the cue that triggers the innate aversion to incest. This aversion does not merely reflect indifference to sexual relations but also constitutes an active repugnance to even thinking about intercourse with genetic intimates: "Sexual indifference is combined with the positive feeling of aversion when the act is thought of."[26]

The Westermarck hypothesis also indicates that all children who are reared together from an early age, regardless of their genetic relationship, should not be sexually attracted to each other later in life. Examples include unrelated age peers who are raised in close quarters when they are very young, adopted but genetically unrelated siblings who grow up together from early ages, or infants with different parents who are both raised in blended families. In addition, the hypothesis implies that genetic intimates who do *not* spend their early years in close proximity will not experience this biological signal and so will be less likely to become incest averse.[27]

Westermarck was most concerned about incestuous feelings (or lack thereof) among people in sibling-like relationships. His argument, however, extends to sexual aversion among parents and children. Several decades after Westermarck, British psychiatrist John Bowlby showed that early attachments prevent the development of erotic instincts between parents and children as well as between siblings. Westermarck's emphasis on sibling relationships and Bowlby's focus on parent–child connections share the quality of close, but sexless, ties among people who bond when both parties (sibs) or one party (parent–child) is very young. Relationships that arise before approximately age 2 or 3 years are fundamentally asexual throughout life. Conversely, the absence of early attachment or association increases the probability that biologically grounded mechanisms of incest aversion will fail to develop.[28]

A vast amount of evidence among both humans and nonhumans supports Westermarck's thesis. It explains the findings noted previously: Primate siblings reared together almost never mate, mothers and their mature male offspring avoid sex, and species featuring close bonds between fathers and daughters avoid incest. Indeed, all primate species that closely associate with genetic intimates during early childhood avoid mating with them as adults.

The Westermarck hypothesis also has the interesting corollary that genetically *unrelated* animals that are reared together will not mate when they reach sexual maturity. Laboratory experiments that vary who mates with whom confirm this prediction. For example, researchers raised female mice born within one genetic litter in a different genetic litter. When these mice became sexually mature, they were given the choice of mating with genetic brothers with which they were not raised or with genetically unrelated males with which they were reared. The females were more likely to mate with their genetic brothers that they had not grown up with than with their unrelated "brothers." The genetic cue for sexual avoidance is activated through close proximity at very young ages, even among animals that do not actually share genes. Animals reared together, regardless of their genetic relationship, will reject each other as mates, most likely because they use the instinctual formula of avoiding sex with those that smell like family members that is acquired through common rearing at early ages.[29]

Studies of humans also indicate that the Westermarck effect holds among children who were reared together, regardless of their genetic connection. Anthropologist Melford Spiro's research on Israeli kibbutzim during the historical period when children were reared communally found an absence of sexual desire among unrelated people of the same age. "In not one instance," Spiro concluded, "has a sabra [an Israeli Jew born in Israel] from Kiryat Yedidim married a fellow sabra nor, to the best of our knowledge, has a sabra had sexual intercourse with a fellow sabra." Another anthropologist, Joseph Shepher, examined nearly 3000 marriages of young adults who were reared on kibbutzim and did not find a single sexual relationship among members of the same peer group who had lived together since birth. The Israeli studies are especially notable because there were no cultural sanctions against sexual relationships among unrelated adults who had been raised together as children. Shepher noted, "There is absolutely no sign of formal or informal pressure or sanction against heterosexual activity with the peer group either from the educators or parents or from the members of the peer group itself." Therefore, members of these kibbutzim would not have learned to refrain from sexual activities with their peers. Nevertheless, close living conditions at an early age activated a natural instinct toward sexual indifference.[30]

Anthropologist Arthur Wolf conducted another impressive study of the Westermarck effect. Wolf examined more than 14,000 cases of two types of marriage in Taiwan during the late nineteenth and early twentieth centuries. In one, which Wolf calls "minor marriage," young boys and girls were betrothed at very early ages, sometimes at birth, and were raised in the same household. In the other, "major marriages," the parties grew up separately before they married as adults. Presumably because the parties had been reared together during childhood, minor marriages featured fertility rates that were 40 percent lower, divorce rates that were three times higher, and twice as many extramarital affairs compared to major marriages. Social learning cannot explain why participants in minor but not major marriages seem to have developed sexual indifference toward each other. Another study that compared married first cousins in Lebanon who grew up together to those who lived apart as children and to unrelated married people found lower fertility and higher divorce rates among those married first cousins who were reared together.[31]

The Westermarck effect not only explains the mechanism through which incest avoidance arises among both kin and non-kin but also predicts the circumstances under which incestuous relationships do occur. Most cases of incest among genetic intimates should involve parents and children who were not attached during early periods of childhood or among brothers and sisters who were not reared together or are separated by a large age gap. For example, Kathryn Harrison, who wrote a piercing memoir of father–daughter incest, was separated from her father when she was 6 months old and had almost no contact with him until they began an incestuous relationship when she was 20 years old. Incestuous siblings who enter clinical treatment likewise were often separated during early childhood. Incest is also far more likely to occur between step- or foster parents and children they rear after the age of 10 years than among such parents and children who bond at early ages. Stepfamilies that form after children reach sexual maturity are an especially likely source of father–daughter incest. In a notable recent case, film director Woody Allen was vilified when he began a sexual relationship with his romantic partner's adopted daughter (who he later married), although the two had no genetic overlap. Overall, stepfathers account for between half and three-fourths of all father–daughter cases of incest, a far higher rate than their proportion in the population. Conversely, children who grow up with step- or foster parents since infancy do not have higher rates of victimization than those who bond with natural parents.[32]

Most cases of sibling incest also feature age gaps that are large enough to prevent close association during early childhood. Sociologist Diana Russell's study found that brothers who were involved in incestuous relationships were on average approximately 7 years older than their sisters. This age disparity is probably great enough to suppress the Westermarck effect (the same age gap occurred among married siblings in Roman Egypt). Most violations of the incest taboo thus occur where limited or no early childhood attachment exists. Incest among people who have been closely associated since birth is extraordinarily rare.[33]

Natural selection thus produced an innate mechanism toward aversion or sexual indifference to mating among people who were reared together as children. This mechanism arose to prevent inbreeding and continues to be transmitted through cues associated with growing up together.[34] Propinquity that begins before age 3 years is an especially powerful deterrent to later sexual relationships. Even children who are not genetically related but who grow up in "sibling-like" settings such as the initial Israeli kibbutzim or Chinese betrothals in early childhood do not develop erotic feelings for each other, even though their cultures do not prohibit—and in some cases even encourage—such sexual relationships. Incest among biological intimates typically involves fathers who were not attached to their daughters in early childhood and siblings with substantial age gaps who did not experience the Westermarck effect. The majority of "incest" occurs among family members who have no genetic relationship at all. Despite this vast body of evidence, which indicates that people refrain from incestuous relationships because of biology rather than learned injunctions, many resist accepting the biological basis of the incest taboo.

Alternatives to Biological Explanations
Anthropological Explanations of Incest Taboos

For more than a century, anthropologists have been intensely concerned with explaining the incest taboo. "Since the professionalization of anthropology in the nineteenth century," intellectual historian Carl Degler asserts, "probably the most fascinating, not to say relentlessly obsessive concern of students of human behavior has been the prohibition against marriage or sexual relations between certain close relatives." Anthropologists fiercely resisted Westermarck's Darwinian view that incest aversion was a naturally selected trait that was triggered when people were reared together from early ages. The claim that a central moral rule had a biological basis threatened the intellectual foundation of the emerging anthropological discipline. Following

James Frazier, one of the founders of the field, many anthropologists claimed that incest aversion could not be innate because if people naturally resisted incest, there would be no need to so strictly prohibit it. However, all societies have strong incest taboos. The existence of strong prohibitions only made sense, the argument went, if people were inclined to engage in the sanctioned behavior. Instead, anthropologists asserted that the incest taboo was humanly constructed to ensure that people transcended their natural urges toward incest and thus formed bonds with unrelated individuals that maintained group solidarity.[35]

Most anthropologists still assume that incest avoidance arises because of the *social* necessity to ensure that people seek mates outside of their intimate groups. They assert that norms restraining incest extend human connections beyond nuclear families and so bind groups together into larger social units. "Obvious," according to Leslie White, "is the fact that the incest tabus follow the pattern of social ties rather than those of blood." For example, French anthropologist Claude Levi-Strauss argued that people either had to marry into unrelated families or face the situation of being in permanent conflict with them. Therefore, men exchange women in order to build alliances with men in other groups, which in turn will enhance their own security. Incest rules thus provide the foundation for group unity; their roots are social, not biological. Without such rules, people would naturally mate with their close relatives at the expense of forming affiliations with other group members.[36] Sigmund Freud's writings provided anthropologists with the justification for their view that cultural rules arose to restrain innate incestuous urges that threatened the basis of collective solidarity.

Freud's View of Incest

Incestuous urges and their prohibition were at the core of Freud's psychoanalytic theory throughout his long career. According to Freud, infant sexuality was naturally polymorphous and could attach itself to any object, especially parents and, occasionally, siblings. "Psychoanalytic investigations have shown beyond the possibility of doubt that an *incestuous love choice* is in fact the first and regular one," Freud insisted. He maintained the view that society is only possible if social norms force humans to repress their innate inclinations. For him, the incest taboo perfectly illustrated this dynamic because it led people to suppress their most basic impulses. Boys' sexual longings were usually directed at their mothers, although their sisters could also become love objects; females desired their fathers or, less often, their brothers. Strict cultural prohibitions were necessary to counteract the sexual longings that children universally developed and to ensure they were never acted upon. Because these urges were so powerful, their cultural repression created lasting psychic injuries. "The prohibition against incestuous object choice," Freud asserted in one of his last works, "is perhaps the most maiming wound ever inflicted throughout the ages on the erotic life of man." Freud's declaration that children have innate sexual desires for their mothers and fathers starkly contradicts the assertion that people are naturally averse to such longings.[37]

In his first major work, *The Interpretation of Dreams* (1900), Freud organized his theory of psychological dynamics around the inherent sexual conflict he believed existed between children and their parents. Incestuous desires among children were natural and universal. His analysis of dreams indicated that boys wished to kill their fathers and sleep with their mothers, whereas girls sexually desired their fathers and so wanted to eliminate their mothers. "Children's sexual wishes," Freud wrote, "awaken very early and . . . a girl's first affection is for her father and a boy's first childish desires are for this mother." Children viewed their same-sex parents as competitors for the parent for whom they lusted after. Such incestuous and murderous wishes, however, were only natural at a particular stage of human development, generally from approximately the age of 4 years through the age of 6 years. At this point, most people successfully repress their sexual feelings for parents and then transfer them to opposite-sex peers during adolescence. Only neurotics maintain intense, although repressed, sexual longings for parents into adulthood. The incestuous conflicts of neurotics, however, were only more obvious and severe than those everybody experienced.[38]

Freud famously used the ancient Greek playwright Sophocles' myth of King Oedipus, which he believed illustrated fundamental and universal human dilemmas, to justify his conception of incestuous desire. Indeed, Freud believed that his discovery of the Oedipus complex in which children desired to kill their opposite-sex parent and marry their same-sex parent was the towering accomplishment of his career: "If psychoanalysis could boast of no other achievement than the discovery of the repressed Oedipus Complex," Freud wrote toward the end of his life, "that alone would give it a claim to be included among the precious new acquisitions of mankind."[39]

Oedipus was the son of Laius, the King of Thebes, and his wife Jocasta. He was abandoned as an infant because an oracle had warned Laius that his son would grow up to murder his father.[40] Oedipus was rescued and brought up in a different court. When he was grown, he met Laius—who was unknown to him—on the road, quarreled with him, and then killed him. Oedipus eventually became the King of Thebes and married Laius' widow, Jocasta. They conceived four children together without realizing they were mother and son. Eventually, Oedipus discovered that he had murdered his father and slept with his mother, and he pulled out his eyes to punish himself for these abominations.

For Freud, the tragedy of Oedipus was so moving because it revealed a universal human conflict:

> King Oedipus, who slew his father Laius and married his mother Jocasta, merely shows us the fulfillment of our own childhood wishes. . . . Like Oedipus, we live in ignorance of these wishes, repugnant to morality, which have been forced upon us by Nature.

Freud acknowledged the general disgust incest aroused, but he insisted that it stemmed from cultural prohibitions that harshly repressed the expression of natural desires. To him, the Oedipal legend showed that because innate incestuous desires are so opposed to moral norms, they must remain unconscious and evoke vigorous denials that they exist.[41]

Although Freud used the story of Oedipus to support his belief that incestuous desires were not unnatural aberrations but, rather, natural products of universal family dynamics, he seems to have drawn the wrong conclusions from this tragedy. Its central feature is that Oedipus was *unaware* that he was having sex with his mother. When he discovered the true relationship, he was horrified:

> Fathers, sons and brothers flourishing in foulness
> With brides and wives and mothers in a monstrous coupling;
> Unfit to tell what's too unfit to touch

Oedipus's repulsion at his incestuous relationship with his mother is so strong that he uses his mother's brooch to tear his own eyes out. His mother/wife is so disgusted at her unwitting sexual relationship that she kills herself. Far from indicating incestuous instincts, the Oedipus myth seems to show the opposite: the innate horror of incest between parents and children.[42]

Freud also used his interpretations of his patients' experiences to justify his insistence that incestuous desire is natural. His claims underwent a considerable change in the early years of psychoanalysis. Freud initially stated that a number of his female patients told him stories about close relatives, usually fathers, seducing them into having incestuous relations when they were very young. He soon repudiated this view, however, and subsequently asserted that these accounts stemmed from fantasies rather than from actual parental seductions. Freud stated, "I had in fact stumbled for the first time upon the Oedipus complex, which was later to assume such an overwhelming importance, but which I did not recognize as yet in its disguise of phantasy." The Oedipal complex reproduced perceptual, not experiential, processes. This reversal not only changed Freud's view that patient accounts depicted real events but also redirected the source of incestuous desires from fathers to daughters. The emphasis that incestuous instincts lay in children, not in parents, persisted for the remainder of Freud's career.[43]

How reliable were Freud's interpretations of his patients' childhood memories? Most psychiatrists and social scientists accept his revised position that children had erotic fantasies toward their opposite-sex parents. Many feminist scholars, however, believe that Freud's initial view that the cases of parental incest his patients recounted were real and not imagined was correct. For example, psychiatrist Judith Herman asserts, "He gained the trust and confidence of many women who revealed their troubles to him." In their view, Freud rejected his original interpretation because the fact that male adults, not female children, had incestuous desires challenged his traditional patriarchal values.[44]

Neither of these contrasting interpretations of Freud's cases seems to be accurate. In fact, patients did not spontaneously recount scenes of parental seduction, whether real or imagined, to Freud. Instead, he admitted, "One only succeeds in awakening the psychical trace of a precocious sexual event under the most energetic pressure of the analytic procedure, and against enormous resistance."[45] Freud went on to describe how patients had no memories whatever of these seduction scenes but "only the strongest compulsion of the treatment" evoked them. Most of his patients knew nothing about their supposed sexual activities with relatives before they entered treatment and, indeed, they vigorously *resisted* Freud's interpretations. However, for Freud, denials of incestuous longings provided evidence of their presence. Indeed, the more strongly people protested, the more intense their desires were likely to be. "By that reasoning," psychologist Steven Pinker notes, "we may conclude that people have an unconscious desire to eat dog feces and to stick needles in their eyes." In other words, there was no way to falsify his theory.[46]

Freud seems to have first developed his theory regarding the instinctual basis of children's sexual longings for their parents and then induced his patients to confirm his view. Indeed, patients opposed Freud's interpretations, which they eventually came to accept with the greatest reluctance, if at all. Freud scholars Mikkel Borch-Jacobsen and Sonu Shamdasani concluded, "It rather appears that [patients] retrospectively confirmed his theoretical hypotheses, only *after* he had suggested the latter by insistent questions, encouragements, admonishments and the reframing of reality.". The incestuous accounts of Freud's patients were more likely to be iatrogenic products of his own suggestions than either their own experiences or fantasies.[47]

The evidence from the Oedipal legend and case studies of his patients that Freud presented as support of his position that incestuous desires are common at best shows that such desires occasionally occur. They do not indicate that such fantasies are common, much less universal. Moreover, Oedipus and his mother were separated at birth so that neither would have developed a natural aversion to incest; even if Freud's interpretation were true it would only apply to the small proportion of people who do not experience the Westermarck effect, not to the vast majority who do. For the most part, Freud's work shows that when analysts are insistent enough, some of their patients will accept their interpretations. Psychoanalytic theories that assume that incestuous desires are natural (although culturally repressed) provide a thin reed to challenge the biological basis of incest avoidance.

The Ubiquity of Incest in Feminist Theory

The views of feminist scholars pose a third challenge to the notion that incest aversion results from biological universals. Until the 1980s, almost everyone assumed that the strength of incest taboos accounted for the rare violations of these prohibitions. At this time, many feminists began to claim that incest was far more common than was generally believed. The first paragraph of psychiatrist Judith Herman's *Father–Daughter Incest*, often considered as the foundational text of the feminist anti-incest movement, states,

> Female children are regularly subjected to sexual assaults by adult males who are part of their intimate social world. The aggressors are not outcasts and strangers; they are neighbors, family friends, uncles, cousins, stepfathers, and fathers. To be sexually exploited by a known and trusted adult is a central and formative experience in the lives of countless women. This disturbing fact, embarrassing to men in general and to fathers in particular, has been repeatedly unearthed in the past hundred years, and just as repeatedly buried.

The claims of Herman and others that male family members commonly force incestuous relationships on female relatives has gained widespread acceptance. If true, it thoroughly contradicts the evidence that genetic intimates naturally avoid having sex with one another. How is it possible to reconcile the feminist view with the assumption that an innate biologically based aversion ensures that incest among genetic intimates is extremely rare?[48]

Before the 1980s, only a few highly flawed studies tried to estimate the prevalence of incest. Alfred Kinsey, who provided extraordinarily high estimates of most culturally disapproved sexual behaviors, reported that approximately 1 in 100 fathers or stepfathers engaged in incest. "Incest," Kinsey observed, "occurs more frequently in the thinking of clinicians and social workers than it does in actual performance." Anthropologist Joseph Shepher's summary of the small, and often speculative, extant studies gave "liberal" estimates of mother–son incest at 4 out of 10,000, sibling incest at 4 out of 1000, and father– or stepfather–daughter incest at 1.6 out of 100. Herman studied victims of incest who entered clinical treatment and so was unable to use her data to estimate how often incest occurred in the population that did not seek therapy. In contrast to the claim quoted previously, however, the data she presented from other studies indicated that less than 1 percent of natural or stepfathers sexually abused their daughters.[49]

The best data about the occurrence of incest in the population stems from a study that was published soon after Herman's book appeared. In the late 1970s, sociologist Diana Russell interviewed 930 women in San Francisco. She defined "incestuous abuse" as "any kind of exploitive sexual contact or attempted sexual contact that occurred between relatives, no matter how distant the relationship, before the victim turned eighteen years old." Her most cited finding is that 38 percent of these women reported having been sexually abused in such relationships before they turned age 18 years. Indeed, when adults were taken into account, "every second female in San Francisco has been sexually abused."[50] These were far higher rates of sexual abuse than any previous study had uncovered. A closer look at this study's findings regarding incest, however, reveals rates among genetic intimates that were comparable to previous, far lower, estimates.

Russell found that percentages of any kind of sexual contact or attempted contact perpetrated by biological fathers, brothers, uncles, and male first cousins were 2.9, 2.1, 5.1, and 2.9 percent, respectively. A more restrictive definition of incest as completed or attempted sexual intercourse or oral sex between biological fathers and daughters or brothers and sisters, however, indicates rates of less than 1 percent for each type of relationship. Mother–son or aunt–nephew relationships were virtually nonexistent. This study also reinforces research that stepfathers are far more likely than natural fathers to perpetrate incest. Compared to natural fathers, stepfathers were reported to commit greater than eight times more sexual abuse, leading Russell to conclude that "stepfather–daughter incest is far more prevalent and severe than biological father–daughter incest."[51]

These findings actually *contradict* the assertion of widespread incest and lend support to the notion of strong natural constraints against incest among genetic intimates. They do not support Herman's assertion that "fathers in particular" should be embarrassed about how commonly they sexually assault their daughters. The high rates of divorce and remarriage that bring together nongenetically related stepparents and children as well as stepbrothers and stepsisters who lack the restraining impact of the Westermarck effect are likely responsible for any recent increase in incestuous relations. The relatively frequent prevalence of incest in stepfamilies illustrates a mismatch between very close physical proximity brought about by changing family constellations marked by parent–child and brother–sister relationships that are not tempered by biological restraints established in early years.

Although the findings of Herman, Russell, and other feminists do not indicate that incest among genetic intimates is common, they do demonstrate the dire consequences of incest for its victims. Intense trauma accompanied the rare occurrence of incest. Males initiated almost all cases; typical victims were females who tried to resist the advances of their stepfathers or older brothers. Victims experienced intense shame and guilt and a host of psychological and social pathologies. For example, incestuous experiences traumatized to an extreme or considerable extent the vast majority of victims of fathers (81 percent) and brothers (60 percent); only a few victims reported little trauma. Daughters who were victimized by fathers almost invariably experienced "fear, disgust, disbelief, confusion, anger, and shame." Incestuous relationships with cousins produced far less suffering: Only approximately one-third of women who were sexually involved with cousins reported negative effects. The families in which incest occurred were usually grossly disturbed and also featured other forms of abuse, neglect, and abandonment. Herodotus anticipated these dreadful consequences of incest for its victims in his description of the Egyptian king Mycerinus, who "conceived a passion for his daughter and violated her, and distress at the outrage drove her to hang herself . . . and her mother cut off the hands of the servants who had allowed the king access to her."[52]

Conclusion

Aversion to incest among genetic intimates is natural, universal, and biologically grounded. It indicates how biology can powerfully influence social definitions of normal and abnormal behavior. Natural selection provided humans (among other species) with an innate aversion toward forming sexual attachments with persons with whom they were reared. Far from desiring sex with genetic intimates, people are biologically inclined to feel repugnance about having sex with them. Because this aversion is innate, it does not need to be taught but is transmitted through cues associated with association and attachment in early childhood. The abhorrence of incest is a universal instinct that has not changed over time and is not subject to fashionable trends: Virtually all groups regard incest between parents and children or between siblings as unnatural and dysfunctional. Had he considered incest among genetic intimates, even the ancient Roman playwright, Terence, might have reconsidered his iconic statement: "I am a human being. I consider nothing that is human alien to me" (*Homo sum, humani nihil a me alienum puto*).[53] Social norms regarding sexual relationships among people who share less than one-fourth of their genes are far more varied so that the exact lines between normal and abnormal familial sexual relationships are cross-culturally diverse.

It is possible that future societies might abandon the incest taboo. However, it is unlikely that any relaxation of social norms would lead to an explosion of, or even much of an increase in, rates of incest. Were social definitions to change, humans would still be predisposed to avoid mating with those whom they shared close attachments or associations during early childhood. If a group did want to promote incest, it would be wise to follow the advice of physicist C. L. Lumsden and biologist E. O Wilson and ensure that brothers and sisters (and, one could add, parents and children) were raised apart while simultaneously promoting cultural norms urging them to procreate together.[54]

A major question for the study of normality and abnormality is whether the biological innateness underlying incest aversion exemplifies or is an exception to the relationship between human nature and cultural norms. Chapter 3 considers a practice—patterns of naming children—that illustrates the opposite pole of this relationship. Naming processes are purely cultural phenomena that have no biological underpinning, vary enormously across different groups, and undergo rapid transformations when social values change. If incest aversion reflects an almost purely Darwinian dynamic, choices of first names mirror the sort of exclusively cultural practice that Herodotus emphasized.

3 FIRST NAMES

Remember that a person's name is to that person the sweetest and most important sound in any language.

—DALE CARNEGIE, *1936/2009, p. 105*

Doubtless today's Brittany will name her daughter Delores.

—PEGGY ORENSTEIN, *2003*

Few, if any, phenomena are as central to our identities as our first names. They are, as Dale Carnegie noted, "the sweetest and most important sound" to us. Although people do not choose their own names, most cannot imagine themselves with a different name; almost all people maintain their given names throughout their lives. Names have cultural meanings but no biological aspects. While children receive names from their parents, genes have no influence on naming patterns, which pass from generation to generation through purely environmental channels. They display the diversity between groups and ability to change rapidly over time that Herodotus considered as hallmarks of cultural practices. Names are uniquely human—no other species has personal names (although, of course, humans give names to members of other species). Despite the fact that our given names have no natural grounding, they are universal. Herodotus noted that the Atarantes (a North African people) were "the only people in the world, so far as our knowledge goes, to do without names." This possible (and unlikely) exception aside, children in all societies receive names.[1]

Because naming processes are exclusively cultural, they vary widely across different groups. For most of Western history, names were narrowly constricted to preserve distinctive traditions so that a small range of names was applied to everyone within each culture. Names were important ways to ensure that religious, communal, and familial values were preserved across generations. The decline of collectively oriented societies ended rigid rules regarding names. Different naming conventions did not replace customary patterns. As Western societies came to be more individualistic, names became important ways for parents to assert the specialness of their children. Naming practices are now associated with *fashion*, a process that rejects previously popular norms and adopts new ones. Unlike customs, which are deeply rooted and change very slowly, fashions go quickly in and out of style and so do not persist. Naming patterns now change rapidly as names that are popular at one time become uncommon at another.

Yet, naming practices are unlike fashions in areas such as clothes or music that are tied to and promoted by commercial interests that profit from changes in fashionable products. In these other areas, individuals frequently discard old commodities and purchase trendy new ones. In contrast, parents name their children only once and after that time do not rename them to keep up with new styles. Another quality that distinguishes names from other types of fashion is that they are free; no commercial interests manufacture, copyright, advertise, or profit from any particular name. Financial resources neither help nor hinder people from giving their child any particular name. Because no economic group benefits from naming patterns, none promote one name or another. These properties ensure that individual parents have an unusual degree of freedom to give their children whatever name they choose, regardless of any economic restraints.[2]

This chapter considers how cultural norms operate in the absence of biological influences. Although names can be normal or abnormal, they cannot be biologically natural or unnatural. How names become common or uncommon and oscillate between these statuses thus provides a rare window for looking at purely cultural influences on normality and abnormality. Despite the nearly unlimited choices that parents have to pick any name they like for their children, the names they select strongly conform to cultural norms and socially structured dynamics. While people think that their naming choices result from their own decisions, they often turn out to replicate what multitudes of total strangers also choose. Definitions of what are regarded as normal and abnormal names reflect fundamental social processes related to tradition and choice, assimilation and separation, and conformity and uniqueness. Even in the most individualistic groups, names still reflect collective patterns of behavior associated with generation, gender, social class, and ethnicity, among other factors.[3]

From Tradition to Choice

Names reflect the social structures and cultural values in the groups in which they appear. The master trend underlying changing naming patterns during the course of the past two centuries in the West is growing individualism: the declining influence of extended family, group, and communal ties coupled with the increasing importance of individuals as the primary units of social structure and cultural values. During this period, naming patterns changed from passing on group traditions to emphasizing individuality.[4]

Before the nineteenth century, connections to families, religions, ethnicities, regions, and other collectivities defined individual identity. The importance of extended kin and communal groups dwarfed that of particular selves. Since that time, the primacy of family ties declined as individuals became more autonomous, geographic mobility increased, and the number of people living outside of familial households expanded. Cultural values reflect these social structural changes. Beliefs and practices that encourage the autonomy, equality, and dignity of individuals flourished. Naming patterns correspondingly shifted from reflecting collective to individual values. The result is that a far greater number and diversity of first names exists now than ever before.

Tradition

Customary constraints over naming practices were far more important in the past than they are at present. Before the nineteenth century, most given names stemmed from family history. Children would routinely receive the same name as a parent, grandparent, or godparent, ensuring the continuity of names over extended periods of time. When Herodotus wrote, for example, sons usually took the same names as their paternal grandfathers or fathers. The Greeks typically used just one name but when traveling would often add the place where they resided (e.g., Timon of Athens). In Ancient Rome, first names reflected only around 17 choices, although no legal restrictions required this small number. Romans commonly used first names followed by their mother's and father's family names (e.g., Marcus Tullius Cicero).[5]

The practice of using surnames largely disappeared after the fall of Rome. Before the fourteenth century, few Europeans had surnames; most were known by a small number of first names. Christian names could be supplemented by their occupation (e.g., Miller), physical characteristic (Little John), or particular locale (Alan a Dale). Most people lived in rural areas or small villages where this naming system sufficed to distinguish one person from another. Family names were generally limited to members of wealthy and aristocratic lineages. Surnames only became common in Europe around the fifteenth century when new centralized states required some means to systematize, among others, property, tax, inheritance, and marriage records. Anthropologist James Scott notes, "Imagine the dilemma of a tithe or capitation-tax collector faced with a male population, 90 percent of whom bore just six Christian names (John, William, Thomas, Robert, Richard, and Henry)." Most surnames arose from such administrative efforts at standardization and came to be passed on routinely from generation to generation.[6]

The first systematic records of Christian naming patterns stem from England beginning around 1500. They indicate that at this time, through the following two centuries and beyond, most people shared their first name with many others. Almost everyone had one of a very small number of names, usually drawn from traditional familial and biblical names (which often overlapped considerably). Between 40 and 50 percent of English children born between 1538 and 1700 received one of the three most popular names. Twenty-one percent of all boys born in 1610 were named John, and an additional 23 percent were named William or Thomas. More than 80 percent of boys were given one of the 10 most common names. Girls also shared names across generations. In 1600, nearly one-fourth of British girls were named Mary. Mary remained the most popular name in 1800, although by that time only slightly more than 10 percent of girls received this name.[7]

Before the nineteenth century, name sharing was of overwhelming importance. The practice of naming children after godparents, parents, or grandparents ensured continuity across generations so that few changes occurred over time. One study of naming in four English parishes in the sixteenth and seventeenth centuries showed that from 52 to 90 percent of children had the same name as a godparent. Sons were more likely than daughters to be named for relatives. This study concluded, "The most salient feature revealed by the close scrutiny of the most commonly used boys' names is a richly conformist tapestry of name-patterning, a model of clarity and regularity of use." Indeed, from 1590 through 1700, traditional English names comprised more than 90 percent of all given names.[8]

The initial English settlers brought this pattern to America. The vast majority of men in the new colonies were named after someone within their immediate family. In 1587, two-thirds of the men and boys in North Carolina's Raleigh Colony shared the most common five names. Among the 101 males, 24 were named John, 16 Thomas, 10 William, 8 Richard, and 7 Henry. More than half of newborn girls in the Massachusetts Bay Colony were named Sarah, Elizabeth, or Mary.[9]

Many names also reflected religious sources because parents often gave their children names of saints (which often coincided with traditional family names). For example, in sixteenth- and seventeenth-century England, more than half of children received names found in either the Old or the New Testament. Between 40 and 50 percent of boys and between 20 and 50 percent of girls were named after some figure in the New Testament. In some periods, up to 90 percent of names stemmed from religious sources. The strength of customary norms meant that the stock of available names was very limited. Because so many children were named after family members, naming patterns changed very little over different generations.[10]

Individualism

For most of Western history, tradition dictated naming patterns. Familial and religious naming conventions maintained considerable power into the twentieth century, when they began a steep decline. Conformity to customary naming patterns sharply declined during the past century and especially during the past 20 years. The weakening of extended familial and religious influences paved the way for parents to give their children a vast variety of names that express their personal preferences unattached to previous traditions. For example, although Biblical names (e.g., Noah, Jacob, and Sarah) remain popular, at present it is the least, not the most, religious parents who use these names. Biblical names have been disassociated from traditional values and are used because of their pleasing sounds rather than their religious significance. Divergence, rather than continuity, across generations has become the norm.[11]

During the course of the nineteenth century and accelerating rapidly during the twentieth century, the decline of extended family ties, urbanization, and the growth of a large middle class associated with greater individualism spurred a vast expansion of names. In England, by the mid-nineteenth century, various fashionable trends began to replace traditional naming patterns, especially for girls. Names of flowers such as Daisy, Violet, or Lily became common; slightly later, names reflecting precious jewels such as Ruby and Pearl emerged. Another example stems from a study of names in Richmond, Virginia, during the period between 1913 and 1968, which showed a sharp decline in the number of boys with "Jr." or "III" attached to their names. In 1930, white fathers who had such a suffix were three times more likely than those without one to transmit it to their male child. By 1968, twice as many fathers with a suffix terminated rather than transmitted it when naming their male children. Despite the decline of traditional naming patterns, common names continued to be the most popular ones through the first half of the twentieth century. Boys, in particular, preferred shared masculine names, whereas those with unusual names reported high levels of dissatisfaction with them. Names that occurred too frequently, however, such as John, lost some of their appeal.[12]

The rate of turnover in the number of different names greatly accelerated during the final several decades of the twentieth century as striving for a degree of distinctiveness came to guide naming practices. Names that had been common in the past became rare, whereas those that became widespread were uncommon in previous generations. In the United States during the 1950s, 63 percent of boys and 52 percent of girls received one of the 50 most popular names. By 2004, this proportion fell to 35 percent of boys and 24 percent of girls. Strikingly, not a single name that was among the top 10 most popular girls names in 1960 remained in the top 10 in 2000. In England, where the top 3 names had accounted for nearly half of all names before the nineteenth century, by 1994 the top 3 names for boys (Jack, James, and Daniel) were given to only a combined 8.5 percent of boys. In that year, only 4.2 percent of boys received the most popular name, James. Only 3.4 percent of girls were named Emily, the most widespread female name. The top 10 female names encompassed just 10 percent of all names, a comparable number to the single most popular name in 1800.[13]

A study of a small town in Germany during the period from 1894 to 1994 also illustrates the steep decline in the number of children named for relatives. Whereas one-fourth of children received the same name as a parent in 1910, by 1994 this figure declined to just 3 percent. This study also documents a decrease from 69 percent to just 28 percent in the number of names of religious origin. Conversely, in 1894, 32 percent of names in this small German town were unique, a figure that increased to 77 percent 100 years later. A Belgian study conducted in 2005 and 2006 found that more than 80 percent of students reported that their first names derived from sources that were unrelated to either family or religious sources.[14]

Once tradition ceases to have an impact on naming patterns, what factors do influence them? One influence lies in idiosyncratic social and historical circumstances during the period when a child is born. In the twentieth and twenty-first centuries, names of popular celebrities, including musicians, film stars, sports heroes, or characters from well-known movies or television shows, have become common sources of names for both girls and boys. Names that suddenly become fashionable can reflect an identification with popular cultural figures such as Dylan (after the singer Bob Dylan), Anderson (TV news reported Anderson Cooper), Madison and Trinity (after characters in the movies *Splash* and *The Matrix*, respectively), or Marie-Claire (after the magazine). For example, the popular basketball player Shaquille O'Neal received a unique name when he was born in 1972: In the 2015 NFL draft, 3 players among the first 155 selected were named "Shaquille" or "Shaq." After the television show *Gray's Anatomy* first aired in 2005 and became popular, the use of one of its main character's names, Addison, increased from 106th to 28th place among girls' names. New trends also develop around general themes, such as naming children after luxury products (Chanel, Armani, Lexus, and Porsche), biblical names (Rebecca, Sarah, Joshua, and Noah), or places (Paris, Brooklyn, and Dakota).[15]

In addition, celebrities create new pathways of naming because the names they give their children instantly become widely known and imitated. For example, after the singer Britney Spears named her son Jayden in 2006, this name soared in popularity. In 2005, Jayden was the 54th most common boys name; by 2007, it increased to 18th place and since 2009 has been among the 10 most popular names. However, because all potential names are freely available to all parents, regardless of their fame, celebrities are under particular pressure to find unique and impressive-sounding names for their children. Often, these names are so idiosyncratic that they are not promising sources of imitation. Recent examples include Blue Ivy Carter, the daughter of singers Beyonce and Jay Z; Bronx, the son of Ashlee Simpson and Pete Wentz; Apple, the daughter of Gwyneth Paltrow; Blanket, the daughter of Michael Jackson; Jermajesty, the son of Jermaine Jackson; Pilot Inspector, the son of actor Jason Lee; and North West, the daughter of celebrity Kim Kardashian and singer Kanye West.

The number of other people who are choosing a name also affects whether it will be adopted. In recent years, people have been able to use the Internet to uncover naming practices and can consult websites where they can solicit opinions about their proposed names from strangers. Perceptions of collective naming patterns are more often a force for avoiding rather than imitating common names. The overuse of a certain name drives others away from using the same name: Most parents do not want the name they have chosen for their child to turn out to be a cliché. At the same time, a totally unique name might seem to be too abnormal. New names generally are not revolutionary departures from common naming patterns but use variations on existing themes, such as slightly different spellings (e.g., Jayson and Jacen; Amy and Aimee) or minor changes in sounds (e.g., Jackson and Jaxson; Karen and Karin). People often try to identify a distinctive name that does not sound too different—one that makes a personal statement without being too adventurous.[16]

Variations in Naming Patterns

First names reflect fundamentally social processes related to tradition, conformity, and individuality that evolve over time. These macro impacts produce the general shapes of naming patterns. Historical circumstances, media influences, and avoiding names that are too common all have some current impact over collective naming patterns. , Much variation, however, exists within these master trends. Although fairly strict customary rules tied to preserving familial and religious traditions that governed naming patterns for most of history crumbled in the latter part of the twentieth century, naming remains profoundly tied to cultural processes. Factors associated with generational, ethnic, social status, and gender dynamics have powerful influences over the names that parents give their children.

Generation

Generational processes that are similar among the same age groups but that differ from previous and future age strata profoundly shape current naming practices. How up-to-date or anachronistic a name sounds has become a major influence on collective naming processes. The influence of tradition reverses itself as names that sound old-fashioned are scorned; names that are fashionable during one period seem out of date at another and so drop out of use. For example, modern-sounding names in the early twentieth century—such as Clarence, Francis, and Henry for boys or Ethel, Gladys, and Edith for girls—later became associated with an older generation and were viewed as antiquated. However, as older generations die off, the passage of time can bring names that were once modern and then out of date back into fashion. When the generation that had, first, trendy names and, then, obsolete ones, is forgotten, their names become potentially modern and reusable. Some names—for example, Walter, Max, Joseph, or Sam for boys and Grace, Esther, Sophie, or Eleanor for girls—that went out of style because they had been old-fashioned are revived and become chic once again. "Doubtless," commentator Peggy Orenstein predicts, "today's Brittany will name her daughter Delores." Yet, other once popular names, such as Elmer, Chester, Mildred, or Gertrude, have not (yet) revived. Why some, but not other, formerly common names are resurrected is unknown.[17]

Perhaps the best general rule at present is that most parents want to give their child a name that sounds up-to-date but that also stands out to some extent. Yet, because naming patterns change rapidly, most people do not know what others are naming their children simultaneously with their own naming. They are often surprised to find that choices they thought were distinctive reflect the same choices that other parents are making. Consider the following Facebook exchange that a mother who had named her first son Milo initiated in 2012:

> What the F? When we named our son "Milo," the name wasn't even in the top 200!!!!
>> Everyone trying to be different in the same way.
>> Asher was on our list, too. Argggh. Can't escape it!
>> Whoa! Every single name we were considering (Micah, Asher, Violet, Maisie, etc. etc.) is on that list—wtf! Is there no escaping the zeitgeist??
>> Same experience for us. Beckett wasn't in the top 500 and now it is 34!
>> I love that everyone is trying to be different the same way . . .

Even when people seek idiosyncratic names, they often wind up selecting the same ones as many other, unknown parents are choosing at the same time.

My own experience with naming reflects this pattern. When my first child was born in 1981, my wife and I named her Rebecca. To our knowledge, we did not have any particular reason—no one in either of our families was named Rebecca, we were not looking for a Biblical name, we did not know any other Rebeccas, and we were not aware of any celebrity with that name. Somehow, Rebecca just sounded like an appropriate first name for a girl that she, we, and everyone else would like. We had no idea that we were picking one of the most popular names (number 12) at the time. Indeed, by 1993, Rebecca was the single most popular name for girls. No lobbying organizations for Rebecca existed, no advertisements or billboards promoted the name, and we received no rebates because we used it. We just *liked* the name, not knowing that multitudes of unknown others had the same preferences at the same time. Powerful cultural forces influenced our choice of names, but we had no idea that they were doing so.[18]

The same phenomenon occurred when my next daughter, Jessica, was born in 1982. We named her after my wife's grandmother, Jessie, who had recently died, believing that her name stemmed from this familial source. Yet, although Jessica had not appeared among the top 200 girls' names during the 1950s or 1960s, in the 1970s it had, unknown to us, become the 11th most popular name. By the 1980s, Jessica had become the most popular name for girls. A similar process occurred with our third daughter, Stephanie. This name was fairly rare while I was growing up during the 1950s, ranking only 119th in popularity. By the 1960s, it had risen to 45th, and it was the 9th most popular name in the 1970s. By 1987, when Stephanie was born, she bore the 6th most common name. At a time when the Internet did not provide a window to see what others were naming their children, we were unwitting participants in the zeitgeist of the time.[19]

In 2011, Jessica gave birth to my first grandchild, Jackson. This seemed to me to be an unusual name because I had only ever heard of two Jacksons—one a colleague for many years and the other the well-known singer, Jackson Browne. I liked the name but thought it was somewhat odd, perhaps because it is also a last name (e.g., Michael Jackson). I was stunned to find out that Jackson was the 23rd most popular name that year and had climbed to 16th by 2013.[20] The "zeitgeist" seems to be a very powerful, if unconscious, force in naming patterns.

What accounts for the changing frequency of names across time? Just a few years before, few people liked the name Rebecca (or Jessica, Stephanie, or Jackson), but only a few years later it had become commonplace. The name's sound, which is identical in different periods of time, did not vary. Yet, its appeal had drastically changed. The same sounds that comprise a name at one time take on different desirable or undesirable connotations at another time. For example, "Jennifer," which was the single most popular name in each of the 15 years between 1970 and 1984, had tumbled to 191st place by 2013. By the latter year, Rebecca (178th), Jessica (163rd), and Stephanie (195th) had all lost their cache, which future generations might or might not restore. Some names become old-fashioned and go out of style while others emerge as hip and appropriate. The result is a huge and unpredictable turnover of names, almost none of which reflect tradition and continuity.[21]

Currently, girls' names that end in "a" (i.e., Annika, Ava, Ella, Emma, Maya, etc.) are fashionable. Boys' names that begin with "J" (e.g., Jayden, Jackson, and Justin) or end with an "er" (e.g., Asher, Carter, Cooper, Harper, and Sander) have become widely held. It is probable that in the future, even in the near future, girls' names ending with "a" and boys' names beginning with "J" will sound out-of-date and be avoided. The normativity of certain sounds is a purely cultural phenomenon that constantly changes at an ever more rapid pace. It seems impossible, however, to predict what names will retain their popularity in future generations and which will seem unfashionable in coming years.[22]

Ethnicity

Names not only reflect processes related to generational dynamics but also are important markers of ethnic (as well as religious and national) identities. Recent decades have featured high rates of immigration across national borders, more contact among diverse ethnicities, and the globalization of communications media. These processes have greatly expanded familiarity with other cultures. Some ethnic groups use naming patterns to reject old identifications and adapt to mainstream values; for others, names help maintain distinctive identities that separate them from the dominant culture.

One way in which the naming process buttresses conformity is when parents from new immigrant groups use names to help their children assimilate to mainstream identities. Migrants whose names drastically differ from typical names in a host society often give their own children names that allow them to conform to conventional values. Using names as tools for integration inverts their use to buttress tradition—assimilating groups reject their own traditional names and adopt ones that represent sharp breaks from their past. Conversely, preserving traditional names can be a valuable resource for ethnic or religious groups that want to maintain separation from the culture of host countries.

German author Thomas Mann's story, *Tonio Kroger*, illustrates how ethnically distinct names that stand out from conventional patterns can be profound sources of discomfort. The title character, although having a German father and living in Germany, has a Spanish mother who named him after her brother, Antonio. Tonio's best friend tells him,

> I call you Kroger because your first name is so crazy. Don't mind my saying so, I can't do with it at all. Tonio—why, what sort of name is that? Though of course I know it's not your fault in the least.

Mann goes on: "Tonio's mouth twitched. He pulled himself together and said: 'Yes, it's a silly name—Lord knows I'd rather be called Heinrich or Wilhelm.'" Tonio himself reflects: "Hans could not stand his name—what was to be done? He himself was called Hans, and Immerthal [another friend] was called Irwin; two good, sound, familiar names, offensive to nobody. And Tonio was foreign and queer." Tonio's un-Germanic name is a source of shame, embarrassment, and stigma.[23]

The power of names as sources of acceptance and rejection led them to become a prominent vehicle through which groups and individuals asserted their similarities to or differences from conventional identities during the twentieth century. In the United States, names allowed new ethnic groups to assume American identities, assimilate into mainstream culture, and establish their normality. In the first half of the twentieth century, most new immigrants used names from British, German, and Scandinavian groups that were long-standing and high-status groups as models for their own naming processes. Indeed, 19 of the 20 most popular names among these three groups were also among the most popular names for the remaining White groups that came to the United States during this period.[24]

Some immigrant groups, which emigrated from countries with naming patterns that were similar to those of the host country, commonly retain their former naming patterns. For example, Kevin, Patrick, and Brian or Katherine, Elizabeth, and Mary are common names in both Ireland and the United States. Other immigrant groups use names in the new society that combine sounds that occur in the country of origin and are also appropriate in the new country. Anthony, Joseph (Giuseppe), and Mark (Marco) are Italian examples.[25]

In contrast, immigrants from non-Western cultures bring naming practices that are often very distinct from dominant patterns in the host country. Because the sounds associated with most names are highly bound to particular languages, the names of immigrants can sound wrong and seem alien, un-American, and foreign in the new environment. In such cases, their names often stand out as highly unusual. For example, the five most popular first names for South Korean boys in 2012 were Min-jun, Ji-hu, Ji-hoon, Jun-seo, and Hyuun-woo. For girls, Seo-yeon, Min-seo, Seo-hyeon, Ji-woo, and Seo-yun topped the list.[26]

As a consequence, East Asian groups are especially likely to adopt American names at a rapid pace. Among Chinese, Japanese, and Korean immigrants, 12, 16, and 12 of the 20 most popular names, respectively, are also among the most popular names given to Whites. Americanized names help children (and adults) fit into their new society. One college professor reports,

> Although my father was White, my mother was a Japanese American and a native Californian who, because of her ancestry, was incarcerated in an internment camp during World War II. She named me Gordon Charles Hall because she wanted me to assimilate.

Similarly, after the September 11, 2001, terrorist attacks, a surge of name changes occurred among people with Muslim names who wanted to adopt more Americanized-sounding ones. Channels of normality run in a single direction: Immigrant groups commonly adopt names from mainstream culture, but the reverse process is rare.[27]

The surnames of immigrants also are likely to stand out from common family names in the host country. As with first names, people who change their surnames for reasons other than marriage almost invariably discard names identified with their original ethnic groups and take on mainstream names. Whereas a number of current Howard's were once Horwitz's, it is doubtful that anyone ever changed their last name from Howard to Horwitz. Such changes allow people to hide their ethnic origins and to seem more normal. Name changes are especially common among entertainers whose original names sounded too ethnic. For example, Kirk Douglas (father of Michael Douglas) changed his name from Issur Danielovitch Demsky. It is barely conceivable that the change would have been in the opposite direction.[28]

Using names as vehicles to achieve normality is not limited to ethnic groups. Transsexuals who have changed their gender from male to female or from female to male represent another example of how names provide pathways to assimilation. One of the most important processes involved in transforming one's sex is taking a gender-appropriate new name. A newly minted female stated that among the various transitions involved, such as changing one's voice to a higher register and learning how to shop for women's clothes, "the centerpiece was the name change."[29] Transgender people who do not already have androgynous names almost invariably change their names to conform to their new sex, either through adopting a totally new name (Caitlyn from Bruce) or modifying their original name (Roberta from Robert). In one celebrated recent case, Private Bradley Edward Manning, who pronounced himself a transsexual after his conviction for violating the Espionage Act, adopted the name Chelsea Elizabeth Manning.

Although ethnic groups typically use names to become more culturally normal, names can also serve as a way of asserting distinctive group identities. One example is found among Mexicans and other Hispanic groups, which have traditionally retained customary names after migrating to the United States—for example, Jose, Juan, or Carlos for boys and Maria, Isabella, or Sophia for girls.[30] One common Hispanic name, "Jesus," retains its popularity (106th overall in 2013) despite the almost complete avoidance of this name among non-Hispanic groups.

The most prominent illustration of using names to uphold distinctive group identity is found among African Americans during the past half-century. During the 1960s and 1970s, black names began to reflect the rise of a distinctive cultural consciousness. Some well-known figures changed their names to deliberately dissociate themselves from mainstream white culture. In 1964, heavyweight champion boxer Cassius Clay became Muhammad Ali. A few years later, star basketball player Lew Alcindor renamed himself Kareem Abdul-Jabbar. By 1970, a typical baby born in a black neighborhood received a name that was twice as common among blacks as whites. Just 10 years later, an average black name was 20 times more common among blacks than among whites.[31]

In the twenty-first century, the names of black and white children differ enormously. Distinctive names whose sounds associate them with black culture and distinguish them from those of other cultures have become deeply embedded among African Americans. Blacks are far more likely than whites to have unique first names. In 1989, 29 percent of African American girls and 15 percent of African American boys had singular names; the comparable percentages for whites were 5 and 3 percent. By 2000, more than 40 percent of black girls born in California had a name they did not share with a single white girl in that year. Blacks are not only more likely to adopt unique names but also more likely to use characteristic sounds that are associated with their names. "La" is an especially popular prefix for black girls (Latonya, Lakeisha, Latoya, etc.) but is almost unheard of among white girls. The use of apostrophes is also a distinctive aspect of black naming patterns (La'Shika, Sy'rai, D'Sean, etc.). Black naming practices are unidirectional. Whereas many blacks still use names that are also common among whites, whites almost never receive names associated with blacks.[32]

Social Status

Naming patterns provide a window to look at the diverse preferences and processes of imitation across different social classes in the unusual situation in which resources are not a consideration. Names are cost-free and available to everyone regardless of their income, occupation, education, or social position. Nothing prevents anyone from any social class from adopting any particular name. However, certain names become associated with people of different social statuses.

In the United States, some names—for example, Emily, Alison, Lauren, Megan, and Catherine—are associated with more highly educated mothers. Others—for example, Crystal, Tammy, Maria, Angela, and Michelle—are connected to mothers with less education. One subject in a Belgian study reports, " 'When you're called 'Cindy,' a student called Cindy lamented, 'most people assume right off that you are lower class and, more disturbing, probably a bit dumb.'"[33] Some formerly popular names, such as Percy or Chauncey, became so stereotypically connected to snobbishness that they are no longer found among the 1000 most common boys' names.

Higher status parents typically begin new naming trends. They try to distinguish themselves from lower status ones through using distinctive names for their children. One historical example stems from upper-class families in the United Kingdom who often used the mother's family name as the first name for a child. This practice diffused to the United States, where surnames such as Abbott, Lowell, Morgan, and Winthrop marked elite males. The use of surnames as first names has now diffused more widely throughout the population (e.g., Madison, Morgan, and McKenzie). Lieberson and Bell reported that names first appearing in the top 20 names of girls born to highly educated mothers show up a few years later among daughters with mothers who have less education. As higher status naming patterns become known, other classes imitate them and use them for their own children (e.g., Amber, Heather, and Brittany). To a lesser extent, the same process holds for boys' names (e.g., James, Asher, and Henry).[34]

To some extent, names thus reflect cycles that start with higher social classes and diffuse to lower class ones. This downward diffusion on the social class ladder, in turn, leads higher status parents to reject formerly popular names and to adapt new, distinctive naming patterns that are not identified with names that lower class parents have imitated. Once a name acquires an association with the lower classes, higher status parents will abandon it and seek out names that distinguish their children from those of lower status groups. These new names will once again downwardly diffuse and so on. This movement across classes goes in one direction: Names associated with higher status people are later adopted by lower status ones but lower status names do not become common among higher status groups.

Social class also affects gender-related naming practices. Higher status parents are more likely to give their daughters androgynous names that are used for both boys and girls. In addition, they gravitate toward girls' names that are less frilly and sound more serious. For example, Lauren, Megan, and Erin end with "n" sounds that seem less "feminine." Parents with more education are also more likely to give their daughters names that indicate strength, such as Elizabeth or Catherine, which are associated with powerful queens. Conversely, lower status parents are more prone to give their daughters names that sound more stereotypically feminine, such as Cindy or Tiffany, and that often have long *ee* endings.[35] Likewise, more educated mothers use less conventionally masculine names for their sons (e.g., Julian), whereas those with less education are more likely to use more traditional male names (e.g., Joe). Although social class is one important source of different naming practices, it pales in comparison to the powerful influence of gender on names.

Gender

Despite the increasing uniqueness of names, the traditional importance of gendered distinctions in naming patterns persists. Indeed, the most conspicuous information that first names convey is the sex of an individual. Different sound patterns are associated with female and male names, and the sounds of most girls' and boys' names differ considerably. During the first decade of this century, five of the most popular eight girls' names ended with a "schwa-like" sound—Emma, Olivia, Hannah, Isabella, and Samantha—compared to just one boy's name, Joshua. In 2013, all six of the most popular girls' names (Sophia, Emma, Olivia, Isabella, Ava, and Mia) ended in "a." The "ee" sound is also more associated with the ending of female than male names (e.g., Ashley, Amy, Chloe, and Emily). Boys' names with "ee" sounds (Stevie, Joey, Johnnie, etc.) are usually, although not always, nicknames reserved for the very young and then change to more mature sounds as boys get older (Steve, Joe, and John). Girls' names beginning with a hard "k" sound became popular during the 1990s (Caitlin, Courtney, Kylie, and Kaylee). Conversely, nearly 90 percent of boys' names end with consonants compared with less than half of girls' names. During the 2000s, all but one of the most popular names for boys (Jacob, Michael, Joshua, Matthew, Daniel, Christopher, Andrew, Ethan, Joseph, and William) ended in consonants compared to just three for girls (Abigail, Madison, and Elizabeth).[36]

The best way to test the gender-linked meaning of sounds is through studying unique names that have not been used before and so have no preexisting gender-typed connotations. In a particularly imaginative study, Lieberson and Mickelson asked people what sex 16 unusual names (e.g., Cagdas, Chanti, and Furelle) represented. They found that linguistic cues have strong gendered associations among both blacks and whites. More than two-thirds of respondents agreed on the sex of 14 of the 16 names: On average, almost 80 percent gave the same answer. Names ending with "a" or vowel sounds are normal for girls but not for boys (e.g., Tamitra and Shatrye). Almost 95 percent of respondents guessed that "Lamecca" was a girl's name, showing the powerful association of "a" endings with female gender. Despite the general weakening of rigid gender-role expectations, naming patterns remain strongly gender-specific with explicit sound patterns associated with girls and boys names, respectively.[37]

One gender-linked naming phenomenon that dates back centuries is that names for girls move in and out of fashion more rapidly than boys' names. An early example stems from England from 1570 through 1700 where a substantially greater turnover of girls' versus boys' names occurred. Female names were less enduring than male names because tradition was more likely to be perpetuated through male offspring. Relatively recently, a study of nearly 200,000 names given to children born in New York between 1973 and 1985 showed that whereas 45 percent of white boys received one of the 20 most common names, only 31 percent of white girls did so. Six percent of girls compared to 4 percent of boys had unique names. The rate of turnover in the 20 most popular names was also considerably higher for girls. To some degree, girls' names are thus more reflective of variety and fashion, whereas boys' names are more reflective of tradition and continuity across generations.[38]

The most striking aspect of gendered patterns in naming is the strength of sex segregation, especially for boys. Lieberson and Mikelson's study of naming patterns in New York between 1973 and 1985 found that not a single name among the 100 most popular boys' names overlapped with any of the leading 100 girls' names. As with social class, names that cross from one sex to another move in a one-way direction. Names first associated with girls almost never become typical names for boys. Names originally given to boys, however, do sometimes cross over to become names for girls (e.g., Shirley, Leslie, Hilary, Stacy, and Tracy). Parents find androgynous names more appealing for their daughters than for their sons. When a formerly male name does become associated with girls, however, it quickly diminishes in popularity among males (e.g., Casey and Dana). For example, after the actress Kim Novak became very popular in the late 1950s, the use of "Kim," a formerly common male name, virtually disappeared for boys. Androgynous names lose their appeal far more quickly for boys than for girls.[39]

The study of names that are not clearly gender-linked provides especially good insights into normal and abnormal naming processes. Examples include Jordan, Casey, and Dakota or, earlier, Frances/Francis, Marion/Marian, or Jean/Gene. Lieberson, Dumais, and Baumann studied the names of all white children born in Illinois between 1916 and 1983 to examine the degree of overlap in names for boys and girls. Androgynous names were those that appeared among the top 200 names given to both sexes. Three characteristics typify androgynous names. First, they lack gender-typical sounds that are associated with the name, such as an "a" at the end. Second, they often have distinct spellings for the same name (e.g., Tracy/Tracie, Adrian/Adrienne, and Jesse/Jessie).Finally, they are not usually traditional names and so lack historical connections to either gender.[40]

Androgynous names are very rare. Although the degree of overlapping names between boys and girls can theoretically vary from 0 to .50, Lieberson and colleagues found that the index of androgyny never exceeded .03 during an 80-year span. That is, no more than 3 percent of children who shared a name were of different sexes. Moreover, in contrast to other naming trends, this tiny level remained almost constant during this period. These researchers also indicated that androgynous names were unstable and over time became names favored by only one sex, usually females.[41]

The degree of gender segregation in names is astonishing. Indeed, a total segregation of the top 100 girls' and boys' names exists. "It is literally impossible," Lieberson and Mickelson concluded in 1995, "for any stratification variable to be *more* segregated by the naming process than is gender." In 2013, names remained completely segregated by gender. None of the 100 most popular names for boys and girls overlapped, and only one pair of closely related names—Gabriel and Gabriella—appeared on this list. One other pair—Kayden and Kaylee—feature sounds that are different enough to maintain gender-related distinctiveness. At a time when cultural conceptions of gender and sexuality are undergoing revolutionary changes, the gendered properties of names remain an outpost of tradition. The consistency of strongly gendered names starkly contradicts the vast changes that have otherwise occurred in naming processes. "Names," Lieberson and Mikelson conclude, "signify gender to a far greater degree than they signify race or class."[42]

The stability of gender-linked first names is even more surprising because it so thoroughly contrasts with the changing gender patterns of surnames for women. For most of Western history, women adopted the last names of, first, their fathers and, later, their husbands. During the twentieth century, a tremendous change occurred in the way that American women identified themselves after marriage.[43] Before the 1960s, women almost always referred to themselves as "Mrs. Husband's Name" (e.g., Mrs. John Smith). This followed the common English practice of eliminating the wife's family name after marriage, which reflected the dominance of descent through the male line.[44] During the 1960s, the referent "Mrs. Own First Name, Husband's Last Name" (e.g., Mrs. Emma Smith) became more common. In the 1990s, the term "Ms." often replaced "Mrs." so that a women's title would not distinguish between the married and unmarried. Only first and last names appear (Ms. Emma Smith). Nevertheless, approximately 80 percent of women still took the last names of their husbands when they married. Around the same time, hyphenated last names also became common—for example, Ms. Emma Jones-Smith. Such names were far more widely adopted among married women than married men. More women also retain their given first and last names after marriage (e.g., Ms. Emma Jones). The moniker of Mrs. Husband's Name, which was ubiquitous not too long ago, is virtually unknown at present. Moreover, although nothing prevents people from giving children the last name of their mothers rather than their fathers, this rarely occurs. In contrast to the thoroughgoing changes in the naming patterns of married women, the terms used for married men have remained remarkably stable (e.g., Mr. George Smith). The radical changes in female surname patterns make the stability in segregated gender-linked given names all the more puzzling.

Nevertheless, even the perennial sex segregation in naming patterns is beginning to show some cracks. Gender-neutral names such as Amari, Carter, Phoenix, Quinn, Reese, Rory, or Taylor are gaining popularity among both girls and boys. More strikingly, a number of Hollywood celebrities are giving their daughters stereotypically male names such as James, Wyatt, and Dashiel (to date, none seem to be giving their sons stereotypical girl's names). Because naming practices so closely track underlying social and cultural trends, the increasingly fluid attitudes surrounding gender identities suggest that the historically rigid boundaries between boys' and girls' names are likely to weaken in upcoming years.[45]

Abnormal Names

As societies become increasingly individualistic, the range of abnormal names shrinks. One exception is that people consistently avoid names that are associated with animals, such as Fido or Rover. Another is that some names become tainted when they are associated with reviled political figures (e.g., Adolf) or stigmatized minorities (e.g., Oscar Wilde). Some previously common names become abnormal once they are associated with disliked fictional characters (e.g., Ebenezer) or cartoons (e.g., Elmer and Donald). Parents refrain from giving their children such polluted names for fear that both they and their offspring will be stigmatized.[46]

Names associated with marginalized ethnic groups can also become contaminated so that members of other groups avoid them. For example, Jews who immigrated to the United States in the early 20th century adopted mainstream names such as Seymour, Stanley, Sheldon, and Morton that were popular at the time. Once these names became common among Jews, however, other groups stopped using them because they had become symbolically polluted.

Similarly, right-wing political commentators often use Barack Hussein Obama's middle name to associate him with foreign, un-American traits characteristic of alien groups. Names associated with despised ethnic groups can also become a source of ridicule, particularly during wartime. Indeed, nicknames for entire armies are often first names—for example, Fritz, Tommy, and Boris for the German, British, and Russian armies, respectively, in World War II. These names can spread to refer to all persons of the particularly despised group. During the Nazi era in Germany, laws required all Jews without obviously Jewish first names to take the middle names Sara or Israel for women and men, respectively. Names such as "Hymie," "Jose," and "Mohammed" are also commonly used as bullying tactics that associate a particular individual with stereotypical names associated with reviled ethnicities.[47]

Names associated with a different sex are also abnormal. One Italian court would not allow the name "Andrea" for a girl because it is a boy's name in that country, and the court renamed the child "Emma." Similarly, the German agency charged with regulating names rejected "Miatt" because it did not clearly indicate whether the child was a boy or a girl. Whereas girls rarely receive names linked to boys, it is virtually unheard of for a boy to receive a name that is associated with girls. Indeed, one of the last bastions of abnormality in naming practices is to give a boy a name that is associated with girls.[48] Occasionally, a name connected with a male becomes associated with a female. Consider what happened to popular British author Clive James, who was born in Australia in 1939 and named Vivian after a popular male tennis player at the time. Unfortunately for James, in the same year, the actress Vivien Leigh became perhaps the world's best-known actress, thus linking the name to female gender. Several years later, James' mother allowed Vivian to pick a new first name and he chose the more masculine name of Clive.[49]

The boy in Johnny Cash's song, "A Boy Named Sue," was not as lucky as Clive. His father named him "Sue"—"the meanest thing that he ever did." The consequences included his embarrassment when girls laughed at him and violence when boys did so. He determined to "kill that man who gave me that awful name." Once he found his father, the man explained that

> Son, this world is rough
> And if a man's gonna make it, he's gotta be tough
> And I knew I wouldn't be there to help ya along.
> So I give ya that name and I said goodbye
> I knew you'd have to get tough or die
> And it's the name that helped to make you strong.

Nevertheless, Sue concludes,

> And if I ever have a son, I think I'm gonna name him
> Bill or George! Anything but Sue! I still hate that name!

Sue's problem was that a boy with a girl's name is thoroughly deviant.

Names that are normal in one culture can become abnormal when a person moves to another culture. Consider the situation of Riad Sattouf, a French cartoonist of Arab heritage. When he lived in Libya and Syria, his Arabic names had "an impressive solemnity." When he moved to France as a child, however, "they sounded like *rire de sa touffe*, which means 'laugh at her pussy.'" When his teacher called his name in class, the other students would burst out laughing and girls would not date a boy whose name meant "laugh at her pussy." The result was that "I lived a very violent solitude." Riad Sattouf's situation illustrates how the thoroughly culturally relative nature of names can lead a normal name to become abnormal and a source of profound discomfort in another culture, especially when it becomes gender inappropriate.[50]

The importance of having gender-appropriate first names is so strong that it is gaining official recognition. As noted previously, people who undergo sex changes almost always change their first names to conform to their new sex. The civil rights organization Human Rights Watch promotes the right of all transgender people to choose a first name that suits their gender identity, thus buttressing the firm identification of names with one sex or the other. The European Parliament has issued a report urging all member states of the European Union to allow transgendered people to change their names easily, indicating that "the uncertainty concerning a person's identity has huge consequences and could prevent a transgender person from his/her full participation in society, education, employment, travelling."[51]

Only a few names are abnormal enough that they are formally subject to taboos against their use. The United States leaves regulations of names to each state, which very rarely change children's names. Great Britain, too, places no restrictions on parents, although officials can refuse to record names that they consider offensive. A number of other countries, however, have registries that list acceptable first names; parents are forbidden to use names that are not on the approved list. New Zealand's law bans names that could cause offense to a "reasonable" person. Italy forbids names that might "limit social interaction and create insecurity." A Swedish law enacted in

1982 states that "first names shall not be approved if they can cause offense or can be supposed to cause discomfort for the one using it, or names which for some obvious reason are not suitable as a first name." Rejected Swedish names include the retailer "Ikea," the rock group "Metallica," and the letter "Q." However, the most striking aspect of official regulation of names is how rarely it is invoked. Denmark, for example, has a list of 7000 approved baby names but only rejects approximately 250 names (e.g., "anus") of the roughly 60,000 children who are born each year. Parents often give their children uncommon names, but they very rarely choose names that are so abnormal that the state forbids them.[52]

Historically, people usually tried to avoid giving their children abnormal names. The growth of individualism, however, can make unusual first names signs of positively valued uniqueness. Indeed, the excessive frequency of a specific name can be a reason to avoid using it. Conversely, exclusivity is something special rather than something peculiar; rare names can be highly valued, especially in cosmopolitan settings that emphasize the virtues of nonconformity. Parents may believe that a child with an unusual name will become more original, creative, and interesting. For example, a study during the 1970s found that a disproportionately high number of persons listed in the manual *Who's Who*, which recognizes outstanding accomplishments, had unusual first names.[53]

In locales that value independence, even when parents try to make shocking naming statements, they find that their deliberate efforts to apply a strange name do not succeed. The best-known example is that of sociologist Dalton Conley and his wife, who purposely named their children to illustrate the culturally arbitrary nature of names. They named their daughter "E" and their son "Yo Xing Heyno Augustus Eisner Alexander Weiser." According to Conley,

> At the time we thought we were bequeathing to them our values of individuality, free choice, and the questioning of social norms. Perhaps it was also an unconscious social experiment: We forced our children's teachers and peers to see them as individuals by virtue of their names.[54]

However, Conley's efforts to give his children abnormal names seem to have failed. E enjoyed having a unique name and at age 12 years still liked her name. In naming his son, Conley tried to challenge the assumption that ethnic minorities should assimilate to mainstream naming processes and so deliberately gave his White child an Asian name (among others). Yet, even Yo does not seem to be that strange of a name. It has a nice sound, is used as a traditional greeting in many circles, and has no negative connotations. No one would typically be acquainted with the remaining six names (most people are unaware of the middle names of most people they know, other than their close friends). Conley reports that through the time he was a teenager, Yo had not suffered any negative consequences from his unique name. Indeed, Yo was featured on television, in *The New York Times*, and in the popular book *Freakonomics* as an example of a more general trend toward the use of unusual names.

E and Yo seem to be extreme examples of following the trend to give children distinctive names. Had Yo been named "Yolanda" (or "Sue") or had E been named "N" or "W," they might have had very different experiences. Yet, aside from such unusual (hypothetical) cases, which seem so abnormal that they virtually never occur, uncommon names have few or no negative results for those who bear them; in current historical circumstances, individuality is not a handicap. Paradoxically, at the same time as parents strive to give their children distinctive names, the growing tolerance for a wide variety of names makes it difficult for them to avoid choosing a name that will not be considered normal. It is increasingly difficult to find any truly *abnormal* names at a time when somewhat unusual names have become more of a norm than a deviation.[55]

Conclusion

Names illustrate how social norms that are unconstrained by biology change drastically over time and across social space. What is normal in one period becomes abnormal in another and vice versa. Naming practices also show huge divergences across cultures. When people move from one culture to another, the normalness of their names changes as well; although the sound remains the same, a name that had been normal in one culture becomes abnormal in another. The major exception regards the striking consistency of sex segregation in names, which itself is showing signs of breaking down.

Changing naming practices are not random but reflect cultural values and social structures. Whereas names were once ways to retain tradition, they now serve to signal distinctiveness. However, even as naming patterns reflect the rise of individuality and free choice, they conform to broader cultural patterns, as well as to distinct generational, ethnic, social class, and gender variations within different groups. Nevertheless, the processes that make particular names appropriate or inappropriate at a time when tradition has little influence are largely enigmatic.

Naming patterns and incest aversion reflect two cases of almost purely cultural and biological practices, respectively. The first varies widely across groups and changes radically over time; the second is universal and unchanging. Most norms, however, reflect a variety of interactions between biology and culture. Chapter 4 uses the values of courage and cowardice to illustrate how cultural norms are often in opposition to powerful biological forces. These norms extol the unnatural quality of courage and deeply stigmatize natural cowardly responses to danger. Cowardice and courage illustrate biological and cultural dynamics that thoroughly diverge from both incest aversion and naming practices.

4 COWARDICE AND COURAGE

I don't believe there's any man who, in his heart of hearts wouldn't rather be
called brave than have any other virtue attributed to him.

—BRITISH FIELD MARSHALL LORD SLIM, *2004, p. 5*

A man near him who up to this time had been working feverishly at his
rifle suddenly stopped and ran with howls. A lad whose face had borne an
expression of exalted courage, the majesty of he who dares give his life, was,
at an instant, smitten abject. He blanched like one who has come to the edge
of a cliff at midnight and is suddenly made aware. There was a revelation. He,
too, threw down his gun and fled. There was no shame in his face. He ran like
a rabbit.

—STEVEN CRANE, *1895/2005, pp. 56–57*

Henry Fleming, the narrator of Stephen Crane's *The Red Badge of
Courage*, facing his first experience in combat, observes a soldier
who had been full of "exalted courage." At a moment's notice,
however, that soldier's valor dissipated and he "ran like a rabbit."
Fleming himself, observing this soldier, "yelled then with fright
and swung about and directly began to speed toward the rear in
great leaps." Neither Herodotus nor Darwin would be surprised at
Fleming's cowardice. Herodotus described the case of Aristodemus,
who took advantage of an acute inflammation of the eyes and left
the Spartan army before a battle but did not return to it. Darwin,
too, observed how "the instinct of self-preservation is not felt
except in the presence of danger; and many a coward has thought
himself brave until he has met his enemy face to face." He went on
to note that when a man confronts some life-threatening situation,
his immediate instincts lead him "to gratify his own desires at the
expense of others."[1]

Both Herodotus and Darwin also emphasized how the natural
urge to save one's own skin and flee from extreme dangers such as
battle is one of the most reprehensible social behaviors. Aristodemus
arrived home to be met "with reproach and disgrace; no Spartan
would give him a light to kindle his fire, or speak to him, and he

was called a Trembler." The scorn heaped on Aristodemus stemmed from the demands of Spartan culture: "Whatever he commands they do, and his commandment is always the same: It forbids them to flee in battle, whatever the number of their foes, and requires them to stand firm and either to conquer or die." Another soldier who survived and returned to Sparta "found himself in such disgrace that he hanged himself." No less than Herodotus, Darwin understood that the power of social values is such that they can supersede even the strongest natural instinct to stay alive. He observed that all societies showed more esteem for courageous than for prudent behaviors. Courage, Darwin wrote, "has universally been placed in the highest rank" of values, but "prudence . . . which does not concern the welfare of others, though a very useful virtue, has never been highly esteemed." The honor that all groups render to the courageous and the scorn they heap upon the cowardly are so powerful that they often override the innate desire for self-preservation.[2]

Cowardice and courage illustrate particularly interesting relationships between what is biologically natural and unnatural, on the one hand, and what is culturally normal and abnormal, on the other hand. Self-preservation in threatening situations, which often involves fleeing from danger, is a basic biological instinct. Cultural norms, however, intensely shame men who act in cowardly ways. Conversely, courageous behavior where men sacrifice themselves to benefit genetically unrelated people is biologically unnatural but culturally esteemed. The inversion of cultural values and natural traits that cowardice and courage exemplify indicates how biological and cultural forces can operate in thoroughly divergent ways.

Explanations of Self-Sacrifice

The fleeing soldiers that Steven Crane portrayed acted naturally. All organisms, even the simplest biological creatures, strive to avoid dangers that threaten to kill or cause serious harm to them. Consider stentors, which are one-celled organisms that attach themselves to rocks in ponds. Around 1900, American geneticist Herbert Jennings showed that these tiny creatures instinctively flee when toxins are added to the water in which they live. Relatively recently, psychiatrist Eric Kandel won the Nobel Prize for his work demonstrating how *Aplysia*, sea slugs with extremely simple nervous systems, have innate mechanisms that lead them to withdraw into their cavities for protection when predators approach. Such findings, along with many others, indicate that defensive reactions to immediate danger are perhaps the most basic instinct in all living organisms. Conversely, steadfastness or moving toward danger without a high probability of overcoming one's adversary are not natural behaviors.[3]

Evolution created mechanisms in all organisms that signal danger and so allow them to avoid or flee from risks that can harm or kill them. Humans, no less than stentors and snails, must make appropriate responses to dangerous situations to stay alive. According to John DeForest, a soldier in the American Civil War, "Self-preservation is the first law of nature. The man who does not dread to die or to be mutilated is a lunatic." DeForest could not have known the reason for his "law of nature," but it is now well accepted that it develops because organisms that can stay out of harm's way are better able to live and reproduce than those that cannot. Moreover, survivors spread successful harm avoidance genes into future generations so that they become widely prevalent. Although different individuals vary greatly in their tendencies to become afraid when danger arises, people (and other organisms) do not naturally expose themselves to life-threatening situations. Conversely, the inability to become afraid in the face of danger typifies psychopathic, not normal, personalities.[4]

Yet, consider the behavior of American soldiers in the Second Battalion 502nd Parachute Infantry, in action against the Germans in Holland during World War II:

> But the machine-gun fire cut into them, sometimes setting the hay afire, sometimes wounding or killing the men behind the hay. These misfortunes stopped hardly any but the dead and the wounded. One man went down from a bullet. I heard someone yell, "Sergeant Brodie, you're next!" Another man behind the hay pile answered, "Brodie's dead, but I'm coming," and he jumped and ran ahead.[5]

Unlike stentors and snails, soldiers (as well as police, firefighters, and other first responders) run toward, not away from, potentially lethal situations.

Courageous behaviors pose a particular problem for evolutionary explanations, which rely on the innate drive of genes to perpetuate themselves: Consciously moving *toward* situations that pose a high risk to one's life cannot be a naturally selected, genetically transmitted trait. Under typical circumstances, people do not risk their own lives and the chance to propagate their genes. However, there are some situations in which biologically grounded traits can explain why people (among other organisms) would give up their own lives to save those of others: Self-sacrifice enhances genetic transmission when the overall survival of one's descendants exceeds the loss of one's own genes. Geneticist William Hamilton developed the general formula that shows the conditions in which altruistic behavior maximizes genetic transmission: r (relatedness) $\times b$ (benefit) $> c$ (cost). The closer the genetic relatedness between people and the greater the number of kin involved, the more likely individuals will act in altruistic ways. For example, female kill-deer, which are small birds found in North and Central America, pretend to have broken wings when they see predators approaching their nesting off-spring. These displays increase risks to mother birds but draw the predators away from their nesting babies and so enhance overall fitness levels. Another geneticist, J. B. S. Haldane, memorably noted that he would sacrifice himself to save two of his brothers or eight of his cousins.[6]

Shared genes, however, can only predict altruism toward kin. The puzzle of explaining altruistic behavior toward genetically unrelated people has been called the "central problem" of evolutionary theory. Biological anthropologist Robert Trivers partially solved this puzzle when he demonstrated how expectations of reciprocity lead people to act altruistically on behalf of non-kin. Humans are likely to engage in selfless behaviors when they expect that those they assist will provide benefits to them in the future that are equivalent to or exceed their own contributions. In most circumstances, people will sacrifice their short-term interests in order to maximize their long-term benefits. Indeed, the norm of reciprocal altruism is a foundational principle of human groups.[7]

However, neither genetic relatedness nor reciprocal altruism can explain why people would risk their own lives to benefit those who share no genes and who are also unlikely to reciprocate their sacrifice. For example, the popular movie, *Saving Private Ryan*, depicts a situation in which eight soldiers try to rescue one unrelated man. Two are killed during the mission, and four others die soon after. Hamilton's, Haldane's, Trivers', or any other genetically based formula cannot account for such actions. Tendencies to act in self-sacrificing ways that benefit non-kin without expectations of reciprocity are unlikely to be genetically transmitted.

There is a large gap, therefore, in evolutionary explanations: Why would people risk their own lives so that strangers can survive? Soldiers rarely make sacrifices for their relatives, are usually in their prime reproductive years, and render their own orphaned progeny more vulnerable to harm. Nor can they expect that those for whom they risk their lives will provide them with future benefits. Instead, nature leads humans (and all other organisms) to avoid situations that threaten death or serious harm to them. Therefore, as the eighteenth-century French philosopher Montesquieu starkly stated, "A rational army would run away."[8]

The natural tendency of humans to shun life-threatening situations poses a fundamental social dilemma. Reasonable people are unlikely to want to sacrifice their lives. Cowardice, placing self-interest above one's social duties, comes naturally to people; they must, however, learn to act courageously and risk their own lives to benefit some higher good. "No soldier desires not even to save his country, to be torn in pieces by a shell, made a disfigured and hopeless cripple. A man of sense is not built that way," wrote one veteran of the American Civil War. Yet, many perils pose threats to groups, not just to individuals. Wars, natural disasters, fires, terrorist attacks, and a host of other calamities create social imperatives to have enough individuals who can overcome deeply rooted natural tendencies to survive and instead move toward, not away from, danger. Because people are naturally designed to maximize their own safety—unless their sacrifices have net gains for the preservation of their genes—societies must find ways to *overcome* instincts of self-preservation among their members.[9]

Darwin suggested one way around this dilemma when he proposed a theory to explain why genes promoting self-sacrificing behaviors that benefit one's group might be naturally selected:

> When two tribes of primeval man, living in the same country, came into competition, if (other circumstances being equal) the one tribe included a great number of courageous, sympathetic and faithful members, who were always ready to warn each other of danger, to aid and defend each other, this tribe would succeed better and conquer the other. . . . Selfish and contentious people will not cohere, and without coherence nothing can be effected. A tribe rich in the above qualities would spread and be victorious over other tribes.

However, Darwin immediately recognized the problem with this group selection hypothesis:

> It is extremely doubtful whether the offspring of the more sympathetic and benevolent parents, or of those who were the most faithful to their comrades, would be reared in greater numbers than the children of selfish and treacherous parents belonging to the same tribe. He who was ready to sacrifice his life, as many a savage has been, rather than betray his comrades, would often leave no offspring to inherit his noble nature.

Moreover, Darwin continued,

> The bravest men, who were always willing to come to the front in war, and who freely risked their lives for others, would on average perish in larger numbers than other men. Therefore, it hardly seems probable, that the number of men gifted with such virtues . . . could be increased through natural selection.

No mechanism could account for how individuals with genes for self-sacrifice are better able to survive and reproduce than ones with propensities to avoid harm. Natural selection would only favor altruistic behaviors that perpetuate individual genes, not those that benefit groups.[10]

This chapter uses wartime combat to illustrate how cultural expectations about normal and abnormal behaviors can *invert* natural and unnatural biological tendencies. Only powerful norms can harness individual actions to the collective benefit of groups, communities, and nations. These norms have two sides: rewards for courage and shame for cowardice. Although courage and cowardice are respectively desirable and undesirable characteristics in all situations, in combat they become mandatory and catastrophic, respectively. Behavior in battle simultaneously arouses humans' most basic fears of death and serious injury and their desires to avoid personal disgrace, act in honorable ways, and support their comrades.[11]

Conceptions of Cowardice and Courage

Courage and cowardice have been perennial themes of Western thought. Classical Greek philosophers set the framework for discussing these traits. Aristotle, in particular, made the most lasting contribution toward understanding the ways that culture could overcome innate tendencies to avoid danger. His basic premise was that fear of dangerous things was natural and "even right and noble, and it is base not to fear them." Indeed, Aristotle considered people who were not afraid when in danger as unusual enough to be insane: "But he would be a sort of madman or insensitive to pain if he feared nothing, neither earthquakes nor the waves, as they say the Celts do not." Courage—acting nobly when fear would naturally lead someone to act otherwise—was therefore unnatural. Societies must somehow produce people who can overcome their natural fears and act courageously even though they experience intense fear. They do this primarily through social pressures that lead men to thoroughly internalize the shameful nature of cowardice and the glorious aspects of courage: "(I)t was the mark of a brave man to face things as they are, and seem, terrible for a man, because it is noble to do so and disgraceful not to do so."[12]

How do social norms come to override powerful natural tendencies and produce men who value courage and despise cowardice even when it means sacrificing their lives? The Greeks connected social norms to the most fundamental aspect of Greek self-identity: one's image as a man (the Greeks rarely discussed women). Indeed, the Greek word for courage, *andreia*, derived from *andr* or adult male. Men desired to win *kleos*—renown, fame, and glory—that motivated them to fight rather than run away. Basic Greek values involved demonstrating courage through willingness to fight, bravery in battle, and steadfastness during confrontations with enemies. The courageous man did not flee from dangerous situations as a coward or effeminate person would because he was imbued with noble ideals about how a man responds to danger. Indeed, the Greeks considered demonstrations of bravery in battle as the highest form of human achievement. The most honorable deaths, says Aristotle, "are those in battle; for these take place in the greatest and noblest danger."[13]

The other side of Greek gender norms was that cowardice, the overt display of fear in threatening situations, was a stigma that men must avoid at all costs. Inappropriate display of fear in wartime was the most shameful possible behavior, leading to ridicule, contempt, and unbearable loss of face. The connection of cowardice to the loss of manhood was an especially powerful motivator of courageous behavior. Shame, in particular, promoted courageous behavior because individual dishonor spread to their families, military units, and cities. Unnatural traits of courage were socially normative; conversely, natural feelings of cowardice became socially disgraceful.[14]

Aristotle probably drew some of his notions about cowardice and courage from early Greek epics. Consider *The Iliad*'s comparison of how cowardly and brave men faced battle. Cowards openly show fear:

> The skin of the coward changes color all the time,
> he can't get a grip on himself, he can't sit still,
> he squats and rocks, shifting his weight from foot to foot,
> his heart racing, pounding inside the fellow's ribs,
> his teeth chattering—he dreads some grisly death.

Although many men fear "some grisly death," only cowards express their underlying feelings and, accordingly, lose all social honor and standing. It was culturally disgraceful to display fear in combat, however natural it might be. Therefore, when men were afraid, their reputation and self-respect depended on concealment. The bearing of courageous men contrasted with the cowardly:

But the skin of the brave soldier never blanches.
He's all control. Tense but no great fear.

Courageous men lived up to social standards through controlling their fear. "Whoever is willing to fight the enemy staying in his rank and does not flee," according to Plato, "he, certainly is courageous."[15]

Social norms regarding courage and cowardice were central to maintaining personal honor. However, they also presented a dilemma for combatants: Ideals of bravery contradicted natural tendencies to act in ways that enhance chances of survival. Achilles posed this essential quandary in *The Iliad*:

I carry two sorts of destiny toward the day of my death. Either,
if I stay here and fight beside the city of the Trojans,
my return home is gone, but my glory shall be everlasting;
but if I return home to the beloved land of my fathers,
the excellence of my glory is gone, but there will be long life
left for me, and my end in death will not come to me quickly.[16]

Achilles' situation starkly sets a "long life" against social "glory."

Greek norms that exalted attaining such everlasting glory usually prevailed over living a long, peaceful life. In Achilles' case, the power of norms regarding comradeship overcame his reluctance to fight. He chooses to avenge his friend Patroklos' death at the hand of Hector, knowing that his actions will lead him to die: "Then let me die at once since it was not my fate to save my dearest comrade from his death." The social importance of maintaining one's honor and avoiding dishonor trumped Achilles' natural survival instincts.[17]

Achilles' antagonist, Hector, faced a similar choice. He responds to the pleas of his wife Andromache that he "not leave your child an orphan, your wife a widow" by saying the following:

All these things are in my mind also, lady; yet I would feel deep shame
before the Trojans . . . if like a coward I were to shrink aside from the fighting;
and the spirit will not let me, since I have learned to be valiant
and to fight always among the foremost ranks of the Trojans,
winning for my own self great glory, and for my father.

For both Achilles and Hector, the disgrace of acting dishonorably outweighed their natural desire to live and return to their families.[18]

Social norms are especially powerful when they tie valued actions not only to personal honor but also to the groups with which people identify. Courageous actions bring glory to collectivities as well as individuals; conversely, soldiers who flee in battle do not just disgrace themselves but also shame their families and cities. At the extreme, these norms even override natural tendencies to grieve the death of close kin. Consider the reaction of Spartan sons, brothers, and fathers when their kinsmen held their places in battle and were slain: "Like glorious victors in a contest they went around exulting." Rejoicing in response to the death of an intimate is particularly unnatural because most soldiers die at the peak of their reproductive years and are unable to perpetuate the genes of the same people (parents, siblings, and spouses) who celebrate their deaths. Conversely, cowardly behavior was the greatest possible humiliation for kinsmen. Because cowards threw away their heavy shields in order to run away, Spartan mothers famously insisted that their sons return "with your shield or on it."[19]

How were societies able to produce men who were willing to overcome their natural sense of self-preservation and act on behalf of group ideals? Aristotle emphasized the necessity of long periods of disciplined training that produced unthinking courageous responses. Ideally, such training began at an early age: "It makes no small difference, then, whether we form habits of one kind or another from our very youth; it makes a very great difference, or rather *all* the difference." The Spartans, in particular, emphasized the importance of early preparation, removing boys from their families when they were 7 years old and raising them in barracks. Because notions of honor and dishonor became such deeply rooted aspects of their characters, men could respond automatically to danger without giving way to fear. Courage, therefore, is more of a learned, acquired trait than a natural instinct. "Man differs little from man by nature," according to one Spartan king, "but he is best who trains in the hardest school."[20]

In addition to training that instilled noble values at early ages, men had to believe that displays of courage were undertaken for good reasons. They acted honorably and avoided acting disgracefully when they believed their cause was just and their actions righteous. Aristotle made this point when he contrasted the behavior of professional with citizen soldiers:

Professional soldiers turn cowards, however, when the danger puts too great a strain on them and they are inferior in numbers and equipment;

for they are the first to fly, while citizen-forces die at their posts. . . . For to the latter flight is disgraceful and death is preferable to safety on those terms.[21]

Unlike professional soldiers, who fear death more than disgrace, truly courageous men act because they know their actions are honorable, not from compulsion, the promise of material rewards, or passion. Devotion to a valued cause helps men to overcome their natural fears.

Aristotle also recognized the compelling power of small, co-present groups to invoke honorable behavior: "Men feel more shame before those who will always be present and those who pay heed to them, as both these groups have been in their sight." Group cohesion within small units of soldiers reinforced the importance of honor because of the fear of incurring the group's contempt for seeming cowardly. Finally, able leadership prevented soldiers from succumbing to their natural fears during battle. Military commanders must exemplify courageous behavior if their followers can be expected to act in similar ways. For example, Alexander the Great was renowned for seeking danger in battle. Later commanders such as Julius Caesar, who led his legions into battle wearing a flowing red cape that made him more likely to be seen and killed, were similarly glorified. In contrast, commanders who seem cowardly demoralized their men. For example, *The Iliad*'s hero, Achilles, refused to fight because his commander Agamemnon disregarded norms of honorable conduct.[22]

Aristotle and other classical thinkers thus assumed that fear was an especially powerful, hard-wired emotion that emerged in response to danger. They also assumed that it was very difficult for conscious, reasoned decisions to override the power of fear. Only strong social norms that shamed natural and esteemed unnatural actions could overcome the compelling force of fearful emotions. Men could learn to control their natural fears when social practices, institutions, and role models make courage normative and cowardice abnormal. These values, which persisted for centuries, cast behavior in extremely dangerous situations within a normative framework in which courage and cowardice were social standards that specified how honorable men should act. Brave men overcame their natural fear "because it is noble to do so and disgraceful not to do so."[23] Yet, Aristotle's analysis also shows how brittle the foundation of courage can be: If any of the elements underlying heroic behavior—for example, a valued cause, group cohesion, and strong leadership—is weak, the entire edifice can crumble.

Courage and Cowardice in Modern Warfare

The Greek template that defined actions in combat as indicators of honorable or dishonorable character traits had a lasting impact on Western views of cowardice and courage. It persisted through the nineteenth century and beyond despite drastic changes in the nature of warfare. Ancient wars were marked by hand-to-hand combat and were limited by what human bodies could accomplish. The industrial era brought about massive increases in firepower that created exceptional dangers for combatants. Nevertheless, social norms regarding the importance of steadfastness in the face of the enemy endured.

The American Civil War

More than 3 million Union and Confederate soldiers fought each other in the American Civil War. Approximately 750,000 men were killed, by far the highest toll of any war in the history of the United States. This war was one of the first to utilize modern weaponry, including heavy artillery, repeating rifles, and high explosives. In addition, physical deprivations associated with poor shelter, inadequate food, widespread disease, and punishing marches on foot tested soldiers' ability to endure. Despite the enormous carnage and physical hardship, understandings of courage and cowardice continued to reflect Classical Greek themes.

Aristotle himself could have written an editorial that appeared in *The New York Times* in 1861 after the surprising defeat of the Union army in the first battle of Bull Run:

> Indeed, the man who does not know the sensation of fear . . . can never be truly courageous. . . . The truly courageous man is he, who being sensible to fear, yet from faithfulness to duty and from self-respect conquers his fear and faces his enemy.

In contrast, the editorial condemned unmanly cowards who faced "disgrace far worse than death. . . . Men pity them; women despise them." Traditional understandings about the naturalness of fear and the need to promote courage and shame cowardice persisted throughout the war.[24]

The same factors that motivated the Greeks—"the complex mixture of patriotism, ideology, concepts of duty, honor, manhood, and community or peer pressure"—also inspired typical combat soldiers during the Civil War.

Although Americans esteemed individualism, self-reliance, and freedom, which contrasted with the collective values of the Greeks, concepts of liberty and democracy were particularly important ideological motivators for both Union and Confederate soldiers. The overriding value of honor and duty "in a word, one's *character*" made men stand and fight. One soldier wrote home after the bloody battle of the Wilderness,

> I am sure if I had acted just as I felt I should have gone in the oppo-
> site direction (i.e., toward the rear) but I wouldn't act the coward.
> I clenched my musket and pushed ahead determined to die if I must,
> in my place and like a man."[25]

Officers, in particular, had to demonstrate personal courage to win the respect of their men. One wrote to his wife, who had urged him to avoid risks, that "an officer has to be very careful of his reputation for courage. . . . When once the troops lose confidence in the bravery of their Commander, they necessarily have an utter contempt for him."[26] Union general Ulysses S. Grant "noticing the reluctance with which the men could be brought to the open embrasure, deliberately clambered on top of the embankment in plain view of the sharpshooters. . . . His example shamed the men into mak-ing a show of courage." Confederate general John Bell Hood went to an even greater extreme when he rode into battle tied to his horse after losing his left arm at Gettysburg and his right leg at Chickamauga.[27]

Avoiding cowardice was perhaps even more important than demonstrat-ing courage in motivating men to act bravely. "Civil War soldiers," historian James MacPherson notes, "went forward with their comrades into a hail of bullets because they were more afraid of 'showing the white feather [a sign of cowardice]' than they were of death." One veteran spoke of avoiding his temptation to flee from battle after his captain told him, "'Hurrah for you! You are one of the 1st Va. I know you'll stand by us to the last!' What could I do under such circumstances? Was I to run and prove myself a coward? No Sir!" Norms of masculinity that emphasized the importance of reputation, honor, and duty prevented the open expression of fear, which was still associ-ated with cowardice. "I do hope," one soldier wrote, "I may be brave and true for of all names most terrible and to be dreaded is *coward*."[28]

The fear of dishonor in the eyes of kin reinforced soldiers' determination to stand and fight. A typical soldier's letter home stated, "I cannot boast of much pluck but I have got my full share of pride and could die before I could disgrace the name I bear." Echoing the Spartans, he added that he knew his wife "would sooner hear of my death than my disgrace." Soldiers' letters often expressed their contempt for the cowardice of others: "What a stigma for men to transmit to their posterity—your father a coward!" The many soldiers who broke down psychologically because of the horrors of war were viewed as cowards: "[They] would have understood that combat stress reaction," McPherson notes of combat soldiers, "was a loss of courage, a loss of the will to go on fighting." The only legitimate wounds were physical, not mental, ones. Moral character still provided the only available lens for viewing soldiers' conduct in battle.[29]

Crane's *The Red Badge of Courage* provides the best literary example of the interplay between courage and cowardice. Its protagonist Henry Fleming's deepest concern is the fear of being labeled a coward. Before his first battle, Fleming wonders if he will run away and face everlasting disgrace: "It had suddenly appeared to him that perhaps in a battle he might run. He was forced to admit that as far as war was concerned he knew nothing of himself." He worries that "those qualities of which he knew nothing should everlastingly disgrace him." When Fleming enters combat for the first time, he yells with fright and begins "to speed toward the rear in great leaps." He feels deep shame because he could not resist his natural instinct to flee. His shame is especially intense because it mistakenly appears he was honorably wounded and has a "red badge of courage."[30]

Henry imagines the ridicule he will receive from his comrades and anticipates: "The whole regiment saying: 'Where's Henry Fleming? He run, didn't 'e. Oh, my! They would doubtless question him with sneers, and laugh at his stammering hesitation." He is in the fortuitous situation, however, that no one else knows he has run away and his apparent wound makes it seem as if he has acted nobly. Henry is able to redeem himself because he is the only person who knows he has been a coward. His self-disgrace leads him to return to his unit and to serve as its standard bearer, the most dangerous possible position. Henry notes, "There was the delirium that encounters despair and death, and it is heedless and blind to the odds. It is a temporary but sublime absence of selfishness." He charges the enemy despite knowing there is little chance of success. The book concludes,

> With the conviction came a store of assurance. He felt a quiet manhood, non-assertive but of sturdy and strong blood. He knew that he would no more quail before his guides wherever they should point. He had been to touch the great death, and found that, after all, it was but the great death. He was a man.[31]

The Red Badge of Courage illustrates the persistence of Classical Greek themes about courage and cowardice. It is difficult for men to act courageously, but they have no choice but to try. Fear in battle is natural, but the power of social norms to shame cowards precludes its open display. However, social definitions of honor are very fragile and can easily collapse, as they do when Henry gives way to his natural feelings and flees during his first battle. Still, his subsequent shame is powerful enough to lead him to fight courageously the next time he has the chance. Ultimately, cultural ideals that define normal and abnormal behavior in combat overcame Henry's natural instinct for self-preservation. Nevertheless, fear remains ever-present and might reappear at any time.

World War I

The moral framework that associated courage with the willingness to die in the service of one's country and cowardice with craven self-interest persisted through the early stages of World War I. This war featured unprecedented firepower, automatic weaponry, and new forms of killing such as poison gas and aerial attacks that greatly increased chances of death and disabling wounds. Erich Maria Remarque's novel, *All Quiet on the Western Front*, vividly portrays life at the front, where "we see men living with their skulls blown open; we see soldiers run with their two feet cut off, they stagger on their splintered stumps into the next shell-hole; . . . we see men without mouths, without jaws, without faces."[32] The war produced previously unimaginable numbers of casualties. At the battle of Passchendaele, for example, 370,000 British soldiers alone died or were wounded. In just 1 day at the Somme, 60,000 of 110,000 attacking British soldiers were killed. By the time the war ended in 1918, both sides had lost a total of 8.5 million men. The war was by far the worst slaughter the world had ever witnessed: Its carnage began to transform traditional notions of courage and cowardice.

Great enthusiasm marked the initiation of World War I. In Britain, men rushed to enlist, showing great national cohesion, self-sacrifice, and patriotism. Rupert Brooke, perhaps the most famous poet of this war, illustrated the prevailing attitude when he wrote the following in 1915 (the same year he died in combat):

> If I should die, think only this of me:
> That there's some corner of a foreign field
> That is forever England.

War age men who stayed out of the military were given white feathers as marks of their cowardice. Those who could not join the military often felt deep shame, as one extreme British case demonstrated:

> At an inquest on the body of Arthur Sydney Evelyn Annesley, aged 49, formerly a captain in the Rifle Brigade, who committed suicide by flinging himself under a heavy van at Pimlico, the Coroner stated that worry caused by the feeling that he was not going to be accepted for service led him to take his life.

Likewise, German youth enlisted because "even one's parents were ready with the word 'coward' for anyone who didn't enlist."[33]

The first battles of the war exemplified traditional notions of courage and cowardice. One poem from the time recounts how a British regiment from Surrey advanced toward the German lines following leaders who dropped footballs:

> On through the hail of slaughter,
> Where gallant comrades fall,
> Where blood is poured like water,
> They drive the trickling ball.
> The fear of death before them
> Is but an empty name.
> True to the land that bore them—
> The SURREYS play the game.

The highest priority in battle remained upholding one's reputation for courage in the eyes of one's peers. Conversely, the relatively small number of soldiers who ran away or refused to fight were not only shamed but also often shot by their own army. Douglas Haig, commander of the British forces, ordered "every position must be held to the last man. There must be no retirement. With our backs to the wall and believing in the justice of our cause, each one must fight on to the end."[34]

However, a new battlefield experience that challenged traditional views of courage and cowardice arose during World War I. The war came to feature trench warfare, in which soldiers had to endure fearsome shell attacks with little ability to take individual action. Soldiers passively faced heavy artillery bombardments for long periods of time without engaging the enemy; they could only try to withstand the salvoes and hope that their own artillery would retaliate. The control of fear became more important than ever.

One soldier noted, "Fear is many-faceted and has many subtle nuances but the terror and desperation endured under heavy shelling are by far the most unbearable." The conditions of trench warfare inevitably changed definitions of courage. "The strongest, fittest, most courageous soldier," military historian Edward Madigan notes, "was just as vulnerable to the threat of death or serious injury as his weakest comrade." Without the possibility of taking action, endurance replaced courage as soldiers' central aspiration. The general exhaustion, depletion, and collapse that prolonged periods of trench warfare produced threatened traditional notions of courageous actions.[35]

As the war ground on, the motivating power of ideals lost its force, and deeply rooted cynicism about the war took root. Paul Baumer, the protagonist of *All Quiet on the Western Front*, soon discovers the way that the horrors of battle could overcome noble sentiments: "While [the older generation] continued to write and talk, we saw the wounded and dying. While they taught that duty to one's country is the greatest thing, we already knew that death-throes are stronger." As belief in any higher cause dissipated, one's comrades were the only resource soldiers possessed that helped them resist the natural terrors of combat. Baumer notes how military training led to the renunciation of personality and "awakened in us a strong, practical sense of esprit de corps, which in the field developed into the finest thing that arose out of the war—comradeship." His comrades

> are more to me than life, these voices, they are more than motherliness and more than fear; they are the strongest, most comforting thing there is anywhere: They are the voices of my comrades. I am no longer a shuddering speck of existence, alone in the darkness; I belong to them and they to me, we all share the same fear and the same life.

The solidarity with his small unit allows Baumer to remain steadfast in the face of enemy fire: "You must, it is your comrades, it is not any idiotic command." However, Baumer also knows how fragile this bond is:

> (A) man perceives with alarm how slight is the support, how thin the boundary that divides him from the darkness. We are little flames poorly sheltered by frail walls against the storm of dissolution and madness, in which we flicker and sometimes almost go out.

A new frame was emerging to understand and deal with the massive number of psychological casualties that World War I produced.[36]

An Illness Frame Emerges

Combat experiences during World War I produced the first cracks in the frame of using character to judge a soldier's actions in battle. Despite the massive number of casualties, as stalemates in battle became commonplace, morale on both sides plunged. Ideals could no longer motivate courageous behavior, cynicism about the war grew, and fear began to overcome the will to fight. The war produced a sudden, unexpected, and huge number of physically healthy soldiers who had psychological wounds. British medical units alone treated tens of thousands of psychic cases. "In this impossible situation," Didier Fassin and Richard Rechtman observed, "where death either through bravery or through desertion seemed inevitable, evacuation on medical grounds was often the only way out."[37]

Initial conceptions of the reasons why soldiers developed psychic symptoms focused on how the shock from exploding shells damaged the nervous system with resulting "shell shock." The term stuck, despite the fact that many affected soldiers had not been near exploding shells but instead suffered from debilitating fear and horror. Most officers and doctors continued to view soldiers who displayed weakness or experienced psychic breakdowns as quitters, exploiters, and malingerers who were "more unworthy than ill." The psychically wounded were grouped with cowards and distinguished from those who suffered from honorable bodily wounds. Psychological damage represented cowardice, which could only be overcome through harsh discipline. "If a man lets his comrades down he ought to be shot. If he's a loony, so much the better," one army neurologist asserted.[38]

Most psychiatrists at the time emphasized how only soldiers with already weak characters were prone to break down in combat. Prominent military physician Lord Moran insisted

> now that I have put aside those who were frightened before they heard a shot, who limped into war half-men, and those who were undone because they were hurt in mind or body, let me ask once more: Can war in time make any man a coward? My answer is that these men apart, the last war most signally failed to turn men of sound stock into cowards.

Normal men who were "of sound stock" did not break down in combat: Only the "frightened," "half-men," and the "undone" were subject to psychological collapse. Lord Moran also noted the general cultural changes that he believed produced men who were more likely than in the past to display cowardly behavior, observing, "Men suffered more in [World War I] not because it was more terrible but because they were more sensitive." He attributed this sensitivity to a more individualistic civilian culture, which no longer idealized men who would willingly die nobly for a higher cause but instead demanded that soldiers be seen as individuals with minds of their own.[39]

The central role of military psychiatrists was to detect malingerers who used their conditions to escape from combat into the safe confines of the hospital. They declared that providing good treatment and compensation to the psychically wounded would reinforce and worsen the condition:

> But there can be no doubt that in an overwhelming proportion of cases, these patients succumb to "shock" because they get something out of it. To give them this reward is not ultimately a benefit to them because it encourages the weaker tendencies in their character. The nation cannot call on its citizens for courage and sacrifice and, the same time, state by implication that an unconscious cowardice or an unconscious dishonesty will be rewarded.

After the war ended, most physicians continued to resist the idea that external traumas caused chronic psychic damage and stressed the rewards that cowards received from diagnoses of shell shock. They also insisted that the loss of a pension posed a powerful disincentive to recovery.[40]

Despite the persistence of a frame that emphasized honorable and dishonorable character traits, a new way of thinking about behavior under extremely dangerous conditions began to emerge among a few physicians. This minority maintained that the horrors of combat, not individual character, led soldiers who were perfectly healthy before the war to become shell-shocked. "The war has shown us one inescapable fact, that a psychoneurosis may be produced in almost anyone if only his environment be made 'difficult' enough for him," anatomist Grafton Smith and psychologist Tom Pear stated in 1917. Most notably, military psychiatrist and anthropologist W. H. R. Rivers found no evidence of preexisting personal vulnerabilities and attributed breakdowns to war experiences. After the war, literary works began to portray characters that were deeply affected by persistent shell shock. A well-known example is Virginia Woolf's *Mrs. Dalloway*, which depicts a World War I veteran, Septimus Smith, as a psychological casualty of the war who displayed symptoms such as numbness, intrusive memories of traumatic combat experiences, and hallucinations of the death of a comrade.[41]

In the United States, prominent psychiatrist Thomas Salmon promoted the view that veterans who had succumbed to the intense stress of wartime combat were normal, patriotic men. He joined with the American Legion to lobby successfully for the establishment of a network of hospitals that provided services for psychically disabled veterans. The social scaffolding that was based on moral views of cowardice and courage since the time of the Greeks had begun to crack. The idea that psychic wounds could be honorable and not signs of cowardice had entered Western culture.[42]

World War II

The aftermath of World War I produced a cultural revolution in attitudes toward courage and cowardice. Tremendous cynicism emerged about the heroic norms that framed wartime conduct. The widespread carnage of the war coupled with its questionable results cast a pall on the sacrifice of millions of young men. Veterans wrote a number of best-selling books, such as *All Quiet on the Western Front, Goodbye to All That*, and *The Sun Also Rises*, that embodied a newly skeptical, critical, and disillusioned view of war, stripping the glory from combat and associating courageous behavior with hackneyed cliques. Ernest Hemingway's observation in *A Farewell to Arms* was emblematic: "Abstract words such as glory, honor, courage, or hallow were obscene beside the concrete names of villages, the numbers of roads, the names of rivers, the numbers of regiments and the dates." As Hemingway also wrote, the war was "the most colossal, murderous, mismanaged butchery that has ever taken place on earth."[43] Belief in any higher cause disappeared. The postwar generation lost its faith in higher values, whether spiritual or secular, which could no longer connect war to heroism, honor, and manliness. Instead, it featured its horrific, futile, and cruel aspects. The cultural framework that used courage and cowardice to override natural fears was breaking down.

Just as the events of September 11, 2001 (9/11), were to do for Americans 60 years later, the Japanese attack on Pearl Harbor overthrew the cynicism of the post-World War I period and revived patriotic ideals about appropriate wartime behavior. The media, government appeals, and widespread enthusiasm among the general public for the war revived traditional ideals of courage and cowardice. A poem written at the beginning of the war captures the initial spirit of soldiers who enlisted: "I was ready for death; Ready to give my all in one expansive gesture; For a cause that was worthy of death."[44]

At the beginning of World War II, most military physicians still considered psychiatric labels to be marks of cowardice and disgrace rather than of illness. They initially emphasized how constitutional factors such as psychopathy, mental instability, and individual defects led soldiers to succumb to the stress of combat. Military psychiatrist Harold Palmer declared, "Why should the neurotic be safe-guarded against the nervous breakdown, any more than the ordinary soldier is safe-guarded against the risk of wounding or death?" Commanders, as well, disdained psychic casualties. General George Marshall believed that the character flaws of psychically disabled soldiers led them to enjoy "a life of leisure with one great goal ahead: to wit, a discharge for physical disability, a comparatively highly paid job as a civilian, a discharge bonus, and eventually pension from the Veterans' Administration Bureau." Similarly, British medical officer Brigadier Morrison posted notices that asserted, "If you are a man you will not permit your self-respect to admit an anxiety neurosis or to show fear." Successful claims of mental illness did not just lead individuals to shirk their duties but also weakened the morale of entire units. American psychiatrist William Menninger noted, "If a soldier made a pretense of being ill and got away with it, every soldier in his platoon knew it, and the morale of each suffered accordingly."[45]

During the course of the war, however, psychiatrists became increasingly likely to display sympathetic understanding for the psychiatric casualties of combat and to emphasize the rarity of malingering. American psychiatrists "underwent a marked change of view, switching from their initial belief that 'a clear cut distinction [could] be made among men as between the 'weak' and the 'strong,' to the view that 'every man has his breaking point.'" In contrast to past wars, open acknowledgments of fear became more acceptable. High proportions of soldiers reported being so scared that they vomited, lost control of their bowels, or urinated in their pants. "I felt nauseated," one marine reported, "and feared that my bladder would surely empty itself and reveal me to be the coward I was." Such symptoms flew in the face of traditional conceptions of manliness. Nevertheless, most soldiers, as well as psychiatrists, came to take the view that psychological breakdowns were genuine diseases and not signs of cowardice.[46]

Physicians began to emphasize how, regardless of individual qualities, remaining in highly stressful situations of danger for prolonged periods of time led nearly all soldiers to have severe symptoms of anxiety or to break down completely. For example, even Lord Moran came to hold the view that each person had a finite amount of courage, which was constantly drained in combat:

Courage is will-power, whereof no man has an unlimited stock; and when in war it is used up, he is finished. A man's courage is his capital and he is always spending. The call on the bank may be only the daily drain of the front line or it may be a sudden draft which threatens to close the account.[47]

Moran's concept, among others, transformed courage and cowardice from aspects of character to ones of circumstances. *All* men would eventually break down if the stress of combat was intense or prolonged enough. Appeals to higher values such as patriotism, democracy, or religion no longer protected soldiers from succumbing to psychic collapse.

Psychiatrist John Appel's research showed that after a long enough period of combat—on average 88 days—even the most courageous soldier would collapse. During the Guadalcanal campaign in the summer and fall of 1942, psychiatric cases accounted for approximately 40 percent of all casualties; in some divisions, this rate was nearly 90 percent. In the Burma campaign of 1942–1943, entire units of the British army succumbed to psychoneuroses. In conformity to human nature, but in contrast to thousands of years of writing about human character, psychic breakdowns after extended periods of combat came to be viewed as natural.[48]

Military psychiatrists Roy Swank and Walter Marchand developed the concept of "combat exhaustion," which was marked by heart palpitations, vasomotor instability, tremors, intense fear and anxiety, and, eventually, hopelessness. However, they considered this condition to be a normal, not a pathological, response to wartime circumstances and, in particular, to the length of the period of combat. Swank and Marchand clearly separated soldiers who broke down because of combat exhaustion from the cowardly, noting that men who developed combat neuroses were "stable and willing," in contrast to cowards, who were "unstable and unwilling." They concluded: "One thing alone seems to be certain: Practically all infantry soldiers suffer from a neurotic reaction eventually if they are subjected to the stress of modern combat continuously and long enough." Indeed, they estimated that less than 2 percent of soldiers can stand combat for long periods of time and noted that "it is interesting that aggressive psychopathic personalities, who were poorly disciplined before combat" comprise this small minority. Much like Aristotle's Celts, these 2 percent were overconfident, believed they were immune from danger, exposed themselves unnecessarily, and were especially aggressive in battle. Unsurprisingly, most were killed. Views of courage and cowardice had radically altered: Breakdowns after extended periods of combat were normal, whereas soldiers who could withstand combat for inordinate periods of time were psychopaths.[49]

The view that combat neuroses could be statistically normal represented a profound moral shift. The fact that so many soldiers broke down during combat made it difficult to blame them for their conditions. It both divorced labels of mental illness from cowardice and largely removed the stigma of these labels. For example, after two hospitalized soldier told General George Patton that they were psychiatric casualties, Patton slapped them across the face and called them cowards. By this time (1943), however, conceptions of cowardice had changed to the extent that Patton was relieved of his command. This incident is telling not so much because Patton considered these soldiers to be cowards but because he was punished for his behavior. It was no longer acceptable for officers to disparage the motives of soldiers who psychologically broke down in combat. Indeed, military policy during World War II encouraged soldiers to understand and even tolerate the cowardice of their comrades.[50]

Courage and Cowardice After World War II

World War II accelerated the transformation from viewing psychic casualties of combat as cowards to regarding them as results of traumatic wartime conditions. Compassionate attitudes toward psychological injuries marked the postwar climate. For example, noted film director John Huston produced a documentary, *Let There Be Light*, which sympathetically portrayed the psychiatrically wounded and the mental health professionals who treated them. Huston equated psychologically disabled soldiers with physically wounded ones. Popular novels about the war, such as Joseph Heller's *Catch-22*, also captured new views of courage and cowardice:

> There was only one catch and that was Catch-22, which specified that a concern for one's safety in the face of dangers that were real and immediate was the process of a rational mind. Orr was crazy and could be grounded. All he had to do was ask; and as soon as he did, he would no longer be crazy and would have to fly more missions. Orr would be crazy to fly more missions and sane if he didn't, but if he were sane he had to fly them. If he flew them he was crazy and didn't have to; but if he didn't want to he was sane and had to. Yossarian was moved very deeply by the absolute simplicity of this clause of Catch-22 and let out a respectful whistle.

Catch-22 merged Aristotle's insights about the naturalness of fear and unnaturalness of courage with the irreverent culture of the 1960s. The military could not allow soldiers to act naturally, which would lead them to avoid combat. Instead, it promoted the unnatural behavior of performing life-threatening actions. The widespread mocking of the ironic relationship between courage and cowardice, on the one hand, and natural and unnatural behaviors, on the other hand, further shook the social foundation of these traits. Ideals that had attached personal sacrifice to collective values since the time of the Ancient Greeks were dissolving.[51]

The generation of psychiatrists who served in the military during World War II took positions of professional leadership in the postwar era. They helped develop the first psychiatric manual for general use outside of mental institutions, the *Diagnostic and Statistical Manual of Mental Disorders* (*DSM*) (1952). It included the first diagnosis—transient situational personality disorders—that recognized traumas stemming from extreme situations such as combat as mental illnesses. This diagnosis encompassed people with no previous history of psychological problems who developed acute symptoms as a way of adjusting to an overwhelming situation. The *DSM-II* (1968) changed this diagnosis to "adjustment reaction of adult life." Adjustment reactions were not long-standing character traits but responses that should "clear rapidly" once the person left the highly stressful environment. Among its brief descriptions was "fear associated with military combat and manifested by trembling, running and hiding." In essence, this definition redefined cowardice as a mental disease, although one that was not likely to endure. This diagnosis, however, did not fit the situations of veterans who returned from Vietnam during the 1970s.[52]

In contrast to the early stages of the two World Wars, the Vietnam War generated little enthusiasm among the conscripts who fought there. Most scorned the idea that they were fighting for a noble cause. They fought because they had no choice; their primary motivation was to stay alive. Widespread alcohol, marijuana, and heroin use helped them cope with a situation in which noble ideals had no resonance. Collective ideologies that exalted self-sacrifice in the name of some higher goal, which had initially motivated soldiers in previous conflicts, had little influence in this war.

Many Vietnam veterans faced problems of readjusting to civilian life after they returned to the United States. Widespread antiwar sentiment led them to be viewed more as victims of an immoral military and political establishment than as cowards or malingerers. The existing diagnosis of "adjustment reaction," which indicated that the condition would clear rapidly once the stressful situation ended, could not encompass the conditions of veterans who were experiencing symptoms many years after the end of their wartime service. The efforts of advocates who embraced the view of combat traumas as normal consequences of extreme situations led to the post-traumatic stress disorder (PTSD) diagnosis in the *DSM-III* (1980).

The PTSD diagnosis excised all references to character. Instead, PTSD was the natural outcome of the "existence of a recognizable stressor that would evoke significant distress in almost everyone." It was based on the environmental model of trauma, which assumed traumatic events produced chronic symptoms in otherwise normal individuals. The horrific quality of events themselves, not preexisting vulnerabilities, was responsible for resulting symptoms. The move away from character was complete: All persons who experienced traumatic events were prima facie victims whose sincerity was not in doubt. Cowardice was a moral impossibility. The new diagnosis transformed men who broke down in combat from cowards to worthy victims who deserved treatment and monetary benefits. Perhaps for this reason, PTSD is one of the few psychiatric diagnoses that are commonly valued rather than stigmatized. Psychiatrist Nancy Andreasen notes, "It is rare to find a psychiatric diagnosis that anyone likes to have, but PTSD seems to be one of them."[53]

PTSD now occupies the moral space where character once resided. One follow-up study in 1988 found that just 1 of 107 veterans of World War II met *DSM* criteria for PTSD. Other long-term studies found that less than 1 percent of several hundred veterans of World War II and the Korean War had a current PTSD diagnosis and only 1.5 percent met lifetime criteria for PTSD. Contrast these rates to results of studies that show that more than 30 percent of Vietnam veterans developed PTSD at some point in their lives (and more than half had some symptoms of this disorder). Researchers estimate that approximately the same proportion of veterans of the Iraqi and Afghan wars will suffer from PTSD. Rates of PTSD have thus increased *30-fold* since wars that occurred in the 1940s and 1950s. A new cultural matrix considers this condition to be a normal and accepted response to trauma that is thoroughly divorced from traditional conceptions of courage and cowardice.[54]

Several factors seem to account for why PTSD displaced courage and cowardice in Western culture as the major framework for interpreting responses to combat. One stems from growing individualism. Historically, soldiers tried to deal with their natural fears through tying their self-sacrifice to collective values associated with communities, nations, rulers, and religions. Modern societies, however, deemphasize communal values based on authority, custom, and faith and stress those that elevate individual rights over duties to a group. This process inevitably weakens the shaming power of cowardice and elevating power of courage that previously helped people overcome their natural aversion to danger. Although occasional exceptions arise, such as the response to the terrorist attacks of 9/11, the collective foundation that supported traditional notions of courage and cowardice has cracked.

The rise of feminism also helps account for the decline of the normative frame of courage and cowardice. For millennia, courage was intrinsically linked to masculinity. Cowards, in contrast, received epithets associated with femininity, such as "pussy," "sissy," or "pansy." Herodotus, for example, described how the Persian cavalry attacked the Greek forces, "taunting them and calling them women." The Greeks required cowards to dress as women for 3 days. Rising female status and influence moves societies "away from a culture of manly honor, with its approval of violent retaliation for insults, toughening of boys through physical punishment, and veneration of martial glory." Related changes in conceptions of masculinity provide more leeway for men to openly express emotional weakness. Moreover, they have made men more amenable to embracing PTSD labels, which resonate with a cultural climate that is more attuned to traditional female concerns with mental health and victimization than with traditionally masculine notions of courage and cowardice.[55]

Finally, PTSD is part of a growing trend to medicalize many forms of social behavior. Recent cultural understandings promote the idea that extreme situations lead to enduring and debilitating psychological consequences in the absence of professional therapeutic interventions. Psychic breakdowns under conditions of extreme stress are viewed as expectable signs of disease, not of weak characters.[56]

Rising individualism, feminization, and medicalization have moved conceptions of courage and cowardice full circle. The exultation of courage in wartime is a dying value in the United States that is largely limited to the South, some rural areas, and small towns. Filmmaker Michael Moore, for example, was met with looks of disbelief when he asked members of Congress if their children were serving in the military. Conversely, mental health advocates argue that troops suffering from PTSD should receive Purple Heart medals that were traditionally reserved for physically wounded soldiers. "The National Alliance on Mental Illness," its executive director asserts, "is drawing a line in the sand with the Department of Defense. Troops with invisible wounds are heroes. It's time to honor them." If Henry Fleming were alive, he might have difficulty understanding what sort of behaviors would be honored and what sorts shamed.[57]

Conclusion

Throughout history, combat has led to fear, horror, and terror. The self-sacrifice that battlefield conditions often demand is biologically unnatural. However, social definitions of conduct in wartime traditionally mandated that honorable soldiers behave courageously in the face of danger and not display outward signs of fear. In addition, these definitions intensely shamed soldiers who gave way to their natural reactions of fleeing from danger. In contrast to social rules about incest for which an innate biological foundation supports cultural values, cultural definitions of courage and cowardice overturn natural and unnatural behaviors in situations of extreme danger.

Because they have no natural foundation, social norms about appropriate and inappropriate behavior in combat are fragile and subject to collapse. Men are highly unlikely to sleep with their daughters, regardless of social norms, but as Henry Fleming found out, courageous intentions can often quickly revert to cowardly behaviors during combat. For most of history, the power of moral duty to some collectivity could often override natural instincts for self-preservation. During the course of the twentieth century and especially since World War I, however, conduct during wartime became less likely to be seen as honorable or dishonorable than as the expectable result of traumatic situations. A widespread view has emerged that men (as well as women) are weak and prone to have lasting mental damage after traumas. Notions of cowardice have virtually disappeared from cultural space, and those regarding courage are wavering. Social changes related to individualism, feminization, and medicalization have paved the way for the emergence of cultural norms that more accurately reflect natural and unnatural actions in combat.

5 OBESITY

In the midst of these temptations I struggle daily against greed for food and drink. This is not an evil which I can decide once and for all to repudiate and never to embrace again, as I was able to do with fornication.

—ST. AUGUSTINE

We do not see what complexion has to do with a man's fitness for an office requiring an active and a well informed mind; but we do see, that gross obesity, as tending to induce mental stupidity, as coarseness of feeling, might seriously disqualify a man for such an office.

—FREDERICK DOUGLASS

"Savages will eat gluttonously and drink themselves insensible whenever they have a chance to," a French food writer noted in 1825. In fact, the same factors that lead "savages" to be gluttons (and drunkards) are universal. Humans have a common biology that leads us to intensely desire food. Savory food has an uncommon ability to create cravings, regardless of our conscious intentions to restrict our appetites. Although different individuals vary in the degree of both their desires and their ability to exert control over their natural gluttony, nature designed us to crave calories. This is because for most of human history biological restraints on food consumption made no evolutionary sense.[1]

Our appetites developed within environments marked by fluctuating and, often, inadequate food supplies. Therefore, evolution designed humans to desire most sources of calories, to consume large quantities of them when they were available, and to store excessive ones as fatty tissue. Natural selection would have favored genes that promoted weight gain over those that were conducive to leanness. However, few people actually became fat over the course of human history because sources of calories were limited and extensive energy was required to get them. Environmental constraints led most people to be thin, despite their genetic tendencies to store fat.

In contrast to the scanty food supplies maintained over thousands of previous generations, modern societies feature abundant, constantly available, and inexpensive sources of calories. In addition, people no longer need to expend energy to obtain food or conduct other routine activities so that excessive calories easily accumulate. Central heating means that layers of fat are not useful in even the coldest climates; air conditioning eliminates the need to perspire. This mix of a food-rich environment with genes that naturally favor fatness has led to a worldwide explosion in the number of very heavy people. Moreover, cultural norms that promote thinness and stigmatize fatness exacerbate the resulting mismatch between human biology and calorie-filled milieus. This double mismatch creates huge tension between innate biology and current patterns of food consumption.

Obesity illustrates how environmental circumstances can lead natural genes to have harmful consequences. It results from an incongruity between an unprecedented social setting that allows for the satiation of human appetites and a biology that emerged under very different conditions of food scarcity and uncertainty. This incompatibility, however, is often mistaken for an individual pathology rather than an expression of human nature. Obesity also shows how our biological heritage can be the source of one of the most culturally devalued conditions. Norms about fatness and slimness for women resemble evaluations of courage and cowardice for men. Thin women, like courageous men, occupy highly valued social statuses that conflict with human biology. Conversely, fat women and cowardly men are products of natural genetically based tendencies.

Unnatural Appetites

Humans are naturally designed to crave almost all sorts of calories. Only a few exceptions to our omnivorous appetites exist. One unnatural type of feeding behavior is to consume fewer calories than are necessary for one's health. Unlike rising weights in modern calorie-rich environments, which result from natural tendencies to crave calories, extreme undereating is a dysfunction of mechanisms that regulate appetite. Assuming that an adequate number of calories are available, no physical health problems suppress appetite, or people are not acting in accordance with some religious, social, or political principle, intentional undereating is highly unnatural. Indeed, anorexia nervosa—the failure to ingest enough calories to maintain minimally sufficient weight—is the most fatal mental disorder, with an estimated mortality rate of approximately 10 percent. Despite the tremendous publicity attendant to anorexia nervosa, the best evidence indicates that this condition is extremely rare: Currently, about 1 in every 100,000 people between the ages of 10 and 39 years develop anorexia.[2]

A second sort of unnatural food consumption involves deliberately eating pathogens that can sicken or kill people. All creatures possess mechanisms that allow them to detect good sources of nutrition and avoid harmful ones. These systems of food rejection evolved to protect the digestive system from ingesting substances that are poisonous, contaminated, or sources of disease. Nematode worms, which have 302 neurons, avoid pathogenic bacteria. Bees remove their dead and diseased members, do not defecate in their nests, and deploy antibacterial mixes that keep parasites out of them. Rats that are given toxic foods show responses that closely resemble the facial responses humans make to disgusting foods.[3]

Humans have retained biological mechanisms of food rejection inherited from other species but add the psychological mechanism of disgust to reinforce aversions to potentially toxic food. Darwin classified disgust as one of six basic emotions that were conducive to survival and reproduction (the others are anger, fear, happiness, sadness, and surprise). Disgust developed as a signal to avoid rotten and potentially poisonous food and to eliminate such toxic foods if they were ingested. Our senses of taste and smell activate emotions of disgust when they sense putrid flavors and repulsive odors. This stimulates our bodies to instinctively withdraw from the sordid object and to develop physiological nauseous reactions and psychological feelings of revulsion. Disgust is found in all cultures and even takes on similar facial expressions that feature a wrinkling of the nose, curling the upper lip, and narrowing the eyes. The adaptive function of disgust is clear: Spoiled foods are likely to be sources of parasites and pathogens and thus a major channel of disease transmission.[4]

Humans (and other living creatures) are naturally designed to avoid foods that appear pathogenic. For example, the famed feral child of nineteenth-century Aveyron in France lived alone in the woods until approximately age 12 years, having no contact with any human culture. He had few food aversions, but nevertheless "a dead canary was given him, and in an instant he stripped off its feathers, great and small, tore it open with his nails, smelt it, and threw it away." His aversion to the odor of a rotting bird could not have been learned but was innate. The common denominator of universally disgusting stimuli—rotten food, some vermin, and excrement—seems to be that they have the potential to cause disease. Bodily waste products are particularly likely to be sources of disgust. After the age of 2 or 3 years, eating feces is universally viewed as a pathological behavior that is typically found only among the most seriously deranged.[5]

In general, people naturally avoid a remarkably limited number of objects of consumption: Other than foods that signal threats to health, almost nothing is unnatural to eat. However, because of the potential dangers of eating disease-ridden food, humans become oversensitive to unusual foods, which leads disgust to spread much more widely than to just intrinsically harmful foods. If offensive objects even touch or resemble a noncontaminated food, they also contaminate that food. When something that is not disgusting looks like something that is, such as chocolate shaped like dog feces or a cake shaped like a toilet bowl, people will refuse to eat it. These reactions are instinctive, do not require conscious thought, and occur even when people know that they are irrational. Just imagining eating disgusting foods can evoke severe aversive emotions.[6]

Like Lot's daughters who broke the incest taboo when no alternative means of reproduction were available, if starvation is the only alternative, people will often eat foods that would otherwise evoke repulsion, such as urine and the flesh of dead humans. Herodotus recounts an illustrative story of the army of the Persian king Cambyses, which attacked the Ethiopians without having adequate food supplies. The soldiers ran out of food, stayed alive by eating their pack animals and grass, but then reached the desert, where they "were reduced to the dreadful expedient of cannibalism," casting lots and eating every 10th soldier. Similarly, American flyers shot down over the ocean during World War II would drink their own urine or suck blood from their comrades' jugular veins. These responses are usually limited to situations in which eating otherwise disgusting foods is the only way to stay alive.[7]

Abnormal Foods

If people are naturally omnivorous, what explains the fact that most of us are quite selective in the kinds of foods we eat? One reason is that disgust mechanisms commonly become connected with idiosyncratic aversive food experiences. Foods that have made individuals sick can become associated with disgust mechanisms and subsequently avoided. Moreover, many people believe that certain foods are disgusting although they have never eaten them and so cannot know what they taste like. Many such food aversions are not natural but stem from personal, and often eccentric, learning histories. For example, I am disgusted by the thought of eating jelly although, to my knowledge, I have never tasted it.[8]

Perhaps the most important reason for the limited range of foods that people actually eat is that almost everyone is influenced by what their cultures consider to be distasteful or forbidden foods. "If you want to know what someone likes to eat the best question is: Where do you come from?" psychologist Paul Bloom observes. Although humans have the same universal receptors for sweet, salty, sour, bitter, and savory tastes, their particular food preferences are often associated with allegiance to a particular group. For example, Herodotus contrasted the Padaei of India who "live on raw meat" with another Indian tribe that "will not take life in any form; they sow no seed and . . . live on a vegetable diet." He also noted the unusual dietary habits of Egyptians, who were forbidden to even touch fish and could not even bear to look at, much less eat, beans. Darwin would not have been surprised at the power of culture to influence food preferences. He noted,

> It is remarkable how readily and instantly retching or actual vomiting is induced in some persons by the mere idea of having partaken of any unusual food, as of an animal which is not commonly eaten; although there is nothing in such food to cause the stomach to reject it.[9]

Traditionally, religion provided the most common source of food prohibitions. Often, different faiths have strict rules that distinguish the pure and clean foods of in-groups from the filthy ones of other groups. Leviticus, for example, is full of examples of "clean" and "unclean" animals. It lays out many food prohibitions, including birds of prey, mammalian predators, and carrion eaters. Land animals that can be eaten must be vegetarian, and fish must have fins and scales. Camels, ostriches, crocodiles, mice, and eels were unclean, whereas gazelles, frogs, grasshoppers, and locusts were clean. These rules served to establish boundaries between the Israelites who would not eat such foods and others who would, although they also helped ensure that potentially toxic foods would be avoided. Muslims, too, avoid pork and drain blood from slaughtered animals, whereas cuisines in traditionally Catholic countries generally embrace pork and other meats with blood. Buddhists avoid all dishes that contain meat. Many states in India punish the possession and sale of beef with penalties of up to 5 years in prison. Such rules serve to both increase solidarity within groups and exclude interaction with other groups.[10]

Although cultural standards about what foods are forbidden or permitted have generally weakened, they remain strong. Other cultures consider as delicacies almost all foods that modern Americans find disgusting, whether cheese with maggots, goat testicles, bull penis soup, cod sperm sacs, or seal eyeballs. Many or most Americans would vomit after finding out they had eaten dog meat, spiders, flies, rats, or human flesh—but each of these activities is normal in some cultures. Street stands in Vietnam sell foods such as cockroaches, spiders, and grasshoppers that would evoke disgust among most Westerners. Psychologist Rachel Herz reports, "In China, chefs can serve you monkey brains from a living monkey sitting at your feet with its skull carved open." In fact, monkey brains, locusts, termites, and flies are good sources of protein, vitamins, and other nutrients. The flavors of these foods are neither inherently repulsive nor gratifying but become so because of cultural tastes. Conversely, many Westerners find cheeses as among the most delicious foods. In contrast, "many Asians . . . regard all cheese—from processed American slices to Stilton—as utterly disgusting and the literal equivalent of cow excrement, which considering that it is the rotted consequence of an ungulate body fluid, is technically correct."[11]

One example of the cultural diversity in food preferences occurred in Europe in 2013 when horse meat appeared in processed foods that were labeled as coming from cows. The British were horrified that small amounts of horse were present in these products. The French, who commonly eat horse meat, were indifferent. Americans, like the British, typically find horse meat repulsive but happily eat lambs, pigs, and cows. Why these animals, but not horses, are acceptable gastronomic choices and why differing food cultures in different countries should define one but not the other as disgusting reflects purely cultural influences.[12]

All groups impose rules regarding what food is permissible or impermissible to eat so that biological mechanisms of disgust become harnessed to cultural norms. Forcing people to eat culturally tabooed food can elicit extreme biological reactions. For example, Muslim soldiers tortured Hindu prisoners by forcing them to eat pork or beef, which violated deeply held religious beliefs. Even the thought of eating disgusting foods such as dog or horse meat can lead some people to vomit or become nauseous. Psychologist Rachel Herz concludes, "In sum, disgust is uniquely personal, highly psychological, culturally malleable, and contextually capricious."[13]

Natural Food Consumption

Underlying the great cultural diversity in what people actually eat is a stark fact: Everyone must eat to stay alive. As St. Augustine noted, he could become celibate but struggled daily with his greed for food. Without adequate nourishment, all organisms become vulnerable to malnutrition, starvation, and many diseases and, eventually, will perish. The drive to survive led nature to select mechanisms that ensured organisms crave food.

Several biological features account for why humans are naturally designed to maximize caloric intake. The large size of human brains, which need a great deal of energy to function adequately, is one reason why humans must ingest large numbers of calories. A second reason is that fatty tissue increases women's reproductive capacities. Third, human infants are much larger than those of other species and require high levels of fat to protect them from starvation and disease. Based on all these factors, natural selection would have favored people, especially women, who ingested fatty foods and stored excess calories as fat in their bodies.[14]

Other reasons for the natural human craving for calories stem from the environment in which the human genome developed. Humans in ancestral settings faced inherent difficulties in obtaining sufficient numbers of calories. During the Upper Paleolithic era, which began approximately 50,000 to 40,000 years ago, hunting, gathering, and fishing were the only ways to obtain food. Foraging groups, geographer Jared Diamond reports, had an "omnipresent concern with starvation as a major risk of traditional life." Aside from tropical climates, adequate nutrition was especially difficult to achieve during long periods of winter. In addition, fluctuating temperatures and rainfall led to unstable food supplies with consequent vulnerability to starvation. Malnutrition and vitamin deficiencies that were risks for many deadly diseases were major reasons why average life expectancy at the time was approximately 33 years (although those who survived until age 15 years could expect to live until about age 50 years). Most of our genetic heritage stems from this period: The biochemistry, physiology, and anatomy of people at that time had few differences with those of present-day humans. In 1988, Eaton, Shostak, and Konner noted that "100,000 generations of humans have been hunters and gatherers; 500 generations have been agriculturalists; 10 have lived in the industrial age; and only one has been exposed to the world of computers."[15]

The caloric environment among early humans featured unpredictable and, often, unavailable sources of calories. The first humans were omnivores, eating whatever calories were available to them. This meant that their diets were heavy in plants, flowers, leaves, nuts, and, if available, fruits and fish because these were the most readily accessible sources of nutrition. During the course of human evolution, animals became more common food sources as improved hunting technologies such as spears, slingshots, and stone tools evolved. At the time, people ate virtually all forms of nontoxic plants and consumed all edible parts of the animals they killed, including hearts, livers, brains, and kidneys.

Another aspect of ancestral environments was that people had to eat foods that were locally available because they had no way to transport perishable supplies across long distances. Outside of the coldest climates, no effective means of preservation existed that would keep food from rotting; animals had to be eaten as soon as they were killed to prevent spoilage. Whenever calories were present, they usually had to be consumed immediately. However, humans were at the mercy of weather conditions that could lead to more than enough food during some periods but inadequate food supplies and consequent risk of famine during others. Therefore, the inability to preserve a profusion of food at one time meant that subsequent food deficits could not be offset.

In such environments in which bonanzas of calories alternated with frequent periods of scarcity, there were major advantages but few disadvantages to ingesting as many calories as possible. One way to enhance chances of survival under these circumstances was to make consuming calories a very pleasurable activity. Nature made eating a gratifying activity through creating reward mechanisms, including the sense of smell, that lead people to crave the idea of eating, to delight in experiences of eating, and to think about consuming more food once they have eaten. Rewards from food became hardwired into the brain's opioid circuitry, which makes eating highly desirable and motivates people to consume more calories when they are available. David Kessler described the cycle of pleasure that eating creates: "A cue triggers a dopamine-fueled urge . . . dopamine leads us to food . . . eating food leads to opioid release . . . and the production of both dopamine and opioids stimulates further eating." Food naturally stimulates us, we respond eagerly to this stimulus, and the rewards we receive lead us to seek out more stimulation. It is difficult to think of a better system to optimize chances of avoiding starvation under conditions of potential caloric scarcity.[16]

Certain types of calories, especially those found in fats, salt, and sugar, were especially palatable sources of energy, so natural selection developed ways to enhance their rewards. Many receptors in the brain and other organs are devoted to taste and smell sensations that make the textures of fatty foods and the tastes of salty and sugary foods naturally appealing. For example, humans have more than 300 olfactory receptors to detect the odors associated with fats. Saturated fats are also essential for a variety of functions, including protecting cell membranes, insulating organs against shock, and facilitating the absorption of many vitamins. Developing fatty tissue (adipose) was particularly valuable because it provides the most efficient way of storing energy in the body, an especially advantageous adaption under conditions of fluctuating food supplies. When excess food was available, people could eat more of it, store it as fat on their bodies, and so preserve its energy for a later time when food supplies were scarce. People who stored fat could survive longer intervals between feedings so that a temporary lack of food would have fewer harmful consequences. In colder climates, fatty foods also helped build up layers of flesh that provided insulation against the weather. Biologists Michael Power and Jay Schulkin state, "Human beings have evolved to be very good at storing fat; fat appears to have been very important in our evolution."[17]

Adequate levels of salt, too, are necessary for, among other functions, adjusting blood pressure levels, regulating bodily metabolism, and maintaining adequate kidney functioning. The biological need for salt, particularly among people in very warm climates who must retain water, is so essential that evolution designed humans to crave its taste. Sugar was also highly valuable in ancient environments. "Thrifty" genes developed that retained sucrose in the blood, allowing people to store glucose as fat and maintain accumulated fat reserves. Excess food energy in times of abundance could be used during later periods of food scarcity—a very beneficial trait in conditions of fluctuating caloric availability. When combined, high-sugar, high-fat, and high-salt foods are even more intensely desired.[18]

Before the industrial age led to the widespread production and consumption of huge amounts of processed foods, however, high levels of salts, sugars, and saturated fats were not common aspects of diets because such highly desirable sources of calories were difficult to obtain. At the time, typical diets consisted of grains, vegetables, fruits, nuts, roots, and wild animals, which had far less salt, sugar, starch, and fat than modern ones. For example, compared to the domestically produced animals people eat today, the animals that early humans ate had approximately one-seventh the amount of fat. It was difficult to satiate cravings for fat, sugar, and salt in ancient environments in which diets featured only modest amounts of these substances.[19]

The other side of the natural craving for calories is that humans in ancestral environments did not require biological mechanisms that limited the amount of eating. The hominid way of life, not biology, prevented obesity. There was little need to set strong upper limits on food consumption because of the combination of limited amounts of food and the large amount of energy expended to obtain it. Under these circumstances, nature created mechanisms designed to maximize caloric intake and storage, not to ensure that people did not consume more calories than they needed.

The development of agriculture during the Neolithic Period approximately 10,000 years ago drastically changed human diets and led to a greater reliance on grains, including, depending on the geographic area, wheat, rice, and maize. In addition, sheep, goats, and, later, pigs and cattle became domesticated and provided more secure sources of meat and dairy products. Although agrarian life led to greater certainty of food supplies, these remained vulnerable to fluctuations in weather, adequate water supplies, and invasive pests. In addition, agriculture made humans dependent on a smaller number of food sources so that famines remained frequent and widespread. Moreover, considerable effort was needed to harvest crops. Aside from elites, few people could ingest more calories than they expended.

The natural craving for calories thus developed as an adaptive response to environments marked by the unpredictable availability of and consequent need for immediately consuming food. The efficient storage of fat protected humans from periodic food shortages and resultant hunger. Maximizing food consumption optimized chances of survival and had few, if any, disadvantages. The general uncertainty with regard to obtaining regular and adequate sources of calories persisted throughout most of human history.

Mismatches

Current calorie-filled environments thoroughly contrast with the conditions under which our natural eating mechanisms emerged. Unlike earlier ways of life, humans in advanced societies do not face alternating periods of feast and famine but instead confront an abundance of constantly available and inexpensive calories. Storing food energy as fat has no positive features when food supplies are adequate and omnipresent. The mismatch between the natural human cravings for calories and the ready possibilities for satisfying these cravings in the modern world creates multiple problems.

The Industrial Revolution in the nineteenth century transformed food production and consumption. The modernization and mechanization of agriculture, as well as the growing use of chemical fertilizers and pesticides, led to much higher crop yields and food surpluses. At the same time, the invention of refrigeration meant that foods could be preserved for much long periods of time than was possible through previous salt-based methods. The development of mass-produced, cheap, and safe canning techniques also enhanced the diets of ordinary consumers. Railroads and other steam-powered forms of transportation abolished the need to produce food locally and to consume it immediately. They also allowed foods to be dispensed widely and, often, globally. Moreover, modern systems of preservation and transportation smoothed seasonal fluctuations as food became readily available at all times of the year.

This revolution in producing, conserving, and shipping food led to widespread changes in food consumption.[20]

A second revolution, this one propelled by advances in food chemistry, began in the 1950s when chemists developed the ability to produce highly desirable, synthetic flavors. Adding chemical ingredients provided the food industry with the ability to imitate the fatty, sugary, and salty foods that humans were naturally designed to crave but that were previously difficult to obtain. Food chemists also exploited humans' natural liking for starchy foods with high caloric density; foods processed from wheat and corn became widespread.

Although the resulting synthetic food products have little actual resemblance to anything that exists in nature, our brains and taste receptors think that they do. For example, the same sweetness cues that led our ancestors to consume nutritious fruits and avoid rancid ones now lead us to consume large quantities of candy, cookies, and cakes. High-fructose corn syrup, one of the most common additives, is more fattening and richer in high-glycemic carbohydrates, which lead to a cascade of plummeting blood sugar, followed by intense cravings for more food that can raise sugar levels, and consequent further eating. Moreover, these calories are promoted not just through ubiquitous advertising but also by parents who try to minimize conflict with their children by allowing and often encouraging them to eat sugary, salty, and fatty foods. Even when healthier and lower calorie foods are available, people prefer these calorie-laden choices. Although resistance to eating processed and artificial food is growing, most people find their instinctual tastiness overrides conscious messages that they are unhealthy. The food industry has successfully tied natural instincts for pleasurable tastes to inexpensive and readily available processed foods. "People say that this is plastic food, that this is very unhealthy, but I like it very much," one satisfied Russian customer of McDonald's summarizes.[21]

These new technologies did not just reproduce highly desirable tastes but also led processed foods to be much less expensive to produce. In 1930, food expenditures in the United States comprised approximately one-fourth of the average family budget; this amount had declined to about 10 percent by 2008. Cheaper additives such as high-fructose corn syrup replaced natural and more expensive ingredients. In addition, the widespread use of pesticides, antibiotics, and hormones lowered the cost of meat production while creating products with considerably higher fat content than those consumed in prior historical periods. The corollary of the low cost of mass producing high-calorie and delicious-seeming foods is that processed foods came to supplant more expensive, but healthier, fresh fruits and vegetables in typical diets. For example, from the 1970s to the present, consumption of fruits, vegetables, and milk has plunged; at the same time, people eat far more bread, pizza, and soda. Another consequence of the cheap production costs of processed food has been a tremendous increase in portion sizes. Since the 1950s, sizes of common food items such as hamburgers, French fries, muffins, and sodas have doubled or tripled. The dramatic decrease in the overall cost of food along with a large increase in portion sizes fueled a growing consumption of calories. In 2000, average Americans consumed 800 more calories each day than they had eaten 40 years earlier.[22]

At the same time as food became more affordable and caloric, it also became more readily available. In contrast to previous historical eras, humans in advanced societies are surrounded by omnipresent sources of calories. During the past century, food production, preparation, and consumption have steadily moved out of the home to commercial sites. Between the 1970s and 1990s, the proportion of calories consumed away from home doubled and now accounts for approximately half of all food expenses, a vastly higher amount than ever before. In the United States, the number of neighborhood food stores and restaurants increased markedly in the 1980s, making highly palatable foods readily available wherever and whenever we might be. McDonald's alone sold more than $27 billion dollars of food in 2015. Convenience stores that are constantly open are around every corner, and vending machines are near most offices and classrooms. The ready availability of high-calorie, processed foods is particularly congruent with the rise of two-parent working families with time binds that enhance the desirability of both buying food that is easy to prepare within the home and consuming more food outside the home.[23]

At the same time as the availability of highly caloric foods vastly expanded, the degree of energy expenditure needed to obtain food plunged. Before the industrial era, the effort necessary to obtain food burned many calories and enhanced muscle tone. Now, however, no exertion is necessary to obtain food or to engage in other routine activities, especially for workers in service industries that are the most rapidly expanding part of the economy. Mechanized travel has replaced foot and bicycle transport. Suburban sprawl means that cars are necessary to move between homes, offices, and shopping. Within the home, couch potatoes flourish as television watching, video games, and Internet surfing become the most common forms of recreation. Modern forms of entertainment coupled with mechanized transportation have led to sedentary lifestyles in which people can obtain and consume as many calories as they like without expending any energy. Physical exertion is now largely a matter of choice: Our environments allow us to barely move to engage in our daily living.[24]

Despite these vast changes in the production and consumption of food, humans still possess the same biology that was designed to cope with environments in which food was scarce, supplies were unpredictable, and high amounts of energy were expended to get food. For most of human history, the limits on food consumption stemmed from external, environmental sources that ensured our biological cravings for calories would rarely lead to dramatic weight gain. The combination of limited and expensive food supplies and the large amount of physical activity in daily life ensured that being overweight was not a major concern. No need existed for internal biological controls over appetites. A biology that developed to maximize caloric consumption under conditions of food scarcity and fluctuating availability now confronts circumstances that feature unlimited, freely available, and inexpensive amounts of calories. The external constraints that used to ensure overeating was rare have crumbled, and humans are left with limited internal constraints that might resist tempting sources of calories. The result is a thoroughgoing mismatch between an environment of abundant calories and our natural craving for them. Current, evolutionarily unique, circumstances lead our biologically driven quest for calories to have many undesirable consequences.

The Consequences of the Mismatch Between Appetite and Environment

During the course of human evolution, genes that promoted food consumption would have been at a selective advantage over those that limited eating. The profusion of cheap, good-tasting, and fattening foods fundamentally transformed the consequences of the natural human craving for calories. The current obesity epidemic results from the confrontation between normal human biology and an environment marked by caloric abundance. Few obese people, probably around 5 percent of the total, have genetic, hormonal, or physiological defects.[25]

Current methods that evaluate the degree of body fat rely on the body mass index (BMI), which is obtained by dividing a person's weight by the square of that person's height. For example, a man who weighs 175 pounds and is 5 feet 8 inches tall would have a BMI of 26.6 ($175/68^2$). Current guidelines state that people with BMIs less than 18.5 are underweight, between 18.5 and 24.9 are normal weight, between 25 and 29.9

are overweight, and those whose BMI is more than 30 are obese. The obese category is further subdivided into obese 1 (BMI, 30–34.9), obese 2 (extreme obesity; BMI, 35–39.9), and obese 3 (morbid obesity; BMI, ≥40). These categories do not refer to their statistical frequency but, rather, to their association with valued outcomes such as living longer and having fewer diseases. According to these guidelines, more Americans—currently approximately 60 percent—are "overweight" or heavier than are "normal" weight.[26]

Levels of BMI in the population have increased considerably in recent decades. Whereas approximately 15 percent of American adults were classified as obese in 1980, rates more than doubled to 33 percent by 2009. The average adult gained more than 24 pounds between the early 1960s and early 2000s. For example, women in their twenties weighed an average of 128 pounds in 1960; their typical weight ballooned to 157 by 2000. The average man gained 30 pounds between 1960 and 2000. Projections indicate that if these trends continue, by 2030 the obese will exceed 60 percent of the population in 13 states, greater than 50 percent in 39 states, and no state will have a rate lower than 44 percent.[27]

Increasing obesity is especially apparent among children and adolescents. The Centers for Disease Control and Prevention (CDC) reports that in 2013 the percentages of 2- to 5-year-olds, 6- to 11-year-olds, and 12- to 19-year-olds who were obese were 12.1, 18, and 18.4 percent, respectively. These percentages are three times greater than comparable figures in 1979. The growing percentage of obese children is particularly problematic because this is the first generation that will be so heavy over such a long period of their lives, with unknown lifelong health consequences. One anti-obesity group, the Trust for America's Health, notes,

> The obesity epidemic is one of the country's most serious health problems. Adult obesity rates have doubled since 1980, from 15 to 30 percent, while childhood obesity rates have more than tripled. Rising obesity rates have significant health consequences, contributing to increased rates of more than 30 serious diseases. These conditions create a major strain on the health care system. More than one-quarter of health care costs are now related to obesity.

The report indicts obesity as a major reason why more than 25 million Americans currently have type 2 diabetes, 27 million have chronic heart diseases, 68 million have hypertension, and 50 million have arthritis.[28]

Obesity is also becoming a worldwide affliction. Rates in western Europe are approaching those of the United States. Even in China, which as recently as the 1960s had faced mass starvation, public health officials proclaimed, "An obesity epidemic is imminent, with more than 20 percent of children aged 7–17 years in big cities now overweight or obese." South Pacific Islanders now have among the highest rates of obesity in the world; on some islands, more than 70 percent of people are obese. One consequence of rising levels of obesity is that rates of global diabetes increased by 45 percent between 1990 and 2013. The World Health Organization has declared that a new pandemic of "globesity" plagues the entire world.[29]

Studies among groups that most closely resemble how ancient hunters and gatherers lived show the dramatic consequences of modern caloric abundance. A number of tribes in New Guinea were among the last recent exemplars of ancient ways of life; Western patterns of food consumption did not reach these hunters and gatherers until the 1960s. Before coming in contact with Western culture, these groups had almost no atherosclerosis, diabetes, or hypertension. Jared Diamond, who studied this area before it was affected by Westernization, reports, "During those early years in New Guinea, I never saw a single obese or even overweight New Guinean." After New Guineans encountered Western culture and began to move into towns and cities, however, their diets radically changed. Diamond states,

> New Guineans who grew up in traditional village lifestyles with limited and unpredictable food availability react to these predictable daily food bonanzas by piling their plates as high as possible at every meal, and inverting the salt and sugar dispensers over their steaks and salads.

Once their caloric environments changed, the traits that had been adaptive in traditional circumstances led to the same negative health consequences that modern Westerners face. The extremely rapid surge of worldwide obesity cannot be due to genetic changes. What has changed is the fact that food environments that in the past would have ensured that our natural tendencies to become obese would never be expressed now lead many people to indulge their naturally voracious appetites.[30]

As Diamond's experience indicates, the hyperabundance of sodium chloride (salt), which traditionally played a useful function in retaining water, keeping blood pressure in balance, and boosting the function of the nervous system, provides one example of the current mismatch of food environments and biological design. These benefits under circumstances in which salt was difficult to obtain led to natural cravings to consume it. Because few sources of salt were available in ancient settings, however, there were limited opportunities to consume excessive amounts. Yet, desires for salt remain in modern conditions in which most processed foods contain high quantities of salt and salt shakers rest on every table. Kidneys that were designed to retain salt, an adaptive function when intake was limited, lead to excessive salt maintenance under modern conditions. The resulting high levels of blood pressure and consequent hypertension are in turn risk factors for heart disease, strokes, diabetes, kidney disease, and almost all cardiovascular diseases.[31]

The human passion for sucrose (sugar) is another example of the consequences of a mismatch between biological design and modern food environments. The average American eats more than 150 pounds of sugar each year, vastly more than in previous historical periods. By comparison, in 1700 the average American consumed approximately 4 pounds. Just as our natural cravings for salt lead to hypertension under the evolutionarily unnatural abundance of salt, high sugar consumption can produce type 2 diabetes. From the 1930s to the present, rates of type 2 diabetes in the United States have increased nearly 10-fold. Worldwide, this disease is increasing by more than 2 percent each year, and current trends indicate even higher growth rates in the future. Diabetes is in turn a major risk factor for many diseases, including kidney failure, stroke, heart attacks, and blindness. Thrifty genes, which retained sucrose in the blood and so were beneficial in prehistory, become sources of obesity and consequent diabetes where excess sugar is freely available and consumed in large quantities, especially among predisposed people.[32]

Paradoxically, the same mechanisms that promoted survival among hunters and gatherers are conducive to developing hypertension, diabetes, and other diseases in societies that feature food abundance. Once the need to store calories in anticipation of food shortages disappears, our genetic heritage becomes highly problematic. The substantial gain in population weight and associated negative health consequences in recent decades are natural results of a human biology that functions in an unprecedented calorie-full environment. Researchers who strive to uncover the causes of obesity through either pathological genes or individual choices will be misled. Heaviness results from a setting that is able to satisfy our naturally gluttonous instincts while at the same time requiring little exertion to engage in life activities. The result has been not only a serious mismatch between natural tendencies and food environments but also a thoroughgoing tension between innate cravings and cultural norms.

The Mismatch Between Natural Food Cravings and Culturally Desirable Bodies

In addition to the mismatch between the natural craving for calories and settings that can easily fulfill this yearning, another mismatch concerns the conflict between heavier bodies and cultural norms about desirable physiques. For most of history, food consumption had little impact on physical appearance and consequent social evaluations because the limited availability and high cost of food ensured that few people would become fat. For example, during medieval times, which were marked by chronic periods of food shortages, eating vast quantities of food was the prerogative of the well-off, signaling a level of prosperity that set them above common people. One thirteenth-century French poem read,

> The clerics were very big and fat
> Because they probably ate a lot
> They were highly esteemed in the city.

Many non-European cultures, as well, held fatness in more esteem than thinness because it was associated with high status. Cultural historian Sander Gilman quotes an example from the diary of a nineteenth-century American consul in Tunisia in 1847:

> The more fatness, the greater beauty as a wife—and, therefore, tender mothers begin at an early age to fatten their daughters. They allow them very little exercise, compel them to eat very rich substances, little past balls dipped in oil, and every kind of food calculated to produce obesity. The result is . . . a lady weighing some three hundred pounds."[33]

In general, however, the modern European era that began during the seventeenth century has been marked by the celebration of slim bodies and denigration of fat ones, especially for women. "Thinness," historian Georges Vigarello observes, "is an uncontested rule across the centuries." In this era, clergy preached against the lack of self-control that gluttonous people displayed, and physicians urged more dietary restraint. Women used constraints such as corsets, girdles, and belts as well as dieting as strategies to fight fat and to emphasize slimness. Heavy men, in contrast, were tolerated and retained respectability as long as they were not grotesquely obese. Those who were obese, however, suffered the same stigma as extremely heavy women. Famed abolitionist Frederick Douglass, for example, contrasted the nobility of race equality with the justified stigmatization of the obese:

> We do not see what complexion has to do with a man's fitness for an office requiring an active and a well informed mind; but we do see, that gross obesity, as tending to induce mental stupidity, as coarseness of feeling, might seriously disqualify a man for such an office.

In 1863, William Banting, an obese English undertaker, wrote about the stigma he faced:

> No man laboring under obesity can be quite insensible to the sneers and remarks of the cruel and injudicious in public assemblies, public vehicles, or the ordinary street traffic. . . . He naturally keeps away as much as possible from places where he is likely to be made the object of the taunts and remarks of others.

Extreme overweight became associated with disease, sloth, uncleanliness, smelliness, ugliness, gluttony, a lack of self-control, and unhappiness that medical or lay interventions should correct.[34]

The devaluation of fatness escalated in the mid-nineteenth century when weight became easier to quantify. At this time, Belgium statistician Adolphe Quetelet developed the first statistical measures of body mass. By the end of the nineteenth century, the spread of mass media and the diffusion of bathroom scales and full-length mirrors allowed people to apply norms that favored thin bodies and stigmatized fat ones to their own bodies. Simultaneously, rising hemlines, scantier clothing, and the growing popularity of beach resorts exposed more bodies to public gaze. Powerful stereotypes associated thin bodies with sexual attractiveness, youth, high status, self-control, and virtue. Conversely, fat people were regarded as lacking in willpower, lazy, and unattractive.[35]

Women are particularly vulnerable to the powerful stigma attached to fatness. Females universally have higher amounts of fat than males because mechanisms that are conducive to fat storage enhanced female reproductive success in ancestral environments. In particular, pregnant and lactating women with excessive fat were more likely to bear children during periods of food shortages, which were common until recent times. Because storing fat was more adaptive for women than men for most of human history, females continue to be more liable to fatness. This was not problematic until cultural standards denigrated and stigmatized fat female bodies as lacking in sexual attractiveness and femininity. Fatness is an especially powerful stigma because it is so visible and almost impossible to hide. Obese people, particularly women, report more depression, less self-esteem, and less life satisfaction than others. Indeed, currently, almost half of obese women report being depressed.[36]

In addition to their disproportionate impact on women, the negative stereotypes surrounding overweight people affect the most marginalized social groups. Because heaviness is no longer the exclusive prerogative of the privileged, elites no longer value larger bodies. In contrast to much of history, abundant and inexpensive calories are readily available to people of all economic means; the poor are now the most likely economic group to rely on cheap, highly caloric, processed foods and to become overweight or obese. Obesity is currently associated with lower- and working-class people and ethnic minorities, and it is viewed as a sign of laziness, irresponsibility, and ugliness. Fat children are often tormented, and fat adults are often looked down upon for their lack of self-control. "The reframing of fatness as unhealthy," sociologist Abigail Saguy observes, "lends medical authority to this century-old dislike for fatness among the elite and white middle classes."[37]

Cultural Norms and Weight

The BMI and other indices of weight are not just measures of biological facts but also reflect cultural norms. Despite the seemingly objective nature of the BMI, social values partially account for why some weights are considered to be "normal" and others "abnormal." Although negative values are placed on higher BMIs because of their association with a host of dire effects, including heart disease, stroke, high blood pressure, type 2 diabetes, joint disease, breathing problems, cancer, and metabolic problems, this association is not straightforward. [38]

No consistent relationship exists between body weight and health risks. *Underweight* people in all age groups have elevated risks for many diseases and higher mortality rates than other weight groups, even after taking into account preexisting diseases that might account for their thinness. Conversely, although BMI places the highest value on people with "normal" weight, *overweight* (but not obese) people (BMI, 25–29) have reduced mortality risks compared to other groups. When particular causes of death are examined, overweight increases mortality from diabetes, kidney diseases, and arthritis but has no association with cancer or cardiovascular disease and actually reduces mortality from other noncancer, noncardiovascular causes. Being overweight also protects older people from developing a number of diseases, such as osteoporosis. Thus, being overweight but not obese has no risks for health and/or mortality and is slightly better than "normal" BMI. Aside from the obese, the value-laden categories of the BMI receive little justification from their association with morbidity and mortality.[39]

There are also reasons to doubt the direst warnings about the impact of an "obesity epidemic." At the same time that weight has been soaring, overall life expectancy in the United States has been increasing from approximately 73.7 years in 1980 to 75.4 years in 1990 and 77 years in 2000. Women at age 50 years could expect to live 27 additional years in 1950, 31 years in 1980, and 33 years in 2007. Fifty-year-old men could expect to live 23 additional years in 1950, 25 years in 1980, and 29 years in 2007. The "public health epidemic" of obesity has not yet influenced overall trends of longevity, although it is possible that its effects will become more dramatic in the future.[40]

In addition, some of the claimed associations between fatness and morbidity result from changing definitions of what both obesity and disease are as opposed to actual gains of weight. For example, in 1998, 25 million Americans became overweight at the stroke of a pen as the CDC changed its definitions of overweight and obesity. A 5 ft. 4 in. tall woman had to weigh 155 pounds to be considered overweight under the old criteria; this weight decreased to 145 pounds under the new guidelines. Overnight, millions of previously normal people became overweight. Similarly, in 1997 the American Diabetes Association and the federal government lowered the standard for diagnosing diabetes from 140 to 126 mg/dl. This redefinition led to more than 1 million new "cases" of diabetes, although most of the people within the new "diseased" range did not have symptoms of diabetes but were only at an elevated risk of getting it. Increasingly looser standards of what counts as devalued conditions account for part of the "epidemic" of obesity and diabetes.[41]

Some critics take the deficiencies and value-laden components of the BMI as indications that the "obesity epidemic" is one of a long line of manufactured or overstated public health epidemics. For example, during the 1950s and 1960s, an intense fear of dietary fat arose because of a supposed association with coronary heart disease. After Surgeon General C. Everett Koop identified saturated fat as the cause of obesity and associated illnesses, including cancer and cardiovascular disease, in 1988, low-fat foods became ubiquitous on supermarket shelves. Historian Harvey Levenstein quotes a leading medical scientist, who stated, "Physicians were overwhelmed by this assault, both from their waiting rooms and their professional journals. A low-fat, low-cholesterol diet became as automatic in their treatment advice as a polite goodbye." The consumption of products including milk, butter, and beef that contained high levels of fat and cholesterol plunged. Later, however, the high-fructose corn syrup that became a prime ingredient in these low-fat foods was itself identified as a prime cause of excessive weight gain. Moreover, subsequent studies showed no association between consumption of saturated fat and heart disease. By 2014, the June 12 *Time* magazine cover proclaimed, "Eat Butter: Scientists Labeled Fat the Enemy: Why They Were Wrong."[42]

Similarly, medical authorities have raised alarms about consuming large quantities of sugar because of its association with numerous diseases. The US Food and Drug Administration, however, determined that "we can now state categorically that there is no evidence at all to link sugar with obesity, diabetes, high blood pressure, hyperactivity, or heart disease." Likewise, although high levels of salt in modern diets have been demonized for increasing rates of high blood pressure, many illnesses, and even deaths, many studies have actually found that consuming low levels of dietary sodium is even worse. Recent decades have also seen unwarranted concerns about dangers from high cholesterol, synthetic sweeteners, and monosodium glutamate, among many others.[43]

It will take several more decades to determine if increasing levels of obesity indicate another in this long line of overstated "epidemics." Currently, however, the increasing number of very heavy people seems to more closely resemble the clear public health damage that tobacco creates than the exaggerated dangers of many past food scares. As the age cohorts most affected by obesity grow old, sicken, and die, the actual health effects—as opposed to the moral revulsion toward fatness—will become clearer.

The Thindustry

The cultural stigma and seeming unhealthy effects of fatness have motivated an obsession with weight loss. The emergence of a gigantic thindustrial complex is another consequence of the glorification of thinness and stigmatization of fatness. A huge weight-loss industry has emerged alongside of the food industry that promotes the consumption of gigantic numbers of calories. Paradoxically, one giant industry promotes the consumption of vast numbers of calories while another (often owned by the same multinational corporations) encourages losing these calories. Almost all food manufacturers now feature large lines of food products promoted as weight-loss aids. Diet drugs, diet support groups, and diet camps, as well as diet foods, have emerged to get people to shed pounds. Popular culture has also become saturated with quests for the most effective ways to lose weight. Stories abound of celebrities' weight gains and attempts at weight loss. For example, Oprah Winfrey's struggles with losing weight have been an ongoing theme for many years. One of the most popular reality programs on television, *The Biggest Loser*, features contestants who compete to lose the largest amount of weight in the shortest period of time.[44]

One result of the simultaneous urgings of the food industry and the thindustry is that many consumers alternate between devouring ever-more calories and trying to shed them. Dieting has become a widespread practice, especially among girls and women. Unsurprisingly, most people find fighting the natural urge for calories extraordinarily difficult. Dieting efforts rarely succeed, most likely because losing weight is not something that humans were naturally designed to do. Nature did not provide strong biological constraints over our appetites so that we must instead rely on willpower to overcome natural instincts. In addition, fatty, starchy, and sugary foods function as stress reducers; eating what is bad for them makes people feel good. Moreover, unlike refraining from smoking, alcohol, or drugs, people cannot simply stop eating. Dieters must overcome natural cravings to eat large number of calories while at the same time consuming a sufficient amount of food to maintain their health. The temptations of the food industry, buttressed by biology, usually trump the strictures of the diet industry, which must fight human nature.[45]

Although some people succeed in building habitual eating behaviors that control eating, far more fail because interventions that aim to induce weight loss must turn natural mechanisms into unnatural ones. "The human body," according to obesity expert Kelly Brownell, "has evolved as a sophisticated regulatory system to protect against weight loss but not against weight gain." The vast majority of people who enter dieting programs do not lose weight over the long term. The power of natural instincts to consume calories usually outweighs the importance of cognitive knowledge that caloric restraint promotes both health and conformity to cultural images of attractiveness. Of course, the weight-loss industry has little reason to desire widespread permanent weight loss, which would bring about its own demise.[46]

The view that obesity is a disease has led to other types of interventions. In 2004, Medicare classified obesity as a disease that it would pay to treat through measures ranging from surgery to diets and psychotherapy. The frustration over the difficulties of dieting has also given rise to an explosion of pharmaceuticals designed to stop food cravings from arising. Interestingly, in the topsy-turvy world of modern food consumption, some of the most effective modes of weight loss stem from their ability to create thoroughly unnatural feelings about food. Phen-fen (a combination of phentermine and fenfluramine that was withdrawn from the market because it was associated with heart valve problems and hypertension) was "the most effective drug therapy [doctors said] they ever had for treating obesity," according to David Kessler. This drug acted to lower the psychic rewards for eating and, thus, the desire to consume more calories. Patients mistakenly believed that their loss of appetite was natural. They would make statements such as the following: "I'm there, the food is there, but I don't feel like eating the food. It used to be that I would see the food and I would go completely nuts, and that doesn't happen any longer." Paradoxically, Kessler quotes a doctor: "Everybody who has ever treated obese people and put them on phen-fen had a patient say to them, 'I felt normal for the first time.' "[47]

In fact, like dieting, chemical interventions rely on thoroughly unnatural mechanisms of appetite control and so do not have high success rates. Three-fourths of people who receive a prescription for diet drugs stop using them after 3 months, and 90 percent stop using them by 6 months. People simply do not like to suppress their appetites, a fact that should not be surprising because our appetites are possibly our most basic instinct. When dieting and drugs fail, more drastic remedies to control obesity, such as surgeries involving gastric bypasses, are becoming increasingly common.[48]

Modern eating patterns are thus doubly mismatched with unprecedented calorically rich environments and with a cultural emphasis on thinness. People (mostly women) must now face circumstances that simultaneously exploit natural tendencies to overeat and stigmatize those that do. The food industry has harnessed nature to its interests: It is inherently difficult for people to resist its omnipresent high-calorie, fatty, sugary, and salty concoctions.

The twin associations of "desirable body image" and "health," however, are powerful countermotivators. In the past few years, widespread publicity about the obesity epidemic coupled with fears about the health impacts of processed foods has led have led to the proliferation of many movements that promote healthier forms of eating. Various food authorities crusade, with some success, against consumption of fat, salt, sugar, meat, processed foods, and food additives. The intake of soda and meat has declined, whereas sales of organic foods have increased. For many, chemical preservatives, salt, and sugar are now equated with poisons, processed foods are equated with a lack of nutrition, and meat consumption is equated with clogged arteries. A slow food movement has emerged that encourages consumption of locally grown and fresh foods. Concern regarding the high amount of dietary fat, salt, and sugar as well as animal products has led more people to become vegans and vegetarians. These movements also tie their food preferences to other moral imperatives, such as the welfare of animals, ending environmental degradation, and decreasing energy use. Whether these concerns will trump the combined power of our natural food tastes and the food industry is an open question.[49]

Conclusion

The relationship between natural mechanisms that promote caloric consumption and food environments and cultural norms has undergone a radical change. For most of history, overeating did not result in negative consequences for either health or body image. Currently, however, unparalleled conflicts have arisen between biological imperatives to eat, calorie-filled surroundings, and cultural norms that promote thinness and stigmatize obesity. In such circumstances, the relationship between what cultures view as normal and abnormal food consumption leads to great tension with how people are naturally designed to eat. Food—once a straightforward source of calories and, sometimes, identity—has become the obsessive and pathological concern of multitudes who try to resolve the historically unprecedented conflict between biology, environment, and culture. The ancient Hippocratic dictum that moderation in all things is generally the wisest course has been discarded in a context marked by extremes of excessive caloric consumption, on the one hand, and efforts to shed calories, on the other hand.[50]

Undoubtedly, the presence of abundant and cheap calories has had some important positive consequences. Aside from the poorest countries and extreme circumstances associated with wars and prolonged natural disasters, no one needs to fear starvation now. Cheap and abundant food especially benefits the poor, who no longer go hungry. Indeed, poor people display by far the heaviest weights of any economic group, although they also have the highest rates of diseases associated with obesity. Working parents, especially working women, and overworked adults in general find that convenience foods make their lives much easier because they spend far less time preparing food.

Nevertheless, evolution might come to have the last word. Biological design and the current food environment are not compatible. Our mismatched food situation, not our natural craving for calories, is the problem that requires fixing. In particular, strategies that promote the control of portion sizes as well as enhance opportunities for physical activity might be easier to implement than ones that try to restrict our naturally insatiable appetites. We have constructed a calorie-filled environment that appeals to our innate urges; building one that requires more exertion might be the most effective counterstrategy to narrow the gap between calorie-rich settings and desires for health and thinness.

6 FEAR

Put a philosopher in a cage of thin iron wire in large meshes and hang it from
the top of the towers of Notre Dame of Paris; he will see by evident reason
that it is impossible for him to fall, and yet . . . he cannot keep the sight of this
extreme height from terrifying and paralyzing him.

—MICHEL DE MONTAIGNE, *1958, p. 449.*

There are . . . for us no instincts—we no longer need the term in psychology.
Everything we have been in the habit of calling an "instinct" today is a result
largely of training—belonging to man's learned behavior.

—JOHN WATSON, *1925, p. 1.*

Contemporary developed societies are the safest, healthiest, and
most prosperous that have ever existed, so we might expect that
their citizens would have low levels of fearfulness. "Hasn't one of
the central accomplishments of modern civilization," Norwegian
philosopher Lars Svendson asks, "been the overall reduction of
fear, by nighttime electrical lighting, insurance policies, police
forces, standing armies, the destruction of predatory animals, light-
ning rods on churches, solid locked doors on all buildings, and
thousands of other small designs?" Indeed, rates of violence seem
to be at their lowest in recorded history. In addition, life spans of
unprecedented longevity mean that few people need to fear dying
before old age. Moreover, amounts of economic security greatly
exceed those typical of eras before the post-industrial period.[1]

Nevertheless, current community surveys reveal extraordinary
high rates of anxiety disorders. Anxiety is the most common class of
mental illness: Almost one in five people report having an anxiety
disorder in the past year, and almost 30 percent experience one at
some point in their lives. These surveys also indicate that the most
frequent type of anxiety disorder is specific phobias that involve
marked fear about some object. The particular things that people
are afraid of are animals (22.2 percent), heights (20.4 percent),

Portions of this chapter are adapted from Horwitz & Wakefield (2012) and
Horwitz (2013).

blood (13.9 percent), flying (13.2 percent), closed spaces (11.9 percent), water (9.4 percent), storms (8.7 percent); and being alone (7.3 percent). The second most widespread anxiety condition is social anxiety, which is associated with situations in which people are subject to evaluations by others. The three most widespread forms of social anxiety are public speaking (21.2 percent), speaking up in a meeting (19.5 percent), and meeting new people (16.8 percent). None of these objects or situations are likely to pose genuine dangers.[2]

What accounts for why so many people intensely fear objectively harmless phenomena? Think back to the case that obesity is not a disease but, rather, a natural product of human tastes for fats, sugars, and salts that enhanced chances of survival in ancient environments. Genes that optimized caloric consumption and stored the excess as fat developed over thousands of generations when sources of calories were usually scarce and always unpredictable. Under current conditions, in which calories are readily available, these ancestral tastes often lead to obesity and associated diseases. The resulting increase in the number of very heavy people does not derive from disordered genes or psychology but from a mismatch between natural biological propensities and modern environments. Tastes for fats, sugars, and salts, however harmful their present consequences might be, are part of our normal genetic inheritance; they are not disorders.

Like our preferences for highly caloric foods, the statistically most common disordered fears, which seem unreasonable and irrational in modern environments, nevertheless result from natural human emotions. Our current fears do not correspond to actual dangers in present situations but seem understandable as reactions that were passed down to us as part of our biological inheritance of fears that did make sense in the prehistoric past. Many currently unreasonable fears arise because natural genes no longer fit the environments in which they must function. Irrational emotions might nonetheless be products of natural physiological responses. Unreasonable, but mismatched, fears raise some fundamental questions about whether or not the results of natural biological forces should be regarded as disorders.

Reasonable and Unreasonable Fears

Commentators from the earliest Hippocratic writings through the present have understood that fear is associated with particular biological sensations. Darwin, for example, observed that danger engenders automatic physical responses:

With all or almost all animals, even with birds, terror causes the body to tremble. The skin becomes pale, sweat breaks out, and hair bristles. The secretions of the alimentary canal and of the kidneys . . . are involuntarily voided. . . . The breathing is hurried. The heart beats quickly, wildly, and violently.

Physiologists including Walter Cannon in the early twentieth century and Robert Sapolsky at present have documented how fright increases heart rate, blood pressure, and breathing, which lead to more efficient transport of nutrients and oxygen through the body. These automatic physiological responses maximize any organism's ability to rapidly react to immediate threats and thus facilitate survival and consequent reproduction in the face of danger.[3]

Humans (among other species) are naturally designed to develop such fear responses whenever they perceive danger. Approximately a century after Herodotus wrote his *Histories*, Aristotle (384–322 BCE) sketched the basic reason for this: "Let fear, then, be a kind of pain or disturbance resulting from the imagination of impending danger. . . . For that is what danger is—the proximity of the frightening."[4] Fear naturally arises as a response to a range of perceived threats to safety, health, family, finances, love, or work. Current dangers range from the mundane worries that arise from parking in a no-parking zone, worrying about missing a plane, or giving a public talk, on the one end, to the extraordinary threats of living in a war zone, facing an impending natural disaster, or experiencing a terrorist attack, on the other end. Aristotle's analysis also implies that proportionality is an essential aspect of natural fear: People develop even terrifying emotions when they face extremely threatening circumstances. Indeed, most people who are in exceptionally dangerous contexts, whether soldiers in a war zone, victims of an impending natural disaster, or mothers with seriously ill children, develop physiological, psychological, and behavioral symptoms associated with fear. Finally, his reasoning leads to the conclusion that because dangers are ubiquitous, so is fear.[5]

In contrast to natural fear that is proportionate to the amount of danger and uncertainty in a particular situation, fear disorders do not result from the contexts in which they arise. The prominent British psychiatrist, Aubrey Lewis, provided a common definition of disordered fears: "There is either no recognizable threat, or the threat is, by reasonable standards, quite out of proportion to the emotion it seemingly evokes." Lewis follows a long tradition of viewing fear disorders as problems of unreasonable perceptions. For example, the eminent seventeenth-century Dutch philosopher, Baruch Spinoza, emphasized how irrational fears are products of faulty thinking that can be corrected through changing cognitive perceptions. Spinoza claimed that "fear arises from a weakness of mind and therefore does not appertain to the use of reason." Relatively recently, cognitive behavioral therapists such as Albert Ellis and Aron Beck have emphasized that erroneous thoughts and beliefs underlie illogical fears. That is, reasonable fears stem from accurate perceptions of danger; unreasonable ones arise when no genuine danger is present. However, it is often not self-evident what are "reasonable" and "unreasonable" grounds for fear, and these greatly differ from culture to culture.[6]

Culture and Fear

Although common human biology underlies fearful emotions, cultural values also explain much about fear. Historians, anthropologists, and behavioral psychologists have shown how cultural rules help define what particular objects and situations are considered to be rational or irrational sources of danger, what cues activate fear responses, and what sorts of things their members worry about as well as the degree of intensity or duration with which they should respond to various threats. It is reasonable to fear whatever cultures emphasize as sources of danger, and standards of reasonableness vary from culture to culture.

For much of the twentieth century, behavioral psychologists adopted the views of John Watson, who proposed an extreme version of the cultural view. Watson claimed that all fears arise from learned conditioning so that people can be taught to fear anything. In one of the best known cases in psychology, Watson and his assistant (and later his wife) Rosalie Rayner exposed an 11-month-old boy, Albert B, to a variety of small animals, including rats, rabbits, dogs, and monkeys, but the boy showed no fear in their presence. However, they discovered that loud clanging sounds from striking a hammer on a steel bar caused the boy to cry, tremble, and display labored breathing. Watson and Rayner then paired the loud noise with exposure to the previously unfeared rat. They did this seven times during a 1-week period, leading Albert to whimper and cry each time. They then introduced Albert to the rat but not the noise. They found that he continued to display his aversive response, which they believed indicated that he had acquired a conditioned fear of rats.[7]

The experimenters indicated that Albert subsequently developed fears of not just rats but also warm, furry animals more generally and even of similar stimuli such as a Santa Claus mask or the experimenter's hair. They thus presumably showed not just that fear could be a conditioned response but also that learned reactions could be generalized to a class of related objects. "It is probable," Watson and Rayner concluded, "that many of the phobias in psychopathology are true conditioned emotional reactions either of the direct or the transferred type."[8] The case of Little Albert initiated a long tradition that examined how environmental rewards and punishments lead to conditioned fears.

Because their cultures teach people what sorts of things they should fear, sources of perceived danger vary widely. Residents of the Massachusetts Bay Colony in the seventeenth century reasonably feared witches, ghosts, and demons. Or, fears of being buried alive dominated nineteenth-century consciousness in the United Kingdom and United States but would be extremely rare at present. Likewise, cultural norms in Western societies in the nineteenth century led masturbation, which was alleged to cause a host of serious diseases or even death, to be a particularly powerful source of anxiety. In the absence of participation in some unusual subculture, fears of demons, witchcraft, ghosts, being buried alive, or masturbation are not reasonable at present. In contrast, prevalent fears among many twenty-first-century Americans, such as many food allergies or germs spread by handshakes, might seem laughable in other cultures.[9]

Moreover, cultures not only provide particular objects of fear but also influence the quantity of fearfulness that is found in given groups. Whereas some cultures, such as the Dobuans of Melanesia, fear a wide variety of objects and situations, others, such as the Tasaday who live in the highlands of the Philippines, have few fears. Indeed, omnipresent fears can umark whole historical periods, such as the late Middle Ages in Europe. Groups with communal norms that emphasize cooperation foster less anxiety than those that promote competitiveness among their members. In addition, cultures that feature consistent and stable meaning systems that offer socially shared interpretations of threatening situations should have fewer fearful members than those that lack these qualities. Other societal factors, such as stressful life conditions, rapid social changes, or economic insecurities that are conducive to anxiety, shape how much fear will arise in various cultures.[10]

Social structures and values also shape the degree of harm that any given state of fear produces. For example, the impairments of social and occupational functioning that psychiatry uses to demarcate social phobias from intense shyness emerge only when group norms reward social engagement and outgoing styles of interaction. For example, our own culture frequently demands that people in certain occupations engage in public speaking to groups of strangers; if this activity provokes intense anxiety, as it is probably biologically shaped to do, our culture then judges that anxiety to be a form of social phobia. Social phobias are less likely to be harmful in groups such as the Japanese that value restrained styles of sociability. Indeed, emotions and actions such as anxiety about humiliation, embarrassment, and scrutiny by others in social situations that Western psychiatrists consider to be symptoms of social anxiety disorder are cultural norms in Japan.[11]

Their cultures also provide people with norms for the appropriate expression of fear. Although common brain circuitry might underlie diverse cultural expressions of fear, fearful people use whatever symptoms their cultural templates make available to them when they display their emotions. For example, symptoms of social phobia among Japanese commonly take the form of a fear of offending others; analogous symptoms among Americans are expressed through intense fear of personal embarrassment. Conditions that are widespread and well recognized in one era, such as hysterical paralyses of limbs or fainting spells, disappear and reappear as another era's panic attacks or social phobia. Cultures also provide people with the tools to exert control over emotions and the thresholds when they are triggered. The ancient Greeks, for example, recognized both the power of fear and the necessity to train soldiers to resist this emotion while in combat. Likewise, cultures can provide ritualistic systems consisting of rules that, when followed, offer reassurance in the face of threatening situations.[12]

Culture thus supplies norms about what particular objects are appropriate to fear; the proper ways to express their fears; and the conventions, norms, and habits that they use to manage their concerns and worries. What is appropriate or inappropriate psychological functioning is often learned from experience. Cultural definitions influence what emotions are considered to be suitable and unsuitable, excessive or deficient, and balanced or unbalanced in given situations. This is why it is difficult and perhaps impossible to define fear disorders without using terms such as "excessive," "unreasonable," "inappropriate," and the like to reflect deviation from sociocultural standards that vary substantially across different cultural contexts. Such terms are not just placeholders until more knowledge is obtained; they are inherent aspects of definitions of dysfunctional fear mechanisms.

Biology and Fear

Despite the powerful role of culture in shaping many aspects of fear, contrary to the claims of Watson and the behavioralists who followed him, most individually learned fears fit into evolutionarily designed categories of threatening objects and situations. Consider Darwin's recounting of his own powerful snake phobia:

> I put my face close to the thick glass-plate in front of a puff-adder [a type of venomous snake] in the Zoological Gardens, with the firm determination of not starting back if the snake struck at me; but, as soon as the blow was struck, my resolution went for nothing and I jumped a yard or two backwards with astonishing rapidity. My will and reason were powerless against the imagination of a danger which had never been experienced.[13]

Despite Darwin's knowledge that he was completely safe, he instinctively reacted as if he was in the presence of a dangerous animal. However, there is no hint that Darwin had ever actually encountered any dangerous snakes, which were almost nonexistent in England during the nineteenth century. As he recognized, Darwin's fear of snakes was not learned but, rather, an inherited, evolutionarily understandable fear that arose because snakes were a common and genuine source of danger during prehistory.

Like other aspects of the human genome, natural fear mechanisms developed in the environment of evolutionary adaption (EEA), which corresponds to the time between 2 million and 10,000 years ago when humans lived in hunter–gatherer societies, first on the African plains and then in dispersed locales. Hominids had much to fear in these ancient environments. During the earliest stages of human evolution, humans lacked powerful weaponry but faced numerous predators that were often larger, stronger, and faster than them. Other animals, such as snakes and spiders, carried venomous poisons at a time when medical remedies were scarce. Dangers were everywhere at the same time that security from threats was weak and often unavailable. Small bands of just 100–200 people faced other hostile groups of humans and other predators, without any government to protect them. Although a range of strategies could be adaptive for dealing with specific circumstances, on average, vigilance, caution, and readiness to flee at a moment's notice would probably have had the greatest evolutionary payoff. The typical fears among modern Americans, however unreasonable they might be, closely resemble the sorts of things that were dangerous in the distant past.[14]

Intense fears of snakes such as Darwin's are usually not justified in modern environments unless one lives in an area populated with poisonous snakes. Considerable evidence, however, indicates that many people inherit or are predisposed to easily learn snake fears, which were adaptive during the period when the human genome was being formed. Even if one is cognitively aware of the unlikelihood of a snake being poisonous, seeing a snake slithering in the grass nearby can cause an automatic fear reaction. Darwin's excessive and unreasonable fear might stem from inherited fear mechanisms that are operating as evolution has designed them to act. Such fears are normal even though irrational in many contexts (i.e., in response to snakes that are known to be nonpoisonous).[15]

Although much fear is clearly natural and some is undoubtedly disordered, it is difficult to clearly classify the most common sorts of specific phobias—such as Darwin's and those noted at the beginning of this chapter that include animals, heights, or blood—on one side or the other of this divide. At first glance, such fears would seem to be unreasonable in most circumstances and so would fulfill the criteria for a disorder. Consider fear of animals. Certainly, an unleashed dog with bared teeth that is chasing you is a genuine source of alarm, but most animal fears are not of this sort. Instead, they typically involve relatively harmless creatures such as spiders or snakes that are rarely dangerous at present. Similarly, fears of high places that generally have guardrails, fences, and other ample protections from falling are rarely realistic. The same is true for the other frequent sources of fear, such as closed spaces, water, storms, or being alone, none of which are related to objects and situations such as guns, automobiles, or electric outlets that can be genuinely dangerous at present. Likewise, the most common forms of social phobias involve speaking to or meeting new people, who are almost never dangerous.

Contrary to Watson's assertion, many intense fears, such as Darwin's snake phobia, are not learned; rather, they are directed at objects that were actually dangerous in the distant past but are not at present. Many common fears appear to be based partly in biological adaptations rather than knowledge about danger or accrued negative experiences. Reason cannot easily overcome these elemental prepared fears. People are pre-prepared to fear some objects more than others: The set of things to which people develop intense fears is overall quite limited and predictable, not a random assortment of objects that the conditioning theory might predict. For example, Little Albert's fear of rats might not have resulted from learned conditioning but instead from a natural predisposition for people to fear small furry animals because they were carriers of diseases in ancient times. Even people who have never seen a snake are apt to be afraid of snakes, whereas almost no one fears lambs. Likewise, few of the many people who refuse to fly have had a bad prior experience with air travel. Many seemingly unreasonable fears of objects and situations are not learned but are products of biological design. Such mismatches between evolutionarily natural fears and what is socially reasonable raise fundamental questions about what is normal and what is not.[16]

The Irrational Aspects of Mismatched Fears

Darwin's fear of a caged, venomous snake not only illustrates how certain types of objects are evolutionarily pre-prepared but also indicates how such fears overwhelm cognitive controls. Darwin realized that his snake fear was unreasonable but was nevertheless unable to control his feelings. He anticipated the idea that fear detection systems operate unconsciously in his speculations that neural signals passing from the brain to the body bypass consciousness. Well before Darwin, philosophers such as Plato, Aquinas, and Hume also noted that reason is a slave to the emotions. The second-century Roman philosopher Epictetus was perhaps the first to recognize the way that natural fear mechanisms were propelled by automatic, unconscious reactions rather than by reasoned, conscious reactions:

> Mental impressions, through which a person's mind is struck by the initial aspect of some circumstance impinging on the mind, are not voluntary or a matter of choice, but force themselves upon one's awareness by a kind of power of their own.[17]

Philosopher Tamar Gendler calls such involuntary mental states "aliefs," a term that refers to mental states involving automatic emotions that override conscious reasoning. Despite beliefs that tell them they are safe, aliefs tell people they are in danger. People who know, for example, that a snake is harmless or that an airplane is extraordinarily unlikely to crash nonetheless act according to aliefs that are more primitive responses to how things seem to us even when we know that our responses are irrational. Moreover, aliefs are highly resistant to change through exposure to empirical evidence. Initial responses to danger are not deliberate choices but reflect unconscious, primitive programs that emerge and function in evolutionarily old brain structures, with little restraint by conscious thought.[18]

Modern biology indicates why this should be the case: The amygdala is wired to preempt thought in dangerous situations because conscious responses are slower than instinctual ones. One reason why innate fears are not reasonable is that fear is often most useful when it is irrationally intense and its triggering threshold is irrationally low. In effect, the best way to design an organism to escape serious threats and live to reproduce is to make some of its normal, biologically designed fears unreasonably powerful in terms of the actual likelihood of threat in any one instance because there will be no further instances if the organism gets it wrong just once. Psychological experiments confirm that subliminal exposure to evolutionarily relevant fear cues such as spiders and snakes, but not to unthreatening stimuli such as flowers or mushrooms, automatically activates physiological fear responses. The normal biology of fear bypasses conscious and rational systems of control in initial stages of response and activates very rapidly when evolutionarily relevant cues are aroused.[19]

Many common fears have this sort of evolutionary basis and may be innate or easily triggered by minimal cues. Such fears are to one degree or another noncognitive—that is, irrational in the sense of not having their source in, or being easily subject to change by, reasoning about the actual danger, as well as sometimes not being easily changeable by new experiences. People typically fear the "wrong things" in terms of the objective probabilities of suffering harm. Few individuals objectively calculate danger by formulas that involve the actual probability of experiencing some injury and the resulting severity of harm from it. The most common specific and social fears illustrate the problematic nature of the reasonableness and unreasonableness of perceptions of danger.

Specific Fears

In ancient environments, small creatures such as snakes or spiders could be poisonous sources of sickness and death. Larger, faster, and stronger carnivores, for which humans were a tasty source of calories, posed another pressing danger: Flesh-eating saber-toothed cats and giant cheetahs were responsible for the deaths of many of the most ancient humans from millions of years ago. The oldest known visual representations, in the French caves of Lascaux, which date back 17,300 years, depict many menacing bison, wild cattle, and hyena, among other intimidating animals. Although experts dispute the meanings of these images, they leave no doubt about the centrality of animals in the earliest portrayals of human history. The first known written documents also give pride of place to animals as sources of danger. A Sumerian cuneiform text stemming from 4000 BC compares an ancient golden age that lacked nonhuman predators:

> Once upon a time, there was no snake,
> There was no scorpion,

> There was no hyena, there was no lion,
> There was no wild dog, no wolf,
> There was no fear, no terror,
> Man had no rival.

In contrast, many Sumerians at the time this text was written found snakes, scorpions, hyena, and the like to be sources of fear and terror.[20]

Aside from animals, fear of heights is the most common specific phobia among modern Americans. This would not surprise French essayist and philosopher Michel de Montaigne (1533–1592), who observed,

> Put a philosopher in a cage of thin iron wire in large meshes and hang it from the top of the towers of Notre Dame of Paris; he will see by evident reason that it is impossible for him to fall, and yet . . . he cannot keep the sight of this extreme height from terrifying and paralyzing him."[21]

Montaigne noted that although he was only "moderately frightened of heights," he shivered and trembled when on top of a mountain, even when he was well away from the edge of the cliff and could not possibly fall off of it. He used philosophers to exemplify the terror many people feel about being in a high place because they presumably illustrate the group who are best able to exert conscious control over emotional states; nevertheless, their rationality completely fails them at high elevations. Height fear results from instincts developed in the distant past when falling from a high place posed a real threat of serious injury or death at a time when protective measures were rare or nonexistent.

In addition to animals and heights, many of the most common specific fears, such as of blood, water, closed spaces, and storms, posed genuine threats in prehistory. Blood, for example, might have signaled the close proximity of enemies. Even air travel, which obviously did not exist when the human genome was being formed, seems to encompass several aspects of biologically shaped fears. It combines fear of being at extreme heights where falling could mean death with fear of entering enclosed spaces where escape is impossible. Currently, Americans are far more afraid of flying in an airplane than of driving in a car, although air travel is many times safer (not a single death occurred in US airspace in 2012, whereas automobile accidents accounted for more than 35,000 fatalities in that year). Such fears could have been useful in ancient periods because they motivated people to stay away from situations that occasionally led to disasters and thus passed on to their descendants genes that also made them more fearful of entering enclosed spaces and climbing to higher altitudes.[22]

G. Stanley Hall (1844–1924), the founder of the American Psychological Association, also emphasized that the most typical fears in his era were remnants of responses to the types of objects and situations that were common when humans evolved in prehistory but that no longer posed threats. He wrote,

> Night is now the safest time; serpents are no longer among our most fatal foes, and most of the animal fears do not fit the present conditions of civilized life; strangers are not usually dangerous, nor are big eyes and teeth; celestial fears fit the heavens of ancient superstition and not the heavens of modern science.

The founder of American psychiatry, Benjamin Rush (1746–1813), likewise depicted the most common "unreasonable" fears as being "thunder, darkness, ghosts, speaking in public, sailing, riding, certain animals, particularly cats, rats, insects, and the like." Freud, too, observed in regard to "the enigmatic phobias of early childhood" such as "fear of small animals, thunderstorms, etc.—there is the possibility that they represent the atrophied remnants of an innate preparedness against reality dangers such as is so well developed in other animals."[23]

What unites most of these fears is that although they are not rational sources of fear in modern environments, they were understandable reactions in the prehistoric past. Fears when being alone at night, unexpectedly confronting a stranger in an open space, or seeing a snake would be cues that long ago indicated possible danger from a predator. However, despite their current unreasonableness, they stem from naturally transmitted brain circuitry that arose millennia ago to respond to realistic threats in ancient environments and so to keep humans safe and alive.

Only minimal cues are necessary to generate such ancestral fears. For example, children, especially those between the ages of 4 and 6 years, still report intense fears of snakes. Indeed, surveys show that snakes are the most disliked animal of all. Small children also often demonstrate extreme fears of darkness, being alone, or animals such as lions or wolves that they are unlikely to actually encounter. Children who have powerful fears of darkness or animals that pose no actual danger to them usually are responding to innate predispositions, perhaps triggered by minimal cues, and not to idiosyncratic learned experiences. Conversely, they are unlikely to have innate fears of current sources of danger such as automobiles or matches. Moreover, it is considerably more difficult to extinguish fears of evolutionarily primed stimuli such as snakes and spiders than conditioned fears to objects such as electrical outlets or guns. The ancient origin of instinctual fears often leads to a tenuous connection between what sorts of objects and situations people fear at present and the corresponding senses of danger that they develop.[24]

Social Fears

Social phobias, the second most common class of anxiety disorders, also seem to stem from responses that were likely natural and adaptive in ancient eras. In the distant past, people lived in bands of 100–200 people, all of whom were well known to one another. Ancestral social structures were small, close-knit, egalitarian groups in which intimates hunted, gathered, mated, and raised children. Group members shared ethnicity, language, lifestyles, and belief systems. Social life involved cooperating and reciprocating relationships with a small number of well-known others. Humans never lived alone but were constantly immersed in tightly knit groups.[25]

Human nature thus developed in the context of all-encompassing small groups. Disapproval or rejection within such groups could be highly consequential for survival. In such small and highly interdependent groups, incurring the negative evaluations of others carried real risks of isolation. A person who was not part of a collectivity would not have been able to live if cut adrift from the group. Fears of ostracism were natural and adaptive when people depended on tightly connected and long-term relationships.

Unsurprisingly, high anxiety about social evaluation and potential rejection became a common part of our nature. It remains so even though such anxiety is no longer as contextually suited to modern societies in which people still fear peer assessments even though they now have other alternatives if any particular group rejects them. For example, many of us become anxious about attending a social event alone, despite the lack of any objective danger involved. One writer describes a typical experience:

I walked into the party alone. Surveying the group of unfamiliar faces, I felt nervous. I stood on the periphery with no one to talk to. It seemed as if everybody was looking at me and, at the same time, as if nobody was looking at me.[26]

Fear of entering settings in which one is unknown to others and must interact with unfamiliar people might have been reasonable in ancient societies where strangers were often sources of danger. Unfamiliar people often posed genuine threats to the sorts of small, tightly bound groups of intimates in which the human genome developed. Strangers were rarely encountered in daily activities; their appearance would typically have been the occasion of suspicion, flight, or violence. In such circumstances, wariness of relationships with those outside of the group was a wise strategy. Fear of strangers would probably have been useful in such environments; thus, people who were afraid of unfamiliar people were more likely than the fearless to live and pass on fearful genes to descendants. Well into the nineteenth century, strangers were rarely encountered in American life, and their appearance engendered considerable anxiety. Marked and persistent fears of unfamiliar people or of possible scrutiny by others might not be reasonable in current settings but still indicate biologically designed aspects of human nature.[27]

Social structures now involve numerous encounters with strangers. Most people live in large communities and cities where they know a very small portion of those they encounter in daily life. Fears of people who do not share one's own social traits are far less adaptive in situations that feature many fleeting relationships with unknown others from highly varying backgrounds. Consider that by far the most frequent current sort of social fears involve speaking in front of groups to people one does not know, meeting new people, and talking with strangers. The extraordinary frequency of fears of public speaking would not have surprised Darwin, who noted that "almost everyone is extremely nervous when first addressing a public assembly, and most men remain so throughout their lives." Well before Darwin, the Ancient Roman philosopher Seneca also observed the natural propensity of people to become anxious when speaking in public: "The most eloquent orator's scalp tightens as he prepares to speak." For some people, the fear of public speaking can become extreme. World War II hero Audie Murphy, who received 32 combat medals including the Congressional Medal of Honor, claimed that he would rather face a machine gun nest than give a speech. Such inherited danger cues about meeting and interacting with strangers are no longer contextually appropriate; nonetheless, individuals are naturally prepared to be more anxious and inhibited with strangers than with intimates. A normal psychological mechanism is operating in an environment that is not the same as the setting for which it was designed.[28]

Consequently, not all irrational or unreasonable fear is pathological. Natural selection did not sculpt human nature according to reasonableness in the current environment but, rather, according to what promoted reproductive fitness in the circumstances in which natural selection took place. The resulting biologically designed fears are part of human nature but do not correspond to what is reasonable now. As many psychologists, philosophers, and scientists such as Seneca, Montaigne, Rush, Darwin, Hall, and Freud have realized, the most common fears are ones that stem from ancient fearful objects and situations. If natural fear mechanisms arise in response to ancient stimuli, then they must have been genetically transmitted across thousands of generations. If so, they would be universal aspects of the human genome. Considerable evidence indicates this is the case.

The Universality of Fear and Anxiety

It is easy to understand why primeval fears developed in ancestral times. Defenses against immediately life-threatening dangers must be any organism's highest priority. People whose fear motivated them to recognize and to avoid situations that threatened harm or death were more likely to survive and reproduce than people who were not able to escape from dangerous circumstances. That is, many fears are not learned through experience or cultural norms but instinctually arise as responses to situations that had been imminently threatening in the EEA. If anxiety had such a basic function to play in responding to ancient environmental dangers, the implication is that it is transmitted as part of the human genome, arises instinctively in the presence of evolutionarily relevant cues, and is present in all cultures. Considerable evidence from studies of other species, infants, and a range of other cultures indicates that fears of evolutionarily relevant dangers are universally found.

Humans inherit proneness to many fears from their evolutionary ancestors. Indeed, Darwin noted how "the fact that the lower animals are excited by the same emotions as ourselves is so well established, that it will not be necessary to weary the reader by many details." He emphasized that fear was probably the evolutionarily oldest emotion that was shared among humans and their distant ancestors alike:

> Fear was expressed from an extremely remote period, in almost the same manner as it is now by man; namely, by trembling, the erection of the hair, cold perspiration, pallor, widely opened eyes, the relaxation of most of the muscles, and the whole body cowering downwards or held motionless.

For example, many snakes pose dangers to nonhuman animals. Numerous mammals are alarmed by snake-like cues despite never having experienced traumatic encounters with snakes. Laboratory-reared monkeys that have never seen snakes are easily conditioned to fear them after viewing films of older monkeys demonstrating intense snake fear. They do not, however, develop fears of stimuli such as flowers or mushrooms when they observe older monkeys responding fearfully to these innocuous objects.[29]

Fear of heights provides another example. It might be called a "prototypical" evolutionarily relevant fear because of the obvious threat from falling to all terrestrial animals. Much experimental evidence stems from studies using the visual cliff, an apparatus that is half board with a pattern and half glass supported several feet above the floor, with a continuation of the board's pattern on the floor several feet under the glass. At the end of the board, there is what appears to be a sudden drop to the floor, although in fact there is a continued solidity of the glass. Results from species including chicks, kids, and lambs indicate the innate nature of height fear. When tested on the first day of life as soon as they could stand and before any learning could take place, no chick, kid, or lamb ever stepped onto the glass on the deep side. When lowered onto the deep side, kids and lambs would initially refuse to put their feet down. They then adopted a defensive posture and their front legs became rigid and their hind legs limp. From this immobile state, they would often leap in the air to the apparent safety of the center board rather than walk on the glass.[30]

Few fears appear more consistently in terrestrial animals: Researchers have noted similar findings with cats, land turtles, dogs, pigs, and neonatal monkeys, to name but a few. Unlike land-dwelling animals, aquatic species such as ducks and water-dwelling turtles, which have little reason to fear a perceived drop, readily cross onto the deep side of the visual cliff. A variety of species thus possess innate fears of heights that appear by the time babies are locomotive. Moreover, these fears are common to all land-dwelling species and therefore must have been inherited through processes of natural selection.[31]

A second line of research that establishes the universality of fear of evolutionary dangers that are no longer realistic sources of fear relies on studies of infants who are too young to be influenced by cultural systems of learning. Notably, many of the things that children fear have ancestral roots. Consider Darwin's observation:

> May we not suspect that the vague but very real fears of children, which are quite independent of experience, are the inherited effects of real dangers and abject superstitions during ancient savage times? It is

quite conformable with what we know of the transmission of formerly well-developed characters, that they should appear at an early period of life, and afterwards disappear.

The hallmark signs of normal fears among children are that they arise at approximately the age at which they would have been adaptive during prehistory. As Darwin observed, fears of strangers and of animals universally arise just when infants start to crawl away from mothers at about 6 months of age and so would have been easier victims for predators.[32]

Freud also emphasized how the most common forms of normal anxiety among young children are fears of being left alone, of being in the dark, and of strangers. Psychiatrist Isaac Marks showed how children developed these fears in a predictable sequence over the course of normal development: Fear of separation and strange adults develops at 4–9 months and persists until approximately the age of 2 years, night terrors and fear of darkness typically arise among children around age 1 or 2 years, followed by fears of animals at ages 2–4 years and of the dark at ages 4–6 years. Marks also noted how his own 2-year-old son was terrified at his first sight of strands of seaweed that looked as if they were snakes. Comparable fears, especially fears of certain animals and of darkness, are found throughout the world.[33]

Recent experimental work also indicates that young children are easily conditioned to fear crawling animals but not, for example, opera glasses. Conversely, children rarely fear things that were harmless in the past but are harmful at present. Only a limited range of phenomena, generally limited to objects and situations that were genuinely threatening in ancient times but that pose little danger now, are biologically prepared sources of fear. For example, parents must make extensive efforts to get children to refrain from crossing busy streets, handling sharp objects, or investigating electric outlets but not to avoid snakes, spiders, and rats. Research with infants also demonstrates how the fear of heights and consequent falling is hardwired and precognitive. This innate fear provides an evolved protection from injuries due to falling—a major cause of injury and death even into adulthood. Montaigne would not be surprised that modern psychology shows that humans, like many other species, are naturally designed to fear high places.[34]

Infants also display much social anxiety. The power of inherited fear of strangers is shown by the fact that infants universally develop this fear when they are about 8 months old and can leave their mothers under their own power, an adaptation that makes evolutionary—if not current—sense. Studies show that infants as young as age 3 months prefer faces of their own race compared to those of other races, as demonstrated by heightened amygdala activity. Fears of strangers that underlie many forms of social anxiety thus seem biologically primed. "The temptation to see the other as hostile and subhuman is always present," according to geographer Yi-Fu Tien, "though it may be deeply buried."[35]

A third source of evidence for the universality of fear stems from cross-cultural similarities in this emotion. Cultures display a remarkable agreement regarding many objects and types of fear, and most feared objects across cultures fall into evolutionarily pre-prepared categories. These universal threats include snakes, heights, novel situations, and encounters with strangers. For example, both the underlying pattern and innate triggers of stranger fear are similar across cultures. A study of six widely varying cultures (Bangladesh, !Kung San, United States, Ladino, Kibbutz, and Mayan) provides an example. It shows that in all cultures, this fear reaches a peak at approximately the same age, with younger and older children showing less frequent fear responses. Such processes reflect evolutionarily grounded fears of unfamiliar persons, although cultural learning buttresses an innate template to fear distant social groups.[36]

Universal, inherited fearful emotions thus underlie the most common forms of anxiety. Generally, people react to cues that lead to responses that had evolutionary payoff in the EEA. However, psychological traits that were adaptive during the EEA are currently adaptive only to the extent that the problems that these traits evolved to solve resemble those that humans currently face. They reflect natural fears of objects and situations that were genuinely dangerous in ancient environments but are no longer realistic threats in current circumstances.

Are Mismatched Fears Mental Disorders?

All cultures distinguish between what they consider to be reasonable and unreasonable fears. However, as previously discussed, many of the most frequent fears stem from natural genetic propensities that no longer suit current circumstances. On which side of the divide between natural and unnatural fears do such mismatched emotions fall?

Certainly, the objects of many biologically naturally fears do not pose any current dangers. In most modern settings, animals rarely threaten humans, groups are culturally heterogeneous, and technology helps us control many external threats. Nevertheless, normal brains are programmed to respond to danger and to produce fear responses that worked effectively during the period when our fear responses were selected, and so people are often afraid of things that often pose no present danger. For instance, as Hall noted, objectively speaking, darkness is the safest time of day. With rare exceptions, such as sudden infant death syndrome, harms rarely happen during the night; people are generally exposed to far more dangers during daylight. However, we—especially children—often retain intense fears of the dark that are evolutionary vestiges of a formerly rational fear of human and nonhuman predators.

The central question is whether fears of such situations and objects that were dangerous in prehistory but pose no current threats should be considered to be mental disorders. Like our taste for unhealthy calorie-laden foods, emotional responses that evolution engineered for recurrent problems in the ancestral world are often not well designed for the modern world. Humans now face very different circumstances than those when emotions developed, such that *appropriately* functioning psychological mechanisms might not produce emotions that are adaptive in present-day conditions. The kinds of dangers that were common in prehistory—wild animals, strangers, rejection by one's social group, and the like—continue to be common sources of fear despite posing threats less often now than they did in the past. Our Stone Age emotional systems might be working properly, but they are doing so in environments in which they were not designed to function. Neurobiologist Joseph LeDoux observes, "We are emotional lizards."[37]

When natural anxieties are problematic and unreasonable, it is very tempting to characterize them as mental disorders to bring medical treatment to bear on the problem. The imprecise borders between natural fears, disorders, and evolutionary mismatches make a precise boundary difficult to justify. Certainly, reactions that developed to allow, for example, zebras to escape from pursuing lions are ill-suited for most modern threats. As Robert Sapolsky demonstrates, physiological reactions that let organisms most efficiently respond to acute dangers are maladaptive ways of dealing with the chronic stressors of modern life, whether long-term economic threats, dissolving marriages, or chronically ill children. The question is whether natural stress responses that have impairing consequences in contemporary circumstances are disorders. Mismatched fears are neither wholly inexplicable like many disorders nor wholly understandable in terms of immediate dangers, leading to a question about how we should label them: Should such mismatches be considered disorders?[38]

An analogy to fear mechanisms that are functioning as they were designed to function but that are maladaptive in current circumstances is the situation in which people are under water or in outer space without breathing aids. In the absence of mechanical forms of assistance, human lungs cannot perform their natural function of taking in oxygen, and therefore certain death will result within a few minutes. Nevertheless, individuals who find themselves in these situations without an air supply do not suffer from a lung disorder: It is just that perfectly normal lungs cannot function in environments that lack oxygen. A mismatch between some mechanism and its current environment does not indicate a disorder when the mechanism remains capable of functioning appropriately within the range of environments for which it was designed to function.[39]

Analogously, naturally functioning emotions that are mismatched with current conditions need to be distinguished from disordered emotions that are caused by toxic environments. For example, evolution did not design the lungs to ingest pollutants from noxious environments. Inhaling such poisons in large amounts or over long periods of time can lead lungs to be unable to perform their natural functions. For example, rescue workers who were exposed to thick dust clouds after the September 11, 2001, attack on the World Trade Center still had malfunctioning lungs 7 years later. External forces have led to a dysfunctional condition.[40]

There are a number of reasons why mismatched fears should not be viewed as mental disorders. One is that natural but seemingly irrational fears do not fit appropriate standards for a disorder. Understanding the distinction between normal and disordered fear requires that we go beyond immediate context to understand both our individual and our species-typical evolutionary history. Mismatched fears may be problematic for us in our current social environments, but they are nevertheless not dysfunctions of psychological mechanisms. They represent how our fear mechanisms were designed to function; nothing has "gone wrong" with our minds. Declaring fears that are disproportionate to actual danger to be disorders mistakenly pathologizes many evolutionarily shaped fears. Human beings are not biologically designed to have only fears that are proportional to actual dangers, although cognitive assessment of danger is certainly one pathway to fear. Biologically designed and innately prepared fears are normal when functioning as designed, whether reasonable or not. Unreasonableness itself is not evidence of a failure of biologically designed functioning and thus is not sufficient for disorder.

Another reason to resist labels of disorders for mismatched anxiety conditions is that they misdirect researchers into believing that the problem occurs due to something going wrong inside the person. Researchers who strive to uncover the causes of such states in disturbances of brain circuitry or information processing within the individual will be misled: Perfectly normal brains produce evolutionarily natural anxiety that results from mismatches with current conditions. Research that attempts to identify what is distinctive about anxiety disorders cannot proceed validly if it conflates groups having natural fears due to biologically designed functioning with those having disordered fears due to something going wrong with such functioning. The ultimate goal of understanding the etiologies of fear disorders cannot be achieved if we cannot distinguish such disorders from normal, nondisordered fears. Overly inclusive categories combining natural and unnatural cases make it impossible for studies to identify etiologies specific to disorder. Therefore, mismatches should be distinguished from disorders because the type of causation is broadly different. In the example cited previously, no physician would think that a dysfunction of the lungs caused a person to drown.

A third reason for not pathologizing mismatched fears has to do with treatment. Clinical decisions may partly depend on whether the anxiety is understood as an intense example of a normal fear or as a failure of fear mechanisms. For example, treating individuals with drugs can be justifiable when they want help in mastering fears that inhibit them from optimal social functioning, but this does not necessarily involve correcting a dysfunction. If the problematic fear is natural, one might be inclined to set a higher threshold for tinkering with overall anxiety functioning and enduring the side effects of a medication than if one believes that something has gone wrong with fear processes that the medication mightcorrect.

Sometimes, however, drug and other treatments can help anxious individuals to overcome their fears and enhance their role performances just as, for example, people who work night shifts and suffer from a mismatch between the hours their jobs demand and their natural circadian rhythms can benefit from sleep medications that minimize the consequences of this mismatch. Treating individuals whose occupations require them to give talks or travel long distances can be regarded as a way to improve social participation, not to correct some disorder. We retain both our humanity and our broadest range of therapeutic options when we recognize that many of our fears are natural and not a sign of mental disorder.

A final reason for separating mismatches from disorders is to avoid confusing psychiatric diagnoses with the control of socially undesirable conditions. Good concepts of mental disorders (and medical disorders more generally) must contain some component that provides a nonarbitrary baseline independent of social values. Calling mismatches disorders implies that one can create mass disorder simply by changing the social environment; whenever human beings fail to satisfy social demands, they can be classified as disordered. If so, then more people can be given the disorder simply by raising the demands of society's technology or otherwise changing social values in ways that some people cannot satisfy. As the pace of technological change increases, the potential for mismatches to generate conditions that are labeled as "fear disorders" is likely to increase. The temptation to medically enforce conformity to novel social demands and values will also increase the likelihood of labeling mismatches as defects in the person. This can impoverish our moral discourse and exert pressure to conform to occupational and social demands that may not be to our liking.[41]

Mismatched fears involve situations in which typical individuals, with their biologically designed emotional reactions, face environments for which they were not designed and in which their anxious feelings may be personally and socially problematic. We may want to adjust natural, but currently disadvantageous, human emotions to minimize stress and to fit more comfortably into novel environments, but retaining the distinction between disorders and mismatches is crucial. Misrepresenting natural fears as mental disorders erodes an important distinction between the social control of undesirable traits and the treatment of disorders. Mental disorders involve the failure of evolutionarily designed functions, not just the failure to perform in a desirable way in current social circumstances. Of course, it is not always easy to make this important distinction between mismatched and disordered emotions.

Conclusion

Despite the unprecedented levels of security, prosperity, and good health in modern, developed societies, people remain highly fearful. Human nature gave us a tendency to fear many things, not only objects and situations that are genuinely dangerous but also ones that pose no present dangers but that were threats during prehistory. The plethora of disorders noted at the beginning of this chapter results from diagnosing biologically prepared tendencies to fear objects such as crawling animals and social situations involving evaluation as psychiatric illnesses. Our fear response mechanisms are not dysfunctional per se, but they are in certain respects poorly structured to face the social organization of the modern world. The overresponsiveness of naturally selected fear mechanisms is the price modern humans pay for maintaining brains developed in circumstances that required many immediate responses to physical threats and to the social exigencies of managing life in small groups of closely connected intimates who rarely interacted with strangers. High levels of fear are the unavoidable result, even now. Moreover, the resultant natural fearfulness can deflect our attention from or fail to alert us to far more dangerous objects and situations that do exist in our current environment.

Optimal scientific progress and proper informed consent when treating anxiety both depend on making these basic conceptual and etiological distinctions. When a condition is considered to be a disorder—and thus there is presumed to be some defect in the individual—medical treatment is generally considered the appropriate response. Although treatment is not limited to medical disorders (e.g., cosmetic surgeries or childbirth), disorder status almost invariably prompts treatment. Calling unreasonable but natural aspects of human nature "disorders" can lead psychiatry to cross the boundary of medicine into the realm of enforcing adherence to social norms.

The inherent blurriness of boundaries between natural and unnatural anxiety gives different cultures much leeway to draw the lines in many different places among the various anxiety disorders, anxiety and other conditions, and natural and disordered anxiety. It is not clear that contemporary psychiatric definitions of disordered and nondisordered fear are better than those that other cultures used in the past. "The line separating healthy from pathological," psychiatric historian Janet Oppenheim notes, "is not sharper to psychiatrists now than it appeared to their Victorian forefathers, and political, ideological, or cultural biases are no less potent in defining normalcy and its opposite."[42]

In particular, current diagnostic criteria generally classify fear that results from evolutionary mismatches as disordered rather than natural. However, knowing that many of our fears are normal can itself relieve some of the distress they cause. If we suffer "impairment" in some social role performance, then we have to decide whether that "impairment" represents a natural response to programmed dangers or instead is truly damaged functioning. If the former is the case, then we might consider changing our roles. When that strategy is impossible, we might want to consider using drugs or other therapies to cope with what is actually a natural emotion. In general, however, although this view does not change the fact that one is fearful, it can help dissipate the shame and social pressures we often feel when we are considered to have a mental disorder. Many of our multitudes of fears are not products of brains that have gone wrong; instead, they are unfortunate, but expectable, aspects of our nature as humans. We retain both our humanity and our broadest range of therapeutic options when we recognize that many of our unreasonable fears are natural and not signs of mental disorder.

7 GRIEF

Melancholy . . . in disposition is that transitory melancholy which goes and
comes upon every small occasion of sorrow, need, sickness, trouble, fear,
grief, passion, or perturbation of the mind, any manner of care, discontent,
or thought, which causeth anguish, dullness, heaviness, and vexation of
spirit. . . . And from these melancholy dispositions, no man living is free.
Melancholy, in this sense is the character of mortality.

—ROBERT BURTON, *1621/2001, pp. 143–144*

Maman died today. Or maybe yesterday, I don't know.

—ALBERT CAMUS, *The Stranger, p.3*

Grief, like fear and tastes for large quantities of calories, is an innate
aspect of human nature. Unlike the topics of the previous two
chapters, however, it is aligned to, not mismatched with, existing
social arrangements. Whereas insatiable appetites and specific and
social phobias emerged as natural responses to ancestral environments but can be seriously impairing under modern conditions,
grief remains an essential way to cope with the loss of an intimate.
Natural tendencies to grieve after the death of a loved one are congruent with cultural values that sanction people who *fail* to grieve.
Moreover, although different cultures express grief in a variety of
ways, emotional indifference is never the appropriate response to
the loss of an intimate. Grief is at the same time biologically natural
and culturally mandated.

Grief as a Natural Emotion

Charles Darwin pioneered the biological study of emotions.
Darwin viewed all core emotions, including sadness, anxiety, joy,
anger, and disgust, as naturally emerging in response to specific
environmental demands. Each emotion has a particular function
that deals with a distinct type of problem. For example, disgust
emerges instinctively to signal people to avoid foods that contain
toxins, and fear arises so that people will recognize and respond

to danger. Darwin also emphasized how distinctive physical expressions accompanied each emotion. Disgust features a wrinkling of the nose, curling of the upper lip, and narrowing of the eyes; fear is expressed through trembling, perspiration, and widely open eyes. Such characteristic expressions serve as communicative signals to avoid poisonous foods or dangerous situations. Humans have a hardwired ability to use facial expressions both to convey their own emotions and to understand the emotions that other people express.[1]

For Darwin, emotions were transmitted as part of the human genome. They developed through processes related to natural selection because people who displayed them in appropriate situations enhanced their chances of survival and consequent reproduction. Although the intensity of core emotions varies widely across different individuals, they are found in all humans and in all cultures. Moreover, they are inherited from earlier species, which displayed similar responses. The functions of the emotions are so basic that they automatically emerge without conscious reflection in response to appropriate environmental stimuli. Because each emotion is designed to emerge in specific circumstances, disorders occur when the emotion arises in inappropriate situations, persists well beyond the situation that evoked the emotion, or features grossly disproportionate and maladaptive symptoms.

Grief, like other core emotions, is biologically grounded and universal. Darwin indicated that the biological foundation of grief was found in the loud cries that human children and offspring of most other animals make as ways of getting aid from their parents. These are accompanied by typical facial expressions, including a drawing down of the corners of the mouth, drooping eyelids, and hanging of the head, that persist among adults. Darwin noted, "In all cases of distress, whether great or small, our brains tend through long habit to send an order to certain muscles to contract, as if we were still infants on the point of screaming out." The universal components of sad facial expressions developed because they elicit sympathy, understanding, and social support from others. People easily recognize these biologically based expressions as signs of suffering and become more likely to provide help to the distressed individual. Grief is so widely recognized as a natural response to a loss that the American Psychiatric Association (APA) uses it in its general definition of mental disorder as the prototype of a nondisordered condition: "An expectable or culturally approved response to a common stressor or loss, such as the death of a loved one, is not a mental disorder."[2]

Grief as a Cultural Norm

In contrast to Darwin, Herodotus focused on how emotional expressions reflect cultural norms that were not universal but differed widely across various groups. He focused on how various cultures displayed their sorrow through diverse mourning rituals. Consider, for example, the Egyptians:

> As regards mourning and funerals, when a distinguished man dies all the women of the household plaster their heads and faces with mud, then, leaving the body indoors, perambulate the town with the dead man's female relatives . . . and beat their bared breasts. The men too, for their part, follow the same procedure, wearing a girdle and beating themselves like the women.

Typically for him, Herodotus contrasted Egyptians' bereavement rituals with those of other cultures. He observed that "in other nations the relatives of the deceased in time of mourning cut their hair, but the Egyptians, who shave at all other times, mark a death by letting the hair grow both on head and chin." The Persian army provided another example. After the death of the esteemed warrior Masistius, "They shaved their heads, cut the manes of their horses and mules, and abandoned themselves to such cries of grief that the whole of Boeotia [a region in central Greece] was loud with the noise of them."[3]

Herodotus also provided counterexamples in which deaths of intimates are celebrated rather than mourned. He noted the custom of the Trausi, a Greek tribe: "When somebody dies, they bury him with merriment and rejoicing, and point out how happy he now is and how many miseries he has at last escaped." He contrasts the jollity a death invokes with the gloom that follows a birth: "When a baby is born the family sits round and mourns at the thought of the sufferings the infant must endure now that it has entered the world, and goes through the whole catalogue of human sorrows." Herodotus also suggests that grief can sometimes result from social norms as opposed to genuine feelings, as in the Spartan ritual occurring after a king's death, in which "men and women together strike their foreheads with every sign of grief, wailing as if they could never stop and continually declaring that the king who has just died was the best they ever had." He had just observed, however, that Spartans are compelled to mourn "under penalty of heavy fine."[4]

Herodotus' views endure in much twentieth- and twenty-first-century social science, which focuses on the thoroughgoing differences in emotions across cultures. Anthropologist Ruth Benedict set the agenda for cultural studies about the emotions, emphasizing that definitions of appropriate and inappropriate emotions derive from local concepts that cannot be generalized across groups. Like Herodotus, she was especially concerned with the cultural relativity of reactions to death. For example, whereas many Western societies focused on the grief that a loss of a loved one generates, many other groups approached death as a sign of danger and contamination. Still others, such as Native Americans on the Northwest Coast, viewed the death of an intimate as an occasion for revenge against the group of the individual they held responsible for the death. Benedict summarized a variety of cultural responses to grief: "Ignoring it, indulging it by uninhibited expression, getting even, punishing a victim and seeking restitution of the original situation." Others, such as the influential historian Lawrence Stone, claimed that grief was a modern invention that did not exist in England and other western European countries before the eighteenth century when declining mortality rates strengthened bonds between spouses and between parents and children. For Benedict and those who succeeded her, normal and pathological emotions have nothing to do with natural functioning but are products of cultural scripts that define suitable and unsuitable actions.[5]

Writers in the tradition of Herodotus emphasize how such pronounced cultural variability is unlikely to have a biological foundation. Culturally specific rules dictate the circumstances that evoke emotions, the kinds of emotions that are felt, and the ways emotions are expressed. In this view, the apparent commonalities in emotional expression that Darwin observed mistakenly impose ethnocentric Western categories about appropriate or inappropriate feelings onto other cultures. Because display rules for the emotions differ so drastically from culture to culture, group to group, and time period to time period, emotions are culturally relative and not universal.[6]

This chapter proposes that the biologically and culturally focused views regarding the emotions are not contradictory. As Darwin stressed, a universal, evolutionarily grounded substrate underlies emotions such as grief. However, as Herodotus observed, different cultures provide divergent norms for how emotions should be expressed. Cultures also provide the conventions that people use to manage and control their emotional feelings. In addition, the particular circumstances that evoke each emotion often differ across cultural contexts. None of these culturally specific aspects contradict the existence of common underlying emotions with parameters that cultural meanings fill. Cultural construction is not antithetical to but, rather, is coordinated with biological design. As the APA recognizes, whatever particular expressions grief might take, it is always a "culturally approved response."[7]

Components of Natural and Unnatural Sadness and Grief

If Darwin was correct in asserting that emotions emerge because of their adaptive functions, then normal grief, as with normal sadness more generally, should have three essential components: It should arise in a specific context, after the death of an intimate; its intensity should be roughly proportionate to the importance and centrality to one's life of the lost individual; and it should gradually subside over time as people adjust to their new circumstances and return to psychological and social equilibrium. Grief processes can also be pathological when grief emerges in inappropriate circumstances; features extreme symptoms such as marked functional impairment, morbid preoccupations, suicidal ideation, or psychotic symptoms; or persists for extraordinarily long periods of time. We consider each of these components in turn.[8]

Context

Emotions are evolutionarily selected to respond to a specific range of stimuli and not to respond outside that range. Grief arises after the loss of a valued intimate attachment that involves closeness, love, and friendship. As long as emotions have been recorded, experiences of grief—feelings of deep sadness that follow the death of an intimate—have been central to portrayals of basic human nature. The intuition that people naturally become intensely sad after a loved one dies is so strong that it is a social norm: People are *expected* to show grief after a close tie dies; those who do not evoke surprise or condemnation. "In our society any man who does not weep at his mother's funeral runs the risk of being sentenced to death," French novelist and philosopher Albert Camus memorably noted about the central character in his novel, *The Stranger*, who was emotionally unaffected by the death of his mother. Biological design and cultural values align in the case of grief.[9]

Gilgamesh, a Sumerian epic dating to around 2100 BC, is widely regarded as the oldest known literary document. It contains profound depictions of the piercing grief that its central character, the king Gilgamesh, suffers. "Hear me," Gilgamesh cries, "O Elders of Uruk, hear me, O men! I mourn for Enkidu, my friend, I shriek in anguish like a mourner." Gilgamesh experiences enormous sadness, cries bitterly, is possessed by restless agitation, and suffers from a sense of worthlessness that leads him to cast aside finery and cover himself with filth. Unable to bear his ordinary social activities, he wanders alone in the desert. In a moving description of grief's expectable effects, Gilgamesh replies to a tavern-keeper who has commented on his condition:

> Tavern-keeper, should not my cheeks be emaciated? Should my heart not be wretched, my features not haggard? Should there not be sadness deep within me! Should I not look like one who has been traveling a long distance, and should ice and heat not have seared my face! . . . My friend, Enkidu, whom I love deeply, who went through every hardship with me, the fate of mankind has overtaken him.

Gilgamesh's repeated use of "should" indicates that he considers grief, however much suffering it entails, to naturally follow the death of a dear friend.[10]

Nearly 1400 years later, Homer composed the founding document of the Western literary tradition. One of *The Iliad*'s central themes is the grief of its hero, Achilles. His reaction on hearing of the death of his friend Patroclus matches the intensity of Gilgamesh's reaction:

> A black cloud of grief came shrouding over Achilles.
> Both hands clawing the ground for soot and filth,
> He poured it over his head, fouled his handsome face
> And black ashes settled into his fresh clean war-shirt.
> Overpowered in all his power, sprawled in the dust,
> Achilles lay there, fallen
> Tearing his hair, defiling it with his own hands.

Such descriptions are common across cultures and historical epochs.[11]

In the fifth century BC, Hippocratic medical writings defined symptoms such as those that Gilgamesh and Achilles displayed as typical of what was then called "melancholia." They characterized this condition in a remarkably similar way as current definitions of depression: "aversion to food, despondency, sleeplessness, irritability, restlessness." However, their definition also emphasized that when these symptoms emerged in appropriate contexts such as the death of an intimate, they should not be defined as melancholic disorders, which only existed when melancholy was disproportionate to its circumstances.[12]

Such Hippocratic-based definitions prevailed for millennia. The most celebrated work on depression, English vicar Robert Burton's *Anatomy of Melancholy*, published in 1621, provided a profound description of contextually appropriate sadness, including grief, which he viewed as a ubiquitous aspect of the human condition:

> Melancholy . . . in disposition, it is that transitory melancholy which goes and comes upon every small occasion of sorrow, need, sickness, trouble, fear, grief, passion, or perturbation of the mind, any manner of care, discontent, or thought, which causeth anguish, dullness, heaviness, and vexation of spirit. . . . And from these melancholy dispositions, no man living is free, no Stoic, none so wise, none so happy, none so patient, so generous, so godly, so divine, that can vindicate himself; so well composed, but more or less, some time or other, he feels the smart of it. Melancholy, in this sense is the character of mortality.[13]

Portrayals of intense, but natural, grief remain central literary themes. Joan Didion's best-selling memoir of her anguish that followed the unexpected death of her husband provides one example: "Grief comes in waves, paroxysms, sudden apprehensions that weaken the knees and blind the eyes and obliterate the dailiness of life." Psychiatrist and anthropologist Arthur Kleinman gives another penetrating portrayal of grief:

> In March, 2011, my wife died and I experienced the physiology of grief. I felt greatly sad and yearned for her. I didn't sleep well. When I returned to a now empty house, I became agitated. I also felt fatigued and had difficulty concentrating on my academic work. My weight declined owing to a newly indifferent appetite.

Novelist Joyce Carol Oates' *A Widow's Story* offers one more recent illustration of the impact of the sudden loss of a beloved spouse. After nearly 50 years of marriage during which Oates rarely spent a night away from her husband, he suddenly fell ill with pneumonia and died 1 week later. Oates describes her despair, inability to eat or sleep, and profound feelings of emptiness. She is unable to feel pleasure even when she learns that two of her books have been nominated for major awards. Such emotions have consistently arisen during the course of history after the loss of a loved one.[14]

Proportionate Severity

The second component of normal grief is that the emotional and symptomatic severity of the response should be of roughly proportionate intensity to the magnitude of the loss that has been experienced. Grief after the death of a distant relative or an acquaintance should generally be minimally disturbing, leading to relatively mild reactions. Deaths of closer relations that expectably occur after long illnesses or that involve relationships that were not deep should generally trigger relatively medium-intensity reactions overall, although they can be quite intense soon after the loss. Deaths of intimates that are unexpected or involve major consequences generally evoke reactions of greater severity, including intense states of deep sorrow, despondency, anguish, pain, numbness, and dejection such as Gilgamesh, Achilles, Joan Didion, Arthur Kleinman, and Joyce Carol Oates experienced. "It is not until we actually experience a profound loss," psychologist George Bonanno observes, "that we really know how intensely sadness can penetrate our being, how all-encompassing and bottomless it can seem." Bonanno's comments echo Robert Burton's much earlier observation that "every perturbation is a misery, but grief a cruel torment, a domineering passion ... when grief appears, all other passions vanish."[15]

Normally bereaved people commonly develop symptoms, including depressed mood, inability to feel pleasure, loss of appetite, inability to concentrate, and insomnia. Most studies indicate that more than three-fourths of bereaved people report crying, sleep disturbance, and low mood, and more than half also indicate loss of appetite in the month following the loss. Among people who have lost spouses, most studies find that between 20 and 40 percent—and some find that more than half—develop symptoms comparable in severity to major depressive disorder (MDD) criteria during the first few months. Rates of depressive symptoms in parents' reactions to the deaths of their children or of adolescents' reactions to the deaths of their parents are even higher, more intense, and longer lasting than those that follow the deaths of spouses.[16]

The intensity of grief generally varies in a roughly proportionate manner with the nature, context, and degree of disruption the loss causes as well as the relational, social, and economic resources individuals possess to cope with their new circumstances. The unexpectedness of the death is one factor that makes people especially prone to intense grief. "It was in fact," Didion reports on the sudden death of her husband, "the ordinary nature of everything preceding the event that prevented me from truly believing it had happened, absorbing it, incorporating it, getting past it." Because deaths of intimates among people who become bereaved at younger ages are less common, they report more symptoms than do older people. In contrast, expected deaths that occur after chronic illnesses produce fewer depression-like symptoms than traumatic or otherwise unexpected deaths. The quality of the relationship with the lost intimate also strongly affects the intensity of the subsequent bereavement. Losses of long-standing, close, and intense relationships are most productive of distress. That is, factors outside of individuals related to their situations and relationships more than their inner capacities are related to the severity of their response.[17]

Persistence

The third and final component of nondisordered grief is that symptoms not only emerge but also persist in accordance with external contexts and then naturally remit when the context changes for the better or as people adapt to their losses. The definitions of melancholia among the earliest Hippocratic diagnosticians made clear that symptoms alone were not sufficient indicators of a mental disorder: "If fear or sadness last for a long time it is melancholia." Natural fear and sadness persist proportionately to their generating context: Only symptoms that "last for a long time" indicate disorder.

The duration of normal sadness after the death of an intimate is highly variable but gradually desists over time. Sigmund Freud emphasized this aspect of normal grief:

> Although grief involves grave departures from the normal attitude to life, it never occurs to us to regard it as a morbid condition and hand the mourner over to medical treatment. We rest assured that after a lapse of time it will be overcome, and we look upon any interference with it as inadvisable or even harmful.

Although Freud asserted that symptoms associated with mourning are both intense and "grave departures from the normal," he nevertheless insisted that grief is not a "morbid" condition. He made clear that suffering was a natural part of responding to the death of an intimate, stressing that grief of even the deepest intensity is naturally self-healing so that with time the mourner returns to a normal psychological state. Indeed, Freud emphasized that it would "never occur to us" to provide medical treatment to the bereaved. Medical intervention, he suggested, could actually harm the grieving person through interfering with natural healing processes.[18]

In support of Freud's contention, relatively few bereaved individuals show serious symptoms for long periods, and most gradually adapt to their losses and recover their pre-loss levels of functioning. In one major study,

42 percent of the bereaved met criteria for depressive disorder after 1 month, but only 16 percent remained in this state after 1 year. Other studies confirm the steep declines in symptoms that arise in the first few weeks after the loss. Approximately 10–20 percent of bereaved persons fulfill *Diagnostic and Statistical Manual of Mental Disorders* (*DSM*) diagnostic criteria for depressive disorder 1 year after the death, and even for many of these, psychological functioning returns to pre-loss levels after 2 years. The vast majority of grief reactions, even those that satisfy current criteria for depressive disorders, are actually transient normal responses to loss, with only a small proportion becoming chronic conditions that are likely disorders.[19]

Whether or not grief endures depends on the degree of social and economic disruption the loss produces and the resources available to cope with these upheavals. In general, people who have better financial resources, more education, stronger family and friendship networks, better health, and fewer other stressors in their lives have greater ability to cope with losses. In the long term, economic deprivation that follows the death of a husband is more strongly associated with the intensity of sadness than is widowhood in itself. The presence or absence of social support that helps cope with the loss is also a good predictor of the duration of grief. Persistent grief, therefore, need not indicate the presence of a disorder but might instead mark the persistence of the stressful situation that accompanies the loss.[20]

Many portrayals of grief emphasize not just its intense painfulness but also how its seeming permanence eventually ends. "This dark experience," Kleinman observes, "lightened over the months, so that the feelings became much less acute by around 6 months."[21] Likewise, Oates' grief unexpectedly lifted after 6 months passed. A few months later, she married for a second time. As Freud emphasized, most people will get over their loss on their own or with the help of family and friends and do not require professional treatment. Evolution designed normal grief reactions, although they might come and go for a period of months or even years, to gradually desist over time.

Disordered Grief

The fact that grief follows an acute loss does not in itself mean that its symptoms must be normal. The response to the death of an intimate can sometimes be of such unusual severity as to produce a breakdown of normal loss response mechanisms and trigger a depressive disorder. Emergence under appropriate circumstances of the loss of an intimate is thus a necessary but not a sufficient condition for the presence of normal grief. Several centuries after the Hippocratics wrote, renowned Greek physician Aretaeus of Cappadocia (ca AD 150–200) recognized this distinction between normal and disordered conditions: "[Melancholic] patients are . . . dejected or unreasonably torpid, without any manifest cause; such is the commencement of melancholy. And they also become peevish, dispirited, sleepless, and start up from a disturbed sleep. Unreasonable fear also seizes them." Aretaeus' definition shows the importance of social context in definitions of natural grief and other deep states of sadness. The same symptoms that emerge in appropriate contexts can indicate a melancholic disorder when they arise "without any manifest cause." Robert Burton, too, distinguished natural melancholic feelings that arise after losses such as the death of an intimate, which are the "character of mortality," from melancholic disorders that arise "without any apparent occasion."[22]

The distinction between contextually appropriate and disordered grief persisted in the diagnostic criteria found in psychiatric manuals before 1980. For example, the *DSM-II* (1968) defined depressive neurosis as follows: "This disorder is manifested by an excessive reaction of depression due to an internal conflict or to an identifiable event such as the loss of a love object or cherished possession."[23] This definition recognized that psychiatrists should not consider as mental disorders reactions such as "the loss of a love object" that are proportionate and not "excessive" to their contexts.

Sometimes, however, the circumstances of loss are so extreme that their pain and disorientation exceed the capacities of natural coping mechanisms and so constitute disorders. Consider the horrific experience of Sonali Deraniyagala, an economist who was vacationing at a Sri Lankan beach resort with her husband, two young sons, and parents when a giant tsunami suddenly developed that killed her entire family (and a quarter million others). The intensity of her symptoms matched the enormity of her loss: She drank copious quantities of alcohol, abused many different kinds of pills, acted out in bizarre ways, and became suicidal. It took many years before Deraniyagala became accustomed to her extraordinary loss.[24]

Although such extreme symptoms might seem proportionate to a sudden loss of such unimaginable proportions, they could warrant a depressive diagnosis because they involve extreme immobilization, morbid preoccupations, suicidal ideation, and psychotic symptoms that have no adaptive qualities. When grief, as in Deraniyagala's case, involves severe symptoms that persist despite the passage of time and changing circumstances, then it can be presumed that an individual's reaction to the death of an intimate has caused a breakdown in psychological functioning. In general, approximately 10–15 percent of the bereaved come to suffer from chronic depressive conditions that may well be disorders.[25]

Beginning with the *DSM-III* in 1980, psychiatric diagnostic manuals drastically changed the criteria for depressive disorder. In contrast to thousands of years of prior medical history, they used overt symptoms instead of the proportionality of symptoms to their context to define this condition. Their criteria specified that anyone who displayed five symptoms—including depressed mood, diminished pleasure, changes in appetite or sleep patterns, psychomotor retardation, fatigue, feelings of worthlessness, inability to concentrate, or recurrent thoughts of suicide—during a 2-week period should receive a diagnosis of major depression (the five must include either depressed mood or diminished interest or pleasure). Nevertheless, these manuals continued to make an exception to their symptom-based definitions in the case of grief: The diagnosis of major depression was not given to bereaved people unless their symptoms were prolonged or were especially severe. Indeed, as noted previously, the *DSM* used grief as the prime example of a nondisordered, expectable condition. Its bereavement exclusion exempted patients from a diagnosis of depression unless their symptoms lasted longer than 2 months, instead of 2 weeks, or included a symptom of marked functional impairment, morbid preoccupation with worthlessness, suicidal ideation, psychotic symptoms, or psychomotor retardation.[26]

An unbroken history of psychiatric (not to mention literary and philosophical) thought up to and including recent psychiatric diagnostic manuals understood that biological and psychological states that might otherwise seem to indicate a mental disorder but that emerged in response to the context of the death of an intimate are natural, not pathological. For most people, bereavement is a normal feature of human experience that will naturally dissipate with the passage of time; in some cases, however, the severity and length of the grieving process can indicate a disorder.

The Universality of Grief

We need not just rely on millennia of medical and literary portrayals of grief to assert that it is an innate aspect of human nature. Darwin focused on three types of evidence—the presence of the emotion among species that arose before humans, among presocialized infants, and in all human cultures—as strong indications that some emotion is universal. Grief meets these demanding criteria.

Continuities Across Species

Darwinj emphasized the commonality of grief between humans and other species, observing that "the power to bring the grief muscles freely into play appears to be hereditary, like almost every other human faculty." Nonhuman primates respond to loss through observable features of expression, behavior, and brain functioning in ways that show clear resemblances to humans. Darwin observed, "So intense is the grief of female monkeys for the loss of their young that it invariably caused the death of certain kinds." He noted, and subsequent observers confirmed, that bereaved apes and humans show similar facial expressions, including elevated eyebrows, drooping eyelids, horizontal wrinkles across the forehead, and outward extension and drawing down of the lips. In addition, both species develop decreased locomotor activity, agitation, slouched or fetal-like posture, cessation of play behavior, and social withdrawal. Chimpanzees make loud distress calls after an intimate dies. Nonhuman primates also react to separations from intimates with physiological responses similar to those that correlate with sadness in humans, including elevated levels of cortisol and ACTH hormones and impairments of the hypothalamic–pituitary–adrenal axis. After the loss of a companion, many dogs show signs such as drooped posture, lack of interest in usual activities, slow movement, sleep and eating problems, and hormonal changes that also characterize bereaved humans. Dolphins stop eating after a mate dies; geese search for a dead companion until they become lost and disoriented.[27]

Studies of other species also show that, as with humans, symptoms of grief that develop after separations rapidly disappear when the situation of loss is resolved, such as when an infant monkey is reunited with its mother. Also, primates in environments that feature readily available mother substitutes rarely exhibit severe or enduring reactions in response to maternal separations. Such transient sadness responses to separation are part of innate coping mechanisms among many species. Similarly, in experimental situations, primates that are given stressors in the presence of companions develop considerably less distress than ones surrounded by strangers. However, prolonged separations and separations marked by profound isolation can produce neuroanatomical changes that permanently affect nonhuman primate brain functioning, analogous to the triggering of genuine depressive disorder in bereaved humans.[28]

Loss Responses in Presocialized Infants

Human tendencies to become sad in certain contexts appear very early—in infancy. Darwin noted how the characteristic mental and physical signs of grief, such as dejection, despair, crying, and weeping, are apparent in very young children. British child psychiatrist John Bowlby conducted influential studies that demonstrated how attachment losses lead to depressive reactions among infants. Bowlby observed that human infants develop sadness responses as a coping mechanism when they are separated from their primary caregivers because they have innate tendencies to need strong attachments and so respond to their loss through signals of distress. Healthy infants who were separated from their mothers initially reacted by crying and displaying other expressions of despair. They protested the separation and searched for their mothers. These responses usually evoked sympathy from the mothers, who responded by attending to their infants' needs.[29]

Bowlby suggested that children who respond to separations with distress are more likely to survive than ones who do not so that expressions conveying sadness became naturally selected. His work indicates that sadness naturally arises after the loss of close attachments before infants have learned culturally appropriate ways of expressing sadness and so is an innate aspect of human nature. Prolonged separations, however, can result in states of detachment, withdrawal, inactivity, and apathy that are similar to the symptoms of grief disorders among adults.

Cross-Cultural Uniformity

The capacity for intense sadness in response to loss appears to be a universal feature found in all human groups. Loss responses with the characteristics described previously are found not only throughout Western history but also in non-Western societies. Darwin was perhaps the first to comment on the universality of sadness responses: "The expression of grief due to the contraction of the grief-muscles, is by no means confined to Europeans, but appears to be common to all the races of mankind." As noted in Chapter 1, Darwin provided a description of grief among the Australian aborigines that was comparable to the appearance of this emotion among Europeans:

> After prolonged suffering the eyes become dull and lack expression, and are often slightly suffused with tears. The eyebrows not rarely are rendered oblique, which is due to their inner ends being raised. This

produces peculiarly-formed wrinkles on the forehead which are very different from those of a simple frown; though in some cases a frown alone may be present. The corners of the mouth are drawn downwards, which is so universally recognized as a sign of being out of spirits, that it is almost proverbial.

Considerable subsequent research confirms Darwin's observations that such expressions, especially the contraction of the muscles at the corners of the mouth, are recognized across cultures as representing grief.[30]

The most important studies stem from psychologist Paul Ekman's research on basic human emotions, including sadness. To test the universality of emotions, Ekman studied facial expressions because they are less susceptible to cultural influences than are verbal reports of emotions. In one type of study, Ekman asked people to show how their faces would look if they felt sad "because your child died." The resulting facial expressions were photographed. In these pictures, sad faces displayed eyes that are downcast with drooping or tense upper lids, eyebrows that are drawn together, jaws that are closed or slightly open, and lower lips that are drawn down. The photographs were then shown to people in different cultures, and they were asked to select from among several choices of narratives about the situation that triggered the pictured emotion (the loss of a child is used for sadness).[31]

Ekman's results indicate overwhelming agreement among persons in different countries about the emotion each photograph expresses. Very high rates of concurrence, ranging from 73 to 90 percent, existed across five different cultures (Japan, Brazil, Chile, Argentina, and the United States); the concurrence was even higher within each particular culture in ratings of sadness photographs. Another study of 10 cultures (Estonia, Germany, Greece, Hong Kong, Italy, Japan, Scotland, Sumatra, Turkey, and the United States) indicated between 76 and 92 percent agreement on facial expressions of sadness.[32]

Even the vast majority (79 percent) of members of the preliterate, isolated, Fore culture in Papua New Guinea, which had not been exposed to any kind of media or to contact with outside cultures, agreed with members of literate cultures on the face that most corresponded to sadness in the story that was read to them. Because Ekman's research in this culture did not rely on the use of Western words, it is immune to critiques that Western preconceptions account for the findings. Ekman's findings indicate that some innate features of expression of sadness are present in all cultures, presumably because they stem from the evolution of humans as a species.[33]

Why Is Grief Natural?

Evidence from other species, infants, and across history and culture indicates that grief after the death of an intimate is a normal feature of human nature. However, the deepest and most puzzling question about grief is: *Why* do people grieve after the death of an intimate? What sort of survival value did this painful and debilitating emotion provide that caused it to be naturally selected? Grieving people must have had some greater ability to spread genes compared to those who do not grieve after suffering the loss of an intimate.

The puzzle is that grieving among people in their reproductive years seems on its face to be harmful to passing genes to future generations. Intensely sad people experience decreased initiative, find less pleasure in life to motivate them, and tend to withdraw from everyday activities. Positive mood, in contrast, encourages activities required to obtain sexual partners, food, shelter, and other resources that increase survival and reproduction. Thus, under ordinary circumstances, consistent levels of negative mood should be selectively disadvantageous. For intense grief responses to have been naturally selected, there must have been some special circumstances in which the benefits of temporarily experiencing such symptoms outweighed the obvious costs. In those particular contexts, and only in those contexts, states of low mood must have increased fitness precisely because they made people less active, less motivated, and so on. The best analogy is to acute pain from an injury, which stops activity but is adaptive because it helps people avoid further tissue damage. In contrast, chronic pain unrelated to any underlying physiological damage would be harmful in the way that depressive disorder is certainly harmful.

In considering grief's function, it is important to keep in mind that the function of a biological mechanism need not be beneficial in the current environment, although it often is beneficial. It must have been valuable in the distant past when the human genome was formed, however, and must thus explain why the underlying mechanism was naturally selected and still exists. What benefit might grief have conferred that led to its natural selection over the course of human evolution? First, note that life spans in ancient Paleolithic groups were quite short; average life expectancies were in the thirties. Experiences of death would have been ubiquitous during this period. Parents would commonly experience the deaths of their children: The best estimates indicate that approximately one-fifth of children died during their first year of life.[34] Spouses would have lost mates while they were caring for young children, and many children would have been orphaned at young ages. Regardless of the exact figures, it is clear that many bereaved people were still in their procreative years. What strategy would best accomplish survival and consequent reproduction in such circumstances?

The most likely explanation is that grief attracts social support. States of social isolation would have been especially threatening in the tightly knit, interdependent human social groups that existed during the environment of evolutionary adaption (EEA), making a positive social response likely. The Australian psychiatrist Aubrey Lewis, following some of Darwin's suggestive comments, was the first to propose that depressive reactions could function as a "cry for help" that calls attention to needy states and elicits social support. The obvious signs that sad facial expressions convey are useful ways to communicate that people need to get help from others. In contrast, people who did not show signs of grieving likely received less support. The withdrawal, inhibition, and vegetative aspects of depression mimic illness and signal others to draw the suffering individual back into the group. Expressions of grief were adaptive because they communicate inner states to other people so that depressed people attract social support after attachment losses. That is, grief successfully shows neediness.[35]

John Bowlby proposed a complementary account of the adaptive nature of grief after losses. For Bowlby, the pain of grief following attachment losses motivates people to vigorously seek reunion with the lost loved one and not to give up the absent tie. Grief at thoughts of loss allowed social bonds to persist during the frequent, temporary absences of one party that characterized hunting and gathering groups in the EEA and thus promoted the maintenance of social relationships. From this viewpoint, grief after the death of a loved one was a by-product of adaptive responses to attachment losses that were not permanent.[36]

The communication of grief after losses of attachment continues to attract support and sympathy from others. Grieving people who have larger and stronger networks of family and friends receive more emotional and material support and help with coping with the demands of daily life than more isolated people. As a consequence, they are less likely to have prolonged periods of extreme intense mourning. Strong collective religious rituals and belief systems also seem to make people less vulnerable to loss. Grief is an ancient emotion that retains its valuable function in the modern world.[37]

Natural grief, however, is also designed so that it will not last for extended periods and thus isolate the bereaved person from sources of social support. Evolutionary processes should provide some limits to the severity of depressed moods after a loss because responses of disproportionately high intensity and duration would not allow people to disengage from inhibited states and return to more productive activities. Nondisordered loss responses cannot encompass gross breakdowns in basic psychological systems, such as delusional and psychotic symptoms, if the individual is to be able to adapt to the new circumstances. With the passage of time, grief gradually wanes and the person returns to his or her normal state. Contextually proportionate sadness responses appear to be a designed, and valuable, aspect of human nature.

Culture and Sadness

The findings that have emerged from studies of primates and very young children and across cultures all indicate that sadness responses are biologically based and not due to social scripts alone. Culture and biological design, however, are not always antithetical to each other; with regard to grief, they are complementary. Culture itself is an evolved human capacity; humans are designed to be capable of a degree of socialization and internalization of social values, meanings, and rules. As sociologist Jonathan Turner has emphasized, people are hardwired to pay attention to cultural symbols, social roles, and interactional needs. Some evolved mechanisms, such as emotions, involve responses to such meanings. Thus, cultural meaning plays an essential and perhaps even designed role in shaping the final expression of grief.[38]

The biological roots of grief in no way preclude important cultural influences on when or how grief is expressed. Culture influences evolutionarily shaped loss responses in a variety of ways. First, cultural meanings influence which *particular* events count as losses. For example, in most social groups within the United States, the failure of a woman to give birth to a male child would not be a reason for intense sadness. In Zimbabwe, however, the meaning of such failure includes a serious decline in social status, undesirability as a marriage partner, and potential divorce. Consequently, failure to have a male child is a source of serious depressive reactions in Zimbabwean women. In India, among the leading causes of suicide are quarrels with in-laws and dowry disputes, which represent major losses in India but would not necessarily bring about such extreme responses in other societies. The fact that such cultural meanings affect the extent to which an event is classified in a naturally given category of loss does not conflict with the fact that the basic categories themselves are given biologically. Nature supplies the template for triggers of loss responses, but culture provides the content for this template.[39]

Cultural values also set the parameters for what are considered proportionate responses to loss. All cultures have display norms or scripts that guide the overt expression of emotion. These provide the scale of intensity and duration of appropriate responses, shape how emotionally expressive people are, and influence which aspects of the response public expressions of the emotion emphasize. Some cultures socialize their members to be highly emotional, whereas others encourage suppression and minimizing emotion.[40]

Many non-Western cultures encourage the expression of sadness in public ceremonies and organized rituals that shape the nature of the display. For example, the Kaluli of New Guinea deal with the loss of an intimate by becoming angry; their anger is turned outward into feelings that one is owed reparations for the loss. Public ceremonies allow for the expression of these feelings in weeping, songs, and the payment of compensation. Yet other cultures as diverse as the Navaho and the Tahitians strongly discourage displays of extreme sadness. Appropriate grieving norms also differ in the West. The traditional Irish wake resembles more of a party than a funeral, with participants celebrating the life of the deceased through consuming copious amounts of alcohol and food. Darwin himself noted,

> With the civilized nations of Europe there is also much difference in the frequency of weeping. Englishmen rarely cry, except under the pressure of the acutest grief; whereas in some parts of the Continent the men shed tears much more readily and freely.[41]

Another example stems from the routine contrast between the psychological expression of grief (and sadness more generally) in the West and its somatic presentation in non-Western cultures. For example, Chinese populations tend to focus, after loss, on bodily feelings of distress that often go along with intense sadness, such as back pain, stomachaches, headaches, and the like. Despite the different outward manifestations, however, common underlying emotions appear to be universal. Chinese patients are aware of the psychological aspects of their feelings, but social norms mandate that they express their problems in somatic terms when they seek help from physicians. Members of these cultures express intense sadness facially and behaviorally as do Westerners, and when specifically asked, they report the same psychological and emotional experiences. Moreover, their symptoms are responsive to the same medications that are prescribed for depression in Western societies.[42]

Cultural norms also affect what is viewed as the appropriate duration of loss responses. At one extreme, among the Navaho, outward expressions of grief are limited to 4 days. The bereaved person is not expected to show grief or refer to the dead person after this short period. At the other extreme,

Mediterranean societies traditionally dictated long periods of mourning for bereaved widows that could last for many years.[43]

It is important, however, to separate cultural norms for expressing emotions such as grief from the experienced emotions themselves. For example, among Iranians,

> if someone in your family dies, you have to really act like you are sorry, to wail and kick, otherwise you'll be accused of having ill feelings toward that person, regardless of what your inner feelings are, especially if you stand to inherit something.

At the extreme, cultural norms can even transform expressions of grief into cheerfulness, as Irish wakes demonstrate. Or, the Balinese respond to bereavement with laughter. However, even when cultural norms dictate expressive responses incompatible with sadness, they recognize sadness as the characteristic underlying feeling; thus, the Balinese believe that sadness is the natural response to loss but that its expression should be combated because it is detrimental to health and leads others to be sad.[44]

The highly varying cultural expressions of sadness are consistent with the existence of a common underlying emotional state. Grief is a universal, innate emotion that cultures channel into various expressions. Culture and biology are not two opposing explanations but, rather, complementary parts of one explanation; each requires the other for comprehensive and coherent explanations of grief responses.

Psychiatry's Abandonment of the Bereavement Exclusion

Both biological and cultural explanations, not to mention common sense, recognize that people naturally grieve after the loss of an intimate. The psychiatric profession, too, recognized that bereaved people would otherwise qualify for a diagnosis of MDD and exempted them from diagnosis unless their symptoms were especially prolonged or severe. In 2013, however, the APA overturned the widespread consensus that grief after the death of an intimate is a natural response. Upending all previous medical, philosophical, and literary understandings, it abolished the previous bereavement exclusion so that experiences of such common symptoms as depressed mood, a lack of pleasure, and sleep and appetite difficulties for a mere *2-week* period now meet the standards for a mental disorder.[45]

The best explanation for why psychiatry abolished the bereavement exclusion seems to be the threat to its broader professional authority. An abundance of evidence indicated that bereavement was not the sole exception to the MDD criteria but actually a *model* for other depressive conditions that arise after losses stemming from such conditions as the collapse of a long-term interpersonal relationship, the loss of a valued job, a diagnosis of a life-threatening physical illness, or the failure to achieve a long-sought-after goal. Such naturally distressing conditions provoke the symptoms of a large proportion of clients in outpatient psychiatric treatment; depression is by far the most common condition that psychiatrists treat. Accepting that many of their patients suffer from normal responses to loss that, like grief, will naturally dissipate over time or after a change in social conditions might force psychiatrists (and other mental health clinicians) to lose a substantial number of customers.[46]

The APA's decision illustrates a sharp regression in understanding how to separate natural from unnatural emotions. Grief after the loss of an intimate is perhaps the clearest case of a distressing emotion that is acting as nature designed it to act. In the absence of the extenuating factors that the now-abandoned bereavement exclusion recognized, it is not a mental disorder. This relapse is particularly disturbing in light of the fact that in our society, the psychiatric profession has the cultural authority and professional power to define which emotions are normal and which are abnormal.

Conclusion

Grief illustrates how biologically based phenomena also have important culturally specific aspects. Portrayals of grief in literature, philosophy, and medicine across millennia of history leave little doubt that humans naturally grieve after the death of a loved one. Moreover, studies of nonhuman primates, infants, and facial expressions across cultures show that grief following the death of an intimate is not specific to Western culture or even to humans. The best explanation for the universal, naturally selected qualities of grief seems to be its ability to attract social support and maintain social relationships. Nevertheless, despite its grounding in basic human nature, culture shapes a number of aspects of grief responses, including the particular events that give rise to grief, the intensity and particular expressions of grief, and the sorts of rituals that groups use to respond to grief. Whatever norms arise to channel grief in different cultures, however, none regard emotional indifference as the appropriate response to the loss of an intimate. Biological design and cultural values align in the case of grief.

The APA's recent decision notwithstanding, most grief, despite its acute painfulness, is not dysfunctional but is a natural response to loss. Psychiatry's pathologizing of grief overturns thousands of years of practical wisdom about a basic human emotion. It even contradicts its own definition of mental disorder that exempts "an expectable or culturally approved response to a common stressor." Grief is a perennial aspect of the "character of mortality," not a mental disorder.

8 SEXUAL BEHAVIOR

It is nature, that is all
Simply telling us to fall in love
And that's why birds do it, bees do it
Even educated fleas do it.

—COLE PORTER, *"Let's Do It"*

No matter gay, straight, or bi,
Lesbian, transgendered life,
I'm on the right track baby.

—LADY GAGA, *"Born This Way"*

The legacies of Darwin and Herodotus diverge sharply in regard to sexual behavior. Darwinian evolutionary processes depend on reproduction. In all species, the driving force of life lies in transmitting genes to future generations; genes that are not passed on will die. In nature, heterosexual intercourse is the only way to perpetuate hereditary traits. Conversely, exclusive homosexuality and other nonreproductive sexual activities are forms of Darwinian suicide. Although many environmental constraints, including ecological conditions, diverse sex ratios, the status of women, legal sanctions, and the shaming of particular kinds of sexual practices, shape optimal procreative strategies, reproduction must be the fundamental evolutionary imperative. Therefore, even when cultural norms permit all kinds of sexual activities, human nature should ensure that most people will be heterosexual.[1]

In contrast to Darwin, Herodotus emphasized the variety of sexual activities across different cultures. For him, sexual behavior was grounded in whatever norms a particular culture promotes, not in universal, biological expressions. Erotic proclivities are not innate but, rather, more closely resemble a blank slate that each culture inscribes with its extraordinarily varied norms. For the past century, social scientists have echoed

Herodotus' focus on the great diversity of sexual practices. Margaret Mead, for example, famously contrasted the free sexual experimentation, relaxed norms, acceptance of marital infidelity, and absence of sexual jealousy among the Samoans she observed with the sexual repression found in the United States during the mid-twentieth century. The great divergence of norms and practices between Samoans and Americans indicated to Mead that nurture rather than nature dictated what sorts of sexual attitudes and behaviors arose in each culture. Since that time, anthropologists and other social scientists have focused on how sexual instincts are extremely pliable and capable of virtually unlimited forms of expression. Heterosexuality is just one of many forms of normal sexuality that also include homosexuality, bisexuality, transsexuality, and, more rarely, asexuality. Prohibitions against such behaviors reflect cultural constructions rather than human nature. One of the most puzzling issues in the study of normality and abnormality is whether various types of sexual activities are biologically natural or culturally arbitrary.[2]

This chapter focuses on historical changes in sexual standards and activities in the United States since World War II as a lens to examine the contrasting views of Darwin and Herodotus. In a remarkably short period of time, views of normal and abnormal sexual practices underwent a revolutionary transformation: Sex shifted from a tabooed to an omnipresent topic. Cultural norms no longer confined approved sexual activity to married partners but came to accept a far wider variety of practices, identities, and objects of desires. Indeed, not to be having sex might be one of the last sources of sexual shame.[3] This era therefore provides an especially good laboratory to see what sorts of sexual practices emerge when cultural norms permit a wide range of activities that are not oriented to procreation.

The chapter also examines whether men and women respond to a more permissive cultural climate in similar or different ways. Finally, it surveys how the relaxation of cultural norms affects the prevalence of behaviors that are not heterosexual. When norms that once prohibited sex outside of marriage, non-heterosexual sex, and sex not oriented to having children change to ones that permit a wide variety of people to enjoy sex, grant equivalence to heterosexual, homosexual, and bisexual practices, and encourage diverse sexual activities, to what extent will behavior mirror pansexual cultural possibilities or maintain heterosexual primacy?

From Sexual Repression to Sexual Expression

Contemporary norms regarding sexuality permit a wide range of erotic activities, view women and men as sexual equals, and, recently, accept homosexual and bisexual behaviors. These attitudes are especially striking because they so starkly contrast with millennia of Western history. Before the twentieth century, despite huge variation within and across cultures, dominant social norms served to suppress sexual activity outside of marriage. This tendency started early, with Adam and Eve. The Old Testament opens with the shameful nature of sex, describing how after Eve and Adam ate an apple from the Tree of Knowledge: "Then the eyes of both of them were opened and they realized that they were naked. So they sewed fig leaves together to make themselves loincloths." The religious tradition initiated in the Garden of Eden continued for thousands of years.[4]

The most eminent spokesmen of early Christianity, such as St. Paul, St. Augustine, and St. Thomas Aquinas, viewed celibacy as superior to marriage and intercourse as a disgusting, albeit necessary, evil. They preached that God designed the sexual organs specifically for reproduction so that the only permissible forms of sex must have that aim. This general rule, often obeyed more in the breech than in practice, limited legitimate sex to married people who desired children. Religious teachings strictly forbade other forms of sex—for example, outside of marriage, with contraception, masturbation, oral, or anal intercourse. Although Christian doctrine repudiated all sexual practices other than marital intercourse with the intent of procreation, it singled out homosexuality as a particularly degenerate form of sex. Indeed, for thousands of years, the church considered same-sex behaviors as perhaps the greatest sexual perversion, emphasizing the passage in Leviticus that states, "If a man also lie with mankind, as he lieth with a woman, both of them have committed an abomination: They shall surely be put to death."[5]

Current views of permissible sex could hardly be more different from the strict normative monogamy promulgated in the Western religious tradition. Cultural portrayals of sex in the twenty-first century reflect a panoply of bisexuality, homosexuality, and transsexualism as well as traditional heterosexuality. Depictions of sex in popular television shows and other media display a far greater variety of practices, diversity of actors, and number of partners than ever before. "We have moved from a culture that told us we were dirty [for having sex]," Rachel Hills summarizes, "to one that tells us we are defective if we do not do it enough." Only stably married people seem not to be having much sex. Cultural theorists distinguish gender, whether people identify themselves as males or females, from biological sex, which refers to anatomical and physiological characteristics. They proclaim that there might be two sexes, but there are many genders; unlike sex, gender is variable rather than binary, malleable rather than fixed, and powerful enough to override any alleged biological forces. In Simone de Beauvoir's canonical statement, "One is not born, but rather becomes, a woman."Moreover, many posit that humans are naturally pansexual. Although social norms channel androgyny into a variety of approved expressions, everyone can potentially enjoy all forms of sexuality.[6]

According to this view, we have entered a "post-sexual" age in which culturally derived gender roles have far more influence than biologically fixed sexual preferences. For example, Facebook allows its users to identify with at least 58 different gender identities. Heterosexual behavior is just one possible choice that prevails because of the power of social norms that promote "heteronormativity" and not because of any biological imperative. Indeed, in the twenty-first century, the cultural referent "gender" has almost entirely replaced the biological term of "sex" to describe whether someone is a male or a female.[7]

From the cultural perspective, Darwinian views of sex are outmoded because changing values and technologies have freed people from evolutionary forces. Natural selection must promote sexual strategies that enhance reproduction, exactly the kind that have withered in modern life. The widespread availability of birth control means that a vanishingly small proportion of sexual relationships results in childbirth: Birth rates have fallen below replacement rates in many Western countries, including the United States. Applied biology has developed to the extent that human reproduction is no longer subject to processes of natural selection: The development of in vitro fertilization techniques means that intercourse is unnecessary for conceiving children and that people of all sexual orientations can have genetically related children. Scrutinizing current sexual behavior and norms affords a particularly valuable way of determining whether bedrock biological forces nevertheless persist once they have become culturally anachronistic.[8]

How Much Sex Do People Have?

Although cultural norms about sex have always been apparent, until the mid-twentieth century little was known about actual sexual practices in the population. Religion, law, and, later, psychiatry defined what kinds of sex people should have, but no one knew how much and what types of sex other people were really having. Early statisticians such as Quetelet had eagerly gathered data on a host of activities ranging from birth and death to marriage and divorce, crime, and suicide, but they did not collect information about sexual activities. Sexually explicit reading material and films were banned or closely censored and were only available through illicit sources. This situation began to change during the late nineteenth century and early decades of the twentieth century as the work of sexual theorists such as Sigmund Freud, Richard Krafft-Ebbing, and Havelock Ellis, the popular new medium of film, and ethnographies such as Robert and Helen Lynd's *Middletown* left no doubt that sexual conduct at the time had little resemblance to repressive sexual norms. During the 1920s, young people, most conspicuously women, began to openly smoke, drink, swear, and question "old-fashioned" values, especially values about sexuality. Although the decades following World War I were marked by growing feelings of sexual liberation, more sexual equality among women and men, and rising divorce rates partly propelled by infidelity, no data existed to document these trends. Much sexual activity clearly took place outside of marriage, but no one knew how much or what varieties of sex were occurring.[9]

Alfred Kinsey's (1894–1956) groundbreaking research during the 1940s and 1950s provided the first large-scale attempt to fill the vacuum of quantitative research about the amount and diversity of sexual behavior. Kinsey's two volumes, *Sexual Behavior in the Human Male* (1948) and *Sexual Behavior in the Human Female* (1953), which together relied on interviews of more than 10,000 men and women, have possibly had more impact on cultural attitudes toward sexuality than any other source. No scientific book of the twentieth century became more widely known than the two reports. Kinsey turned sexual behavior from being an unmentionable topic into a major subject of public debate. "Kinsey's studies," historians John D'Emilio and Estelle Freedman assert, "propelled sex into the public eye in a way unlike any previous book or event had done." Although each volume was more than 800 pages, written in dull, methodical prose, and featured many complicated statistical tables, together they sold hundreds of thousands of copies. "Kinsey," *Time* magazine announced, "has done for sex what Columbus had done for geography."[10]

Although trained as a biologist, Kinsey was no Darwinian. His core belief was that everyone was naturally pansexual; only cultural norms prevented them from exploring a wide variety of sexual activities. He was convinced that people should be able to act on their sexual needs—whatever form they took—without fear or guilt. In his view all sexual practices prominent cultural critic Lionel Trilling wrote at the time: "must be *accepted*, not merely in the scientific sense but also in the social sense, in the sense, that is, that no judgment must be passed on them." Kinsey *inverted* Herodotus' view that "everyone without exception believes his own native customs, and the religion he was brought up in, to be the best." Indeed, the driving force behind his research was his intense loathing of mid-century American sexual norms. He viewed his culture as a repressive force that had to be overcome before people could become sexually liberated. When Kinsey wrote, religion, and to a lesser extent psychiatry, was the legitimate arbiter of sexual decency. The criminal law reinforced religious and psychiatric definitions of appropriate and inappropriate sexuality. Sodomy, birth control, interracial sex, and adultery were illegal in much of the United States. Reducing and abolishing rigid controls on human sexual behavior was the great cause of Kinsey's life. [11]

Kinsey focused on how often people engaged in six practices: masturbation, nocturnal emissions, heterosexual petting, heterosexual intercourse, homosexual outlets, and animal contacts. He treated each of these as equivalent to the others, never assuming that one was more natural or better than any other. In particular, in contrast to Darwinians, he refused to privilege heterosexual intercourse, emphasizing how the five nonnormative types of outlets occurred more frequently than the single normative type of marital sex. His key finding was that "nonnormative sexual activities are, in fact, the statistical norm." Nearly 100 percent of men masturbated and about 85 percent had engaged in premarital intercourse. Approximately 70 percent had visited a prostitute, and 60 percent had oral sex. Half of married men reported extramarital affairs. Thirty-seven percent experienced homosexual contact. Eight percent had sexual contact with animals, a figure that increased to 40 percent for those who lived on farms. Kinsey summarized, "At least 85 percent of the younger male population could be convicted as sex offenders if law enforcement officials were as efficient as most people expect them to be."[12]

Kinsey was particularly outraged at the restrictions placed on premarital intercourse and argued that sex before marriage led to more successful marriages. He also observed that half of married men had intercourse with people other than their wives. The harmlessness of masturbation was another of his dominant themes. At the time Kinsey wrote, masturbation was commonly viewed as a source of disease, immorality, and insanity. "Taken together," two historians of sex concluded, "Kinsey's statistics pointed to a vast hidden world of sexual experience sharply at odds with publicly espoused norms."[13]

Kinsey relentlessly associated more frequent sex with better sex. For example, to him, a man who engaged in intercourse only with his wife was inferior to a compulsive womanizer who had superficial sexual relationships with numerous partners. Renowned cultural critic Lionel Trilling noted,

The Report's own data suggest that there may be no direct connection between on the one hand lack of restraint and frequency and on the other hand psychic health; they tell us of men in the lower social levels who in their sexual careers have intercourse with many hundreds of girls but who despise their sexual partners and cannot endure relations with the same girl more than once.

Or, in response to a lawyer who was defending a man "charged with carnally knowing a pig by the anus," Kinsley responded that such behavior occurred in a large proportion of the population and so was not abnormal. "The book suggests no way of choosing between a woman and a sheep," Margaret Mead memorably noted. [14]

Kinsey's animosity to traditional morality and view that virtually all sex was good sex led him to take a benign view of even child molestation. He ridiculed the concern regarding the sexual abuse of girls: "It is difficult to understand why a child, except for its cultural conditioning, should be disturbed at having its genitalia touched, or disturbed at seeing the genitalia of other persons, or disturbed at even more specific sexual contacts." In fact, Kinsey viewed adults who made sexual advances to young people as victims of children who had unreasonable fears, and he considered the children involved to be "partners," not victims. One particularly notorious case was "Mr. X," a child molester who masturbated infants, penetrated children, and performed a wide variety of sexual acts on preadolescent boys and girls alike. For Kinsey, however, even Mr. X exemplified what sorts of sex someone freed of social constraints would have. Such a person, reports Kinsey biographer James Jones, "would commence sexual activities early in life, enjoy intercourse with both sexes, eschew fidelity, indulge in a variety of behaviors, and be much more sexually active in general for life." [15]

A number of commentators observed that perhaps the major contribution of the Kinsey Reports was to provide people answers to the question "Am I normal?" Before the Kinsey Reports, normal men and women were unaware of the fact that their neighbors, community members, and ordinary people throughout the country were as discontented and critical of sexual norms as they were. The Reports let individuals compare their own behaviors to those of others: "The trouble was that up to now nobody who belonged to the majority that broke sexual taboos could know that he did belong to a majority; hence people felt abnormal and guilty." A popular song in 1948, "Thank You, Mister Kinsey," summarized this accomplishment:

> When I heard the people all talking
> I thought they were only mocking
> I never knew what I could do
> 'Til I got all the facts from you.[16]

Not surprisingly, Kinsey's research generated a huge amount of controversy. Many fundamentalist religious leaders and political conservatives were appalled by his findings and views. For them, Kinsey's work threatened "the basis of decency, the innocence of children, the sanctity of marriage, the honor of women, and the moral fiber of society." More commonly, however, his work was viewed as a groundbreaking triumph of science over custom, modernity over tradition, and realism over moralism. A writer in the *American Journal of Public Health* asserted, "Perhaps the most important conclusion from this whole study is that our conception of what is normal sexual behavior must be radically revised." Another adulatory review in *Harper's Magazine* gushed, "So startling are its revelations, so contrary to what civilized man has been taught for generations, that they would be unbelievable but for the impressive weight of scientific agencies backing the survey." Many came to advocate that Puritanical cultural norms inhibiting and restraining sexual behavior were at the root of Americans' sexual predicament; calls for sexual tolerance became widespread so that natural biological urges could surface. A prominent critic of psychiatry, Alfred Deutsch, wrote,

> Such terms as abnormal, unnatural, oversexed, and undersexed, as used in our legal and moral codes, have little validity in the light of Professor Kinsey's revelations. There is a tremendous variety in the frequency and type of sexual behavior in normal Americans.[17]

Kinsey's work had an extraordinary impact on views of normal and abnormal sexual behavior. Before the reports were published, people knew only that "good" people did not engage in sex outside of marriage but did not know what "average" people actually did sexually. Finding out that sex of various kinds was seemingly frequent made Kinsey's findings normative and thus relieved guilt feelings from millions of people. For those who were not heterosexual, he emphasized the lack of sharp differences between straight, gay, and bisexual people. For young people, he helped create more tolerance for premarital sexual activities and recognition of their intense sexual needs. The notion that women should be virgins when they married came to be seen as thoroughly anachronistic. After Kinsey, sexual life became more free and less of a source of anxiety.

More frequent sexual activity, more varieties of sex, and more sex among a wider range of people became normative. Kinsey's research began a trend toward acceptance of what had long been thought of as abnormal sexuality.[18]

After Kinsey

The Kinsey Reports opened a cultural space for the transition from the prudish, repressive, and stigmatizing standards of the 1950s to the sexual revolution of the 1960s. During this period, American society changed from a place where sexual behavior was covert and unmentionable to one where it was ever-present. Highly visible plays such as *Hair*, novels including Gore Vidal's *Myra Breckinridge*, and artists such as Andy Warhol trumpeted diverse forms of sexuality. From the fields of Woodstock to the pages of *Playboy*, sex became more public, commonplace, and open. Other than Kinsey's research, however, few data documented the actual impact of the loosening of cultural norms.

Although Kinsey's research left the impression that almost everyone was having endless, fascinating, and varied sex, there were ample reasons to question this interpretation. His findings were viewed as especially revelatory because of the huge number of cases he used, which seemed to represent what average Americans were like. "His specimens," one commentator noted, "are not neurotics, psychopaths, or psychotics . . . but average men, who are encountered daily on the street or bus." In fact, however, his sample relied on volunteers, creating the bias that more sexually uninhibited people should be most willing to talk to a stranger about their sexual activities. It heavily overrelied on college students, people from Indiana (where Kinsey lived and taught), gay men, and prisoners. It was not possible to generalize the findings of this group to the wider population.[19]

Moreover, the design of Kinsey's interviewing procedures ensured that subjects had maximal incentives to report, rather than to deny, engaging in some sexual practice. For example, his interviewers did not ask, "Have you ever engaged in masturbation?" but instead inquired, "When did you first masturbate?" If respondents initially claimed they never engaged in some practice, the interviewer expressed surprise: "Yes, I know you have never done that, but how old were you the first time that you did it?" His intimidating style of interviewing and leading questions could easily have elevated the number of people who reported engaging in various kinds of sexual activities.[20]

Finally, there was reason to question Kinsey's analysis of his findings. Despite the nature of his sample and his relentless interviewing techniques, 85 percent of orgasms that married males had stemmed from marital intercourse; females other than their wives provided between 5 and 10 percent of their sexual outlets. These findings suggest that even the men in Kinsey's sample were more sexually restrained than his own interpretations and the general response to the Reports suggest.[21]

Many questions surrounded the representativeness and accuracy of Kinsey's findings. Nevertheless, although sex research became a well-known field after Kinsey, no good, large, and representative studies assessed the actual prevalence of sexual practices until the early 1990s.[22] At that time, the National Opinion Research Center (NORC) fielded a large study of sexual behavior among approximately 3400 Americans. Unlike Kinsey's study, the NORC research was a probability sample that represented the entire nation with a satisfactory 80 percent response rate. In 1993, it was published under the modest title of *Sex in America: The Definitive Study*.

The study was in agreement with Kinsey that statistical data could provide standards for normal sexuality:

> Many people remain unsure of the rightness or legitimacy of specific sexual practices and feel the need to compare what they do with what others do. Is it normal to want your partner to perform oral sex on you? Do other heterosexuals want anal sex? Does fantasizing about group sex place you outside the pale? What can you actually ask your partner to do? Most of us have wondered, deep down, if everyone likes what we like or whether what we want, or what we'd like to try, is odd or is overly staid and conventional.

Its findings reassured those people who were worried that they were "overly staid and conventional." The vast majority of respondents said they had one or zero sex partners in the past year, and very few reported more than two. Moreover, only one-third had sex as often as twice a week, another third said they engaged in sex a few times each month, and the final third said they has sex only a few times a year or never.[23]

Other findings from the study also indicated that American sexual practices were quite restrained. Although considerable premarital sex took place, more than half of 18- to 24-year-olds had just one sex partner in the past year, and an additional 11 percent had no partners. The "paltry number" of respondents who reported having one-night stands stood in particular contrast to media portrayals. Spouses were faithful to each other: 94 percent had just one partner in the past year. "Despite the popular myth that there is a great deal of adultery in marriage," the study indicated, "our data and other reliable studies do not find it." Only slightly more than 10 percent of adults reported having extramarital affairs while they were married. Kinsey would have been shocked that, four decades after his research, Americans said they were over-whelmingly monogamous and heterosexual in their sexual practices. Worse for him, married people were the most physically and emotionally pleased of all groups.[24]

Other studies largely confirmed the NORC findings. A review of four large, representative national studies indicates that although many young people have sex in their teenage years, few have a large number of sexual partners. Depending on the study, between 37 and 53 percent of 15- to 17-year-olds reported having had sexual intercourse. However, about two-thirds of those with sexual experience had fewer than four partners. One large survey indicated that approximately two-thirds of young adults between 18 and 23 years old had one or no sexual partners during the past year; one-third had never had a sexual partner. Another study used two waves of data that surveyed a large number of young adults who had com-pleted at least 1 year of college from 1988 to 1996 and again from 2002 to 2010. It found no increase in sexual behavior during that time and a decline in the number of persons having sex more than once a week. More than half of the group had sex less than once a week, and just one-third had sex with more than one person during the past year. Another study of roughly 1300 young adults interviewed in 2007 and 2008 and again in 2012 and 2013 found that approximately one-fourth of subjects had sex only with the person they eventually married. The average participant had five sexual partners before marriage.[25]

While accurate data about sexual behavior are notoriously difficult to obtain, the best studies do not support media images of increasing amounts of casual sex, one-night stands, and hookups. Monogamy seems to be far more common than media portrayals (and Kinsey's findings) indicate. The reality of sexual behavior appears to diverge considerably from social expecta-tions of constant, diverse, and carefree sex. Instead, quantitative studies show that long-term, serial monogamy is the most typical pattern of sexual practice.

Why haven't people taken more advantage of the opportunities that cul-tural norms now provide for a freer sexual life? One reason for the contin-ued predominance of monogamy might lie in the emotion of jealousy. As Darwin noted,

Nevertheless from the strength of the feeling of jealousy all through the animal kingdom, as well as from the analogy of the lower animals,

more particularly of those which come nearest to man, I cannot believe
that absolutely promiscuous intercourse prevailed in times past.

Humans are not promiscuous because they and their sexual partners naturally become jealous when their relationship is threatened by additional
sexual involvements. Jealousy thus functions to protect monogamous
bonds, to deter sexual infidelity, and to signal a potentially adulterous
partner that he or she should refrain from entering a new relationship.
According to classicist Peter Toomey, "Jealousy is the glue that holds
the sexes together—for the benefit of the family and the survival of the
species." This ancient emotion has not lost its power in modern societies: Sexual freedom, when put into practice, still arouses the wrath of the
betrayed partner. Most people, it seems, forego extra-partner relationships
because of the vast emotional and logistical complications they entail
as well as the strength of the social norm that one should not cheat on
one's lover. Humans have yet to find ways to take advantage of the cultural
freedom to engage in sex with a variety of partners while simultaneously
retaining enduring relationships. The natural power of jealousy sabotages
the cultural promotion of sexual liberty.[26]

Men and Women

The views of Darwin and Herodotus particularly diverge in regard to the
different sexual strategies of men and women. Because intercourse is the
only way to transmit genes, Darwinians take heterosexuality for granted.
Instead, they emphasize what they assume are striking differences in male
and female mating strategies and sexual behaviors. Although evolution drives
both sexes to desire to pass their genes on to future generations, reproduction has drastically different consequences for each sex. In particular, biology
has programmed males and females to take into account how much parental
investment they must make to conceive and rear a child.[27]

The consequences of sex take place within female bodies so that male
genes can be propagated within many females. Each time a male has sex with
a new partner, he has the chance to get his genes into the next generation so
that intercourse with many partners is usually his optimal reproductive strategy. In addition, men have many millions of sperm so that each ejaculation
has little impact on overall reproductive fitness. Moreover, males use minimal
resources when they transmit genes, often just a few moments of insertion
and ejaculation. In almost all species, males show less selectiveness in having

sex than females because they have little to lose when they try to mate with as many partners as possible.[28]

In contrast to natural male tendencies toward indiscriminate mating, Darwinians emphasize how females are far choosier about with whom they are willing to mate. Males can reproduce many times with different partners in a short period, but biology mandates that females will have roughly the same number of offspring, regardless of their number of sexual partners. In addition, unlike men, women must make a huge investment to have a child. Not only do they face a prolonged period of carrying and then feeding their offspring but also each new successful conception prevents a woman from having another child for many months or years. Therefore, it makes evolutionary sense for women to be very selective about what man is going to help transmit her genes; the quality of their mate counts for far more than the quantity of men with whom they mate. Usually, their primary imperative is to select a man who is likely to make a long-term commitment to defend, protect, and provide resources for them and their offspring. Darwin concluded, "The exertion of some choice on the part of the female seems a law almost as general as the eagerness of the male."[29]

As opposed to Darwin, Herodotus focused on the great diversity of sexual expressions among women as well as men. In stark contrast to the female selectivity that Darwin posited, Herodotus noted that Gindane women in Libya wear bands around their ankles representing each man with whom they have has sex; whoever has the greatest number of bands "enjoys the greatest reputation because she has slept with the greatest number of men." Yet, Thracian women were subject to intensive surveillance by their husbands, who strictly regulated interaction with other men (although they allowed their daughters to have intercourse with any man they pleased). The Greek historian observed that men in the Massagetae, Agathyrsi, and Nasamones cultures use all wives promiscuously; among the latter, all male wedding guests enjoy the bride in turn. Herodotus neither endorsed nor condemned these diverse practices with the exception of the "wholly shameful" practice of the Babylonians, who mandated that every woman must once in her life sit in the temple of Aphrodite and give herself to the first man who throws money at her.[30]

Current gender norms emphasize sexual equality between men and women. For most of Western history, however, social norms and legal restrictions exerted far more control over female than male sexual behaviors. Although trends toward parity had begun earlier in the century, a strong double standard for men and women still existed when Kinsey conducted his studies and remains to some extent at present. Men were highly sexual beings who were allowed, and even expected, to engage in sexual activities outside of marriage; women were assumed to have little sexual enthusiasm and were supposed to refrain from sex with anyone except their husbands.

In contrast to prevailing norms at the time, Kinsey found that women, like men, were highly sexual: 90 percent of his female sample had petted, 66 percent had nocturnal sex dreams, 62 percent had masturbated, nearly 50 percent had premarital intercourse, 26 percent had extramarital intercourse, 13 percent had at least one homosexual contact that resulted in orgasm, and almost 4 percent had engaged in sexual contact with animals. However, his results also indicated that women preferred to have less sex than men and were less sexually responsive and less active in every category. Adolescent girls reported only approximately one-fifth as much sexual activity as adolescent boys; sexual activity among women in their twenties and thirties remained below that of typical adolescent males. Overall, women had far fewer orgasms before marriage than men: A typical woman reported less than 250 compared to the male average of 1500. In this regard, Kinsey's conclusion would not have surprised Darwin:

> There seems to be no question but that the human male would be promiscuous in his choice of sexual partners throughout the whole of his life if there were no social restrictions. . . . The human female is much less interested in a variety of partners.

The nature of Kinsey's data, however, precluded him from knowing whether such female restraint resulted from innate biological tendencies or cultural norms that exerted far more control over women's sexuality.[31]

A thoroughgoing revolution in sexual norms began about a decade after Kinsey published his landmark findings. Although the women's liberation movement of the 1960s contained a number of diverse ideological strains in regard to sexuality, it emphasized how women should be just as entitled as men to have many sexual partners. For example, Helen Gurley Brown, the editor of the popular women's magazine *Cosmopolitan*, encouraged her single female readers to have casual sex with multiple partners, preferably married ones: "Use them in a perfectly nice way just as they use you. . . . One married man is dangerous. . . . A potpourri can be fun."[32] Erotic magazines such as *Playgirl* arose that catered to a newly sexually liberated female audience and featured photos of nude men. Popular films such as *Last Tango in Paris* and *Barbarella* featured sexually liberated female characters. By the end of the century, television series such as *Sex in the City* portrayed women as sexual equals to men and, often, just as sexually obsessed as their male counterparts. At the same time, the widespread use of the pill and other contraceptive devices allowed women to have sex with multiple partners without fear of getting pregnant.

Sexual norms were clearly moving in the direction of parity between women and men. Did changes in actual sexual behaviors reflect these normative changes? The NORC survey in the early 1990s again provides the most comprehensive data on this topic. It indicated that female sexual behavior was far removed from its cultural portrayal. More than 80 percent of married women reported that their spouses were their only sexual partners while they were married. Indeed, approximately half of women born after 1953 indicated that they had sex only with the person who became their husband, although this was considerably fewer than the 84 percent of women born from 1933 through 1942 who made this claim.[33]

To be sure, some of the survey's findings about gender differences in sexual practices were puzzling. Logically, because heterosexual intercourse involves one man and one woman, each gender should report the same total number of heterosexual partners. However, whereas 7 percent of men claimed to have had more than 3 sex partners in the past year, virtually no women reported this many encounters. Thirty-three percent of men but just 9 percent of women reported 10 or more sex partners after age 18 years. The gender disproportion was even greater for adults who claimed to have 21 or more partners: 15.1 percent of men but just 2.7 percent of women reported this many. Moreover, considerably more men than women reported having sexual events lasting more than 1 hour; conversely, women were more likely to recount encounters lasting less than 15 minutes.[34]

These results suggest that many of this survey's findings were normative— either men exaggerated their sexual activities and prowess, women concealed theirs, or both processes occurred. The stark gender discrepancies in reported sexual activities make it impossible to determine the extent to which the findings of this "definitive" survey reflect what men and women were actually doing or what they thought they should be saying they were doing. The results, as one critic of the study suggested, indicate that "normal Americans are driven by their desire to be normal." Likewise, surveys of adolescent sexual behavior show that approximately 35–47 percent of sexually active boys report four or more partners; this figure declines to 20–30 percent among sexually active girls. Young men also report having sex much earlier in a relationship than young women. Separating what is normal from what is normative sexual behavior is far more difficult than the NORC and many other sex researchers recognize.[35]

What accounts for why women's sexual activity has not increased in proportion to the greater liberalization of sexual norms? One reason might lie in the rising economic status of women. In contrast to evolutionary history, many adult women no longer depend on men for resources and support. Under these circumstances, gaining commitment from a man is a less compelling sexual strategy. A woman without a man is, as the old slogan of women's liberation proclaimed, like a fish without a bicycle. Because women are naturally choosier about their sexual partners than men, the growing relative power of women has suppressed the quantity of sexual partnerships that might have otherwise arisen. Another factor contributing to the seeming dearth of sexual activity among women might stem from changing ratios of acceptable male and female sex partners. As women gain economic equality or superiority, the pool of acceptable male partners decreases. For example, the number of college-educated women in their twenties exceeds the number of comparable men by about 33 percent. In most circumstances, female selectivity and male desires for promiscuity might remain strong predispositions, although these strategies now operate in radically different social and cultural contexts.[36]

Homosexuality

Homosexuality presents another striking discrepancy between the views of Darwin and Herodotus. Heterosexuality is such a bedrock evolutionary principle that Darwin never mentioned same-sex erotic behavior. Conversely, for Herodotus, heterosexual behaviors were just one of many possible sexual expressions. For example, his own culture's norms approved sexual relationships between older men and adolescent boys. Indeed, historian Michael Grant notes that among the ancient Greeks, same-sex relationships were "more intense, profound and complex than men's relations with women." Herodotus observed how even Persian men, who were reputed to be extremely macho, quickly incorporated homosexuality into their array of approved practices once they discovered the widespread homosexuality among the Greeks: "Pleasures, too, of all sorts [the Persians] are quick to indulge in when they get to know about them—a notable instance is pederasty, which they learned from the Greeks."[37]

Although a number of nineteenth- and early twentieth-century sexual theorists focused on same-sex relationships, Kinsey was the first to provide quantitative data about these behaviors. Homosexuality was of particular concern to Kinsey. When he conducted his research, children were socialized into rigid sex-linked behaviors: Homosexuality was the opposite of the way men were supposed to act, feel, think, and look. Normal men were rugged, strong, and masculine; homosexuals were caricatured as weak, swishy, and effeminate. However, since early childhood, Kinsey himself had intense homosexual desires. In such circumstances, a boy who felt attracted to other boys could only view himself as a sinner, a criminal, and a pervert.[38]

Kinsey believed that his own experiences reflected his era's more general social repression of sexual desires and, in particular, of homosexual desires. He rejected not only the notion that homosexuality was bad but also that it had any biological foundation at all. His core contention was that humans were naturally pansexual and, although they might be taught that some sexual channels were preferable to others, they had no innate preference for any particular type of outlet. People had equal capacity and desire for erotic relations with others of either the same or opposite sex. For Kinsey, the problem to be explained was why people did not become involved in every form of sexual behavior, not why they preferred a partner of one sex rather than the other. He indicated, "Without social forces that prevented people from acting on their bisexuality, I think most people would carry on both heterosexual and homosexual activities coincidentally."[39]

Although Kinsey loathed psychiatrists, his views were not so different from those of Sigmund Freud, who also believed that humans were naturally bisexual and attracted to both sexes (although Freud thought that exclusive homosexuality could be a type of arrested sexual development). Freud himself had a fairly tolerant view of homosexuality, but most psychoanalysts subsequently came to view same-sex attractions as pathological conditions stemming from inappropriate parenting. In 1952, the first edition of the psychiatric profession's diagnostic manual placed the condition among the "sociopathic personality disturbances" along with transvestism, pedophilia, fetishism, and sexual sadism.[40] Kinsey thus conducted his research in a cultural climate that viewed homosexuality as triply abnormal: It was a grave sin, a serious crime, and a psychiatric disorder.

Kinsey's major empirical contribution was to conceive of heterosexual and homosexual behaviors as continuous rather than dichotomous. He developed a "heterosexual–homosexual rating scale," which is still used, that placed sexual behaviors on a spectrum consisting of 7 points:

0: Exclusively heterosexual, no homosexual
1: Predominantly heterosexual, incidentally homosexual

2: Predominantly heterosexual, more than incidentally homosexual

3: Equally heterosexual and homosexual

4: Predominantly homosexual, more than incidentally heterosexual

5: Predominantly homosexual, incidentally heterosexual

6: Exclusively homosexual

For Kinsey, exclusive heterosexuality was not "normal" but at one end of a continuum with exclusive homosexuality at the other end and a range of combined hetero- and homosexual behaviors in between.[41]

Perhaps the best known finding derived from this scale was the widespread prevalence of homosexual behaviors:

> Since only 50 per cent of the population is exclusively heterosexual throughout its adult life, and since only 4 per cent of the population is exclusively homosexual throughout its life, it appears that nearly half (46%) of the population engages in both heterosexual and homosexual activities, or react to persons of both sexes, in the course of their adult lives.

Given that 40–50 percent of men had homosexual experiences and 37 percent had at least one orgasm from homosexual sex, it was inconceivable to Kinsey that same-sex behavior could be pathological.[42]

Kinsey's finding that homosexuality was a common variant of human sexuality and inference that all people therefore had equal capacities to become homo- or heterosexual directly challenged religious, psychiatric, and legal definitions (at the time, Darwinian views were not significant enough to be a target of Kinsey's ire). What direction sexual behavior actually took followed cultural norms, not inborn tendencies: Kinsey stated, "Patterns of heterosexuality and patterns of homosexuality represent learned behavior which depends, to a considerable degree, upon the mores of the particular culture in which the individual is raised." Although it took several decades for Kinsey's views to become widely accepted, his work had a lasting impact on later efforts to make homosexuality morally equivalent to heterosexuality, and it soon became a touchstone for the gay liberation movement that emerged in the 1960s.[43]

The vast transformation in attitudes toward homosexuality since the time Kinsey conducted his research is one of the most striking developments in cultural attitudes toward normal and abnormal behavior. When Kinsey wrote, same-sex relationships had to be concealed and almost all gay people remained closeted. Because of the strict sanctions against the open display of homosexual behaviors, many of their sexual encounters were initiated anonymously in public restrooms, parks, and bars. Like the other civil rights movements that arose in the 1960s, the gay rights movement formed to end institutionalized oppression and to promote pride in a previously stigmatized and marginalized identity. Although repression against them was still strong at the time, a vibrant gay subculture gradually emerged. Activists embraced and trumpeted Kinsey's statistical findings. By the late 1960s, the gay movement was not just claiming legal equality but also advocating acceptance of homosexuality as an alternative lifestyle.[44]

Gay people congregated in large cities, where nearly 10 percent of men identified themselves as gay. This concentration, coupled with the growing numbers of gays who were "coming out of the closet," greatly heightened their visibility and allowed for the formation of a rich variety of political, social, and cultural institutions. The gay rights movement became especially prominent after 1969 when the police raided the Stonewall bar in Greenwich Village in New York City and were met with fierce opposition. During the 1970s, gay activists joined feminists in asserting that sexual identities were social constructs designed to promote power structures that reinforced "heteronormativity." In their view, heterosexuality was linked to the oppression of women by men, whereas homosexuality challenged existing political arrangements. Prominent gay activist Charlotte Bunch proclaimed, "Feminists must become Lesbians if they hope to end male supremacy." Most advocates argued that gay people should develop their own norms and lifestyles without taking monogamy or lifelong commitment as their standard.[45]

The psychiatric profession, and especially its designation of homosexuality as a mental illness, was among the movement's most prominent targets. In 1968, the second edition of the *Diagnostic and Statistical Manual of Mental Disorders (DSM-II)* characterized homosexuality under "Personality Disorders and Certain Other Non-Psychotic Disorders," specifically under the "Sexual Deviation" category. During the late 1960s, gay activists relied on the research of Kinsey and others to contest the psychiatric designation of homosexuality as a psychopathology. In particular, they drew attention to the harmful effects of psychiatric treatments that aimed to "cure" this condition. Activists emphasized the psychic similarity of homo- and heterosexuals and demanded the deletion of homosexuality from the list of mental disorders. They insisted that any pathology some people displayed did not result from being gay but, rather, from social exclusion and stigmatization. If social norms changed, then homosexuals would be psychologically indistinguishable from others. The activists succeeded when the board of trustees of the American Psychiatric Association approved the deletion of homosexuality from the *DSM* in 1973, stating that "homosexuality ... by itself does not necessarily constitute a psychiatric disorder." At the same time, the board passed a civil rights proposal deploring "all public and private discrimination against homosexuals."[46]

During the 1970s, gay activists proudly asserted their differences with heterosexual culture. Especially in large cities, the gay rights movement became institutionalized, establishing thousands of advocacy organizations, religious institutions, law offices, health clinics, community centers, and cultural venues. They strove to develop a culture that was not constrained by the norms of straight culture, and they refused to privilege institutions such as marriage. Many gay men rejected social norms regarding sexual behavior but militantly asserted an alternative sexuality built around bathhouses, multiple and brief sexual encounters, and a culture that was independent of mainstream practices; gay women engaged in far less visible, usually monogamous, relationships.[47]

Rocked by the devastating impact of AIDS on gay men during the 1970s, dissent arose to the view that gay culture should embrace a promiscuous lifestyle (which would have greatly appealed to Kinsey). Andrew Sullivan's *Virtually Normal* (1996) urged gays to strive for acceptance within mainstream culture. Sullivan argued that two ideals in particular should appeal to gay people: military service and marriage. Although Sullivan's arguments seemed utopian at the time, they proved to be remarkably prescient.[48]

In the twenty-first century, the status of homosexuality underwent a remarkable transformation. Until 2003, same-sex relationships were illegal in 13 states; at that time, the Supreme Court in the *Lawrence v. Texas* case deemed these laws unconstitutional. In 2011, the military was forbidden to discriminate against gay soldiers. Two years later, in *Windsor v. United States*, the US Supreme Court invalidated a federal law denying marital benefits to gay couples who lived in states in which gay marriage was legal. The court also annulled a public referendum in California that banned gay marriages. By 2014, the goal of equality in the military was realized and that of marriage— not long ago a preposterous concept to most heterosexuals and unthinkable even to most homosexuals—seemed inevitable. As recently as 1988, barely 10 percent of Americans approved of gay marriage; by 2013, more than half did so. Two-thirds of people younger than age 30 years support gay marriage so that its eventual institutionalization seems assured in the United States and other Western countries. In 2015, the Supreme Court ruled in *Obergefell v. Hodges* that all states must recognize the right of gay couples to marry.[49]

In a remarkably short time, homosexuality underwent a metamorphosis from a hidden sexual perversion to a widely accepted sexual status. By the beginning of the current century, most laws against gay sex had been repealed, and those that remained on the books were rarely enforced. Mental health treatments that aimed to change gay people's sexual orientation were widely ridiculed and, in some states, banned. Gay sex and sexual desire moved from the bathhouse to suburban respectability. Popular television shows and films frequently feature gay characters in conventional roles. Ironically, gay people are now able to conform to mainstream values at a time when fewer heterosexuals are getting married or enlisting in the military. The rapid and thoroughgoing transformation in attitudes toward homosexuality in the twenty-first century, like those of the Persians in Herodotus' time, appears to support the tenet of the cultural view that rapid changes in even deeply rooted norms are possible.[50]

Although a revolution in normative views of homosexuality has undoubtedly occurred in an extraordinarily brief period of time, less is known about its impact on the actual prevalence of these behaviors. If the NORC study in the early 1990s is to be believed, and it at least provides better representative data than any other study, non-heterosexual sex is relatively uncommon. This survey found that homosexuality was rare: Just 2.5–3 percent men and 1–2 percent of women claimed to be gay. Bisexuals were even less common, with only approximately 1 percent of respondents reporting having sex with both men and women. Even Kinsey, who emphasized the high prevalence of homosexuality in his sample, downplayed the fact that most people who reported a homosexual orgasm had only one or two so that homosexual contacts accounted for only about 6 percent of all orgasms in his study. A survey of almost 35,000 adults undertaken in 2013 by the Centers for Disease Control and Prevention found that just 1.6 percent of the population identified as gay or lesbian and even fewer, 0.7 percent, as bisexual. Most studies, however, provide somewhat higher estimates of around 3–5 percent of the population as gay, lesbian, bisexual, or transgendered. The numbers of people who are willing to identify themselves as anything other than fully heterosexual, even when social norms permit them to do so, are far less than Kinsey (and Herodotus) expected and are more in line with what Darwin might have predicted. Although people are now much freer to become gay, bi, or transsexual, relatively few do so or, at least, are willing to admit they participate in these behaviors.[51]

Is Homosexuality Innate?

Whether certain people are born with same-sex preferences or whether all people are naturally pansexual and so would express homosexual preferences when cultural norms and other contextual factors allow them to do so remains controversial. As noted previously, homosexuality is so irreconcilable with Darwin's theory of evolution that it does not appear in any of his writings. Conversely, this behavior was taken-for-granted among the Greeks when Herodotus wrote. Toward the end of the twentieth century, although many gay activists challenged the notion that sexuality could be understood through the presumptive binary categories of "homosexual" and "heterosexual" and supported a proliferation of multiple, proudly "queer" identities, the idea that homosexuality was as genetically embedded as heterosexuality started to gain traction. Researchers began to apply the techniques of behavioral genetics to investigate the potential heritability of homosexuality.

In the 1990s, articles about the "gay brain" became front-page news as neuroscientific and genetic researchers claimed to identify specific biological bases of homosexual behavior. Neuroscientist Simon LeVay published a study in *Science* reporting that the hypothalamus in the brains of gay men who had died from AIDS tended to be smaller than that in the brains of a comparison group, suggesting that gay men might have a different neurophysiology than heterosexual men. In 1993, Dean Hamer, a geneticist at the National Cancer Institute, reported in *Science* that "it appears that [the chromosomal region] Xq28 contains a gene that contributes to homosexual orientation in males." Hamer's study received widespread publicity, and Xq28 soon became widely known as "the gay gene." Both LeVay and Hamer became public advocates for the notion that homosexuality is a biologically based "normal variant in human behavior." Moreover, they contended that scientific research will "help dispel the myths about homosexuality that in the past have clouded the image of lesbians and gay men."[52]

Although many gay activists initially criticized LeVay and Hamer's research for assuming binary oppositions between homosexuality and heterosexuality, since the 1990s the notion that many homosexuals are "born gay" has attained increasing credibility and acceptance in the gay community. The vast majority of publicly gay men claim that they have always been gay and that their sexual desires are exclusively directed at others of the same sex. Widespread support for biological explanations of homosexuality also exists in the general population. In many writings about homosexual identity, the presumed genetic basis of homosexuality came to replace more voluntary notions of "chosen lifestyle."[53]

Advocates are attracted to the idea that homosexuality is genetically determined because it allows them to oppose arguments of some religious fundamentalists that being gay is an individual choice. These groups assume that if gay people choose their sexuality, they should not have legal protections, and thus strive to keep homosexuals from entering professions in which they might "recruit" students and others into the homosexual lifestyle. They also encourage gay people to enter "reparative" psychotherapies that teach them how to become heterosexual. If, in contrast, homosexuality is genetically determined, then gay people presumably deserve the same rights and acceptance that others have.

The notion of a gene that would ground homosexuality in biology, however, contradicts both cultural and evolutionary views. It challenges the notion that humans are naturally pansexual and only develop distinct sexual identities because of cultural scripts. It is also diametrically opposed to evolutionary theory: How would genes for sexual desire that are directed at members of the same sex—and so are unrelated to reproduction—get passed on to future generations? Gay genes are incompatible with the bedrock principle that natural selection would lead such a gene to disappear eventually because gay people would have fewer children than others. None of the speculations that evolutionary theorists have proposed to account for the possible existence of a gay gene—gay men historically helped care for the children of their kin and the increased consequent survival rate of relatives balanced their own lack of fertility; mothers carry the gay gene and so perhaps it consequently produces more offspring among these women that offsets the lack of fertility among their gay children; and the gene has an usually high rate of mutation—have received empirical support. Although many gay people (because they know they have always been gay) embrace the idea of a gay gene, it is highly unlikely that any gene or genes incline people to focus erotic energy on others of the same sex.

Perhaps the most likely possibility is that sexual orientation is relatively fixed at birth because of hormonal and neurological factors that operate on developing fetuses. In particular, sexual identities and preferences arise during the first few months of gestation through complex processes involving the time-dependent exposure of the nervous system to sex hormones. Experimental work with animals including rodents and monkeys shows that male and female typical orientations and behaviors are associated with high and low levels of testosterone, respectively, during the prenatal period. These processes result in strong predispositions toward heterosexuality in most cases but in homosexuality in a number of others. Once established in the womb, sexual preferences are not easily overcome by subsequent learning experiences and usually persist over the life span. The early hormonal environment, among other factors, could account for why people of all sexual dispositions believe that they "were born this way," why few are bisexual, and why most, but not all, are naturally heterosexual.[54]

Paradoxically, the current acceptance of the "gay gene" has more to do with favorable cultural attitudes toward genetic explanations than with any biological evidence for such a gene. Perhaps the processes of hormonal transmission during pregnancy that affect sexual orientations will be discovered, or perhaps some new theory will emerge. In the end, the most reasonable conclusion at present is that, as evolutionary psychologist David Buss observes, the origins of homosexual desire, identity, and behavior "remain scientific mysteries."[55]

Conclusion

Norms about sexual activities are far freer now than in the past, even the recent past. They proclaim that sex is a positive and fulfilling human experience; that sexual repression is detrimental and should be reduced; that there are a great variety of normal types of sexual experiences not limited to married, heterosexual intercourse; and that a broad range of people, including adolescents, elderly people, and those with disabilities, can have fulfilling sexual lives.[56] They view women and men as equally sexually empowered. Heterosexual marital intercourse has lost its normative centrality, and premarital sex and cohabitation are taken for granted. The shame of having an out-of-wedlock child has vastly declined. Homosexuality is largely destigmatized, and other sexual proclivities, such as transsexualism and bisexuality, are becoming matters of individual choice. Disapproval of homosexuality and other sexual activities has virtually disappeared from psychiatric manuals and legal statutes, and many, although far from all, religions embrace gay people.

Now that norms and laws no longer hinder a wide range of sexual expressions, what sorts of sexual practices actually take place? Sexual encounters among adolescents are common, and because people now marry at later ages, most engage in premarital intercourse. Likewise, high divorce rates mean that people have more partners during their lifetimes. Despite these changes and despite media depictions, the best evidence is that sexual behavior remains much more conventional than Kinsey (and other sex researchers) would have anticipated. Although cultural restrictions over sexual practices have greatly eased, the amount and diversity of sex do not seem to have exploded. Little or no evidence exists that people are much more promiscuous now than in past eras. Few have multiple sexual partners during the same period of time; serial monogamy is by far the most common pattern of sexuality among people who have had more than one partner. Although ancestral mating strategies take place in vastly different cultural, demographic, and ecological contexts, males remain more interested in a greater amount and variety of sex than females. Paradoxically, once homosexuality became normative, gay male culture changed from promoting many sexual partners to embracing marriage and adopting or having children. The opportunity to be normal trumped any purported urge to promiscuity.

Perhaps most surprising, despite increasing social tolerance, it appears that bisexuality, the form of sexuality that Kinsey and, to some extent, Freud thought was natural, is not widely prevalent. Few people—less than 2 percent—claim to be equally attracted to men and women. Sexual orientation does not seem to be fluid: Lifting the cultural veil of sexual repression has uncovered predispositions that seem relatively fixed at birth among most people, who view themselves as born to be either heterosexual or homosexual. [57] In contrast to the expectations of culturally grounded theories of sexuality and despite the development of reproductive technologies that do not require heterosexual intercourse, the vast majority of people still choose to have heterosexual sex and identify as male or female. Although sexual orientations are not as rigid as traditional moral codes believed they were, they are not nearly as variable as Kinsey and "post-gender" theories assume.

Standards that define normal and abnormal sexual practices act on what are apparently strong natural predispositions toward heterosexuality or homosexuality. Although changes in cultural norms allow far more people to openly express their sexual desires and preferences, they have had much less effect in altering these powerful predilections. Despite the far greater normative availability of a diverse range of sexual preferences, the vast majority of people—very roughly, 95 percent at present—remain exclusively heterosexual. If Herodotus has prevailed over Darwin in cultural depictions of varied sexualities, sexual activities still reflect Darwinian tendencies. Even more surprisingly, most are monogamous within any particular time period, perhaps because of the emotion of jealousy. It is an open question whether these propensities can persist in the face of technologies that render intercourse superfluous and of value systems that no longer obligate having children.

If changing cultural norms have not revolutionized patterns of sexual activity, they have completely transformed the degree of harm that non-heterosexual activities entail. For centuries, homosexuals were liable to stigma, shame, isolation, and criminal prosecution. They were forced to either engage in clandestine sexual activities or abstain from acting on their desires. Current cultural norms and legal regulations have eliminated, or at least vastly reduced, the harm stemming from same-sex erotic orientations. Being a gay person at present thoroughly diverges from gay experiences in even the recent past. It is likely that Darwin, as well as Herodotus, would celebrate the ability to have full and free sexual lives that people of all sexualities can now enjoy.

9 DEFECTS AND DIFFERENCES

Without social forces that prevented people from acting on their bisexuality I
think most people would carry on both heterosexual and homosexual activities
coincidentally.

—ALFRED KINSEY, *quoted in Jones 2004, p. 384*

The home is kept pure from incestuous defilement neither by laws, nor
by customs, nor by education but by an *instinct* which under normal
circumstances makes sexual love between the nearest kin a psychical
impossibility.

—EDWARD WESTERMARCK, *1926, p. 319*

This book has considered some perennial issues about how biology
and culture shape what is natural or pathological. One tradition,
which emerged among Socratic philosophers in Classical Greece,
emphasizes how what is natural or unnatural is grounded in universal principles that reflect human nature, is innate, and is relatively
impervious to change. Since the nineteenth century, this naturalist
view has been associated with Charles Darwin's evolutionary theory. An opposing line of thought, which was embodied in the work
of Herodotus and the Sophist school, denies that normality and
abnormality have any natural foundation. Instead, this approach
insists that what is normal or abnormal derives from arbitrary and
highly variable local customs, must be learned, and readily changes
over time. The values of one culture are neither better nor worse
than those of other cultures; they are just different from them. The
issue of whether normality is natural or conventional that Classical
philosophers, scientists, and historians raised remains central to
current discussions of how culture and biology influence what
traits should be regarded as normal or abnormal.

Differences or Defects?

The tradition that Herodotus launched remained dormant until it
resurfaced during the era of the European Enlightenment and, later,

the French Revolution, but it became the dominant way of thinking about normality among twentieth-century social scientists. This group emphasized the variability of social norms, their moral relativity, and their disconnection from any biological grounding. Anthropologist Ruth Benedict summarized the core of this view when she noted "the universal fact that, happily, the majority of mankind quite readily take any shape that is presented to them." Each of the multitudinous possible ways of life was an equally valuable way of being human that reflected different, but not inferior or superior, styles of functioning. "The difference between a homosexual and a heterosexual," novelist Gore Vidal observed in this vein, "is about the difference between somebody who has brown eyes and somebody who has blue eyes."[1]

Alfred Kinsey's studies of sexual behavior epitomize the view that behavioral diversities reflect differences rather than defects. For Kinsey, desirable forms of sexuality ranged continuously from exclusively homosexual to exclusively heterosexual, with every intervening point as normal as any other. All forms of sexual behavior—oral or anal sex, sex between adults and children, masturbation, and, especially, homosexuality—were natural. Kinsey's outlook accords with Benedict's claim that people "in a society that institutionalizes homosexuality will be homosexual."[2] He would have added that if they had not learned oppressive cultural norms regarding sexuality, they would truly enjoy same-sex relationships or any other form of sexual activity.

Currently, the notion that virtually all conditions, whether homosexuality, transgender, deafness, autism, Down syndrome, mental illness, or physical disability, reflect diversities of functioning as opposed to pathologies thrives. Advocates for such groups promote and celebrate a multiplicity of ways of living and at the same time reject the possibility of deriving universal standards of normality and abnormality that can judge human behavior. Instead, they urge the acceptance of differences and oppose efforts to correct them. One website that promotes the normalization of schizophrenia claims that "we believe these experiences are mad gifts needing cultivation and care, rather than diseases or disorders." An anthropologist who studies autistic children similarly asserts, "Autism is less a disease to be hidden than a disability to be accommodated; it is less a stigma, reflecting badly on [families] than a variation of human existence." Such positions focus on the positive values of multiple ways of living as opposed to binary forms of normal or abnormal conditions.[3]

There was a fairly seamless transition from the views of Herodotus to those of current social scientists and disability activists.[4] In contrast, the grounding of naturalism radically shifted from the Socratic emphasis on reason to the biological thrust of evolutionary theory. Since the mid-nineteenth century, biology has been foundational for the view that objective forces underlie what is normal or pathological. Biological tendencies channel cultural norms in certain directions so that judgments about normalcy are not independent from what is natural. The norms regulating social behaviors go beyond customary expressions to reflect deeper laws of human nature.

Current evolutionary theorists ground values in innate aspects of human nature. "The individual," biologist Edward Wilson asserts, "is predisposed biologically to make certain [ethical] choices." Wilson goes on to claim that genetic forces bias cultures toward "the conventions that express the universal moral codes of honor, patriotism, altruism, justice, compassion, mercy, and redemption." Far from arising from particular cultural beliefs, such norms reflect inherited genetic tendencies that arose through processes of natural selection. Neurophilosopher Patricia Churchland likewise asserts, "It is increasingly evident that moral standards, practices and policies reside in our biology."[5]

If Alfred Kinsey is the most representative figure of the perspective that celebrates diversity, the work of Finnish sociologist Edvard Westermarck best typifies the view that cultural norms reflect innate biological forces. Westermarck proposed that natural selection led humans to develop indifference or repugnance toward having sexual relations with those who shared intimate living conditions with them from their earliest years. This instinctual aversion is not just found in all cultures but also is shared with nonhuman primates and many other species. Intercourse with someone who is known to be a close genetic relative is not simply unusual or culturally disvalued but also biologically unnatural. In each respect, Westermarck's conception thoroughly diverges from that of Kinsey.[6]

For most of history, despite some recent tendencies toward reconciliation, the cultural and biological approaches stood in opposition to one another: What is normal and abnormal or natural and unnatural is rooted in either cultural value judgments or in biological functioning. This book, however, illustrated the great *variety* of connections between the two perspectives. Incest provides the strongest example of how natural design shapes social evaluations. Yet, in other instances, cultural forces override instinctive ones; social norms celebrate courageous people who sacrifice their lives for others and ridicule cowards who naturally give pride of place to their own safety. Sometimes biology is simply irrelevant as an explanation for important cultural phenomena such as first names. Grief provides a contrasting example in which cultural evaluations and biological forces correspond: The intense sorrow people develop after the death of an intimate is both naturally designed and culturally expected.

In a number of other cases, natural biological mechanisms are fundamentally mismatched with current social environments. Voracious appetites designed to consume and store calories when food supplies were limited result in unhealthy weight gain when calories are ubiquitous; fears of objects that were genuinely dangerous in ancestral times but are harmless at present can be seriously impairing. The issue of how culture and biology combine to influence sexual behaviors might be the most perplexing of all. Although heterosexuality must underlie the transmission of genes, "natural" sexual behavior is incredibly variable across human groups. Where to draw lines over what is natural or unnatural about each of these topics is often puzzling.

Harmful Dysfunctions

The harmful dysfunction concept provides one way of integrating the notions that disorders have some objective basis and reflect cultural evaluations. Natural selection during the period when the human genome formed led certain traits—for example, avoidance of incest, ravenous appetites, fleeing from danger, and grieving after the loss of an intimate—to be genetically transmitted through thousands of future generations. They are aspects of human nature that need not be learned but instinctively arise when triggered by the appropriate conditions. Moreover, they are difficult to change even when they are no longer adaptive ways of responding to environmental circumstances.[7]

The presence of some biological, psychological, or behavioral dysfunction is a necessary, although not a sufficient, criterion for the presence of a disorder, which also requires a cultural evaluation that the condition is harmful. Edward Wilson's and Patricia Churchland's views notwithstanding, evolutionary design itself is amoral and cannot be used to derive human values; biological functioning is distinct from cultural evaluation. To say that some mechanism is working naturally or unnaturally is not the same as approving or disapproving it. Evolutionary psychologists Leda Cosmides and John Tooby aptly state, "It would be a bizarre medical or psychiatric system that aimed to return everyone to mental health as defined by evolutionary standards." Moreover, the very purpose of norms and laws is to *control*, not to reflect human nature. "If murder is in the nature of man," philosopher Albert Camus observed, "the law is not intended to imitate or reproduce that nature. It is intended to correct it." Cultural evaluations as well as biological performance are each necessary aspects of judgments that some condition is disordered.[8]

For example, Benedict used the example of catalepsy—a state of consciousness that involves trancelike states, hearing voices, losses of voluntary motion, and limbs that remain rigid—to illustrate how what Western cultures consider to be the mental disorder of catatonic schizophrenia a number of other cultures treat as valued conditions. She asserted, "There are well-described cultures in which these abnormals function at ease and with honor, and apparently without danger or difficulty to the society."[9] This assertion remains influential. In 2014, the British Psychological Association issued a report claiming in regard to schizophrenia that

> some people find it useful to think of themselves as having an illness. Others prefer to think of their problems as, for example, an aspect of their personality which sometimes gets them into trouble but which they would not want to be without.

That is, psychoses are not defects but, rather, differences that some individuals might prefer to other ways of being.[10]

In contrast, the harmful dysfunction (HD) analysis indicates that indigenous catatonics or British schizophrenics have flawed internal mechanisms that they or their cultures do not find harmful. They have dysfunctional perceptual systems but not disorders. Neither a dysfunction nor a judgment of harm in itself is a sufficient indicator of a disorder. Both a defect in universal human functioning and a cultural judgment that devalues this deficiency jointly constitute a genuine disorder.

Dysfunctions

A dysfunction refers to the failure of some behavioral or psychological mechanism to perform its evolutionarily designed function. It is not merely a different way of behaving but is a deviation from the way that biology designed humans to function. Among the conditions this book considered, incest provides the strongest example of a dysfunction. Natural mechanisms of sexual attraction are designed not just to respond to specific types of stimuli but also not to respond to the wrong kinds of stimuli. Erotic feelings toward known genetic intimates fall outside of the natural range of sexual arousal.[11]

Limits on the appropriate targets of sexual feelings developed because of their biological costs. The offspring of closely inbred relationships among humans and other species have far greater chances of developing many defects and diseases. Therefore, natural selection led genetic intimates to develop instinctive aversion to sexual intercourse to prevent such relationships. This dislike is universal, innate, and fixed: Incest disgusts almost everyone, regardless of time and place. The condition that triggers repugnance to incest— intimate living conditions when children are very young—has the same impact in all groups and so is not dependent on cultural values. Most people who do have incestuous relationships did not acquire this avoidance mechanism because they did not share close quarters at an early age.

Although cultural values set the boundaries over the degree of genetic relatedness that constitutes forbidden or acceptable sexual relationships, sex between people who share half of their genes is universally tabooed and intercourse between those who share a quarter of genes is nearly so. Circumstances when incest is the only way to transmit genes and so is adaptive to environmental circumstances, such as those in the Biblical story in which Lot's daughters had sex with their father, are extraordinarily rare. The natural abhorrence to incest seems so strong that it is difficult to imagine that changing cultural values would have much, if any, impact on promoting this behavior.

Anorexia provides another illustration of a dysfunction. Evolution designed humans to consume enough calories to maintain their health and to store any excess as fat. Extreme undereating undermines fitness, disrupts reproduction and fertility, and can be lethal. There are no historical precedents for voluntarily starving one's self in the absence of some recognized cultural, religious, or political script. For example, the fasting of holy women in medieval Italy that is sometimes claimed to be a predecessor to today's anorexics is, like vows of silence of monks, explicable through a well-recognized set of sacred beliefs. Although its causes—whether biological, psychological, or social—are currently unknown, anorexia is a dysfunction of mechanisms that regulate appetite and not simply a cultural difference.[12]

Many cases of depression also are dysfunctions of biologically designed responses to loss. Findings from studies of primates, infants, and a wide range of cultures indicate that sadness naturally arises after losses of valued close attachments, most likely because such responses function to attract social support. However, depression that is not accompanied by some loss, initially emerges after a loss but remains intense for prolonged periods after the distressing event occurred, or features symptoms of extreme severity goes beyond normal sadness to indicate that something has gone wrong with a naturally designed mechanism. Such cases, like incest and anorexia, are not just differences in normal functioning but, rather, indicate the presence of a defective response to loss.[13]

The HD perspective also implies that comparable behaviors can be dysfunctions in some cultures but not in others. Consider pederasty—sexual relations involving adults and prepubescent children—which our culture views as perhaps the most reviled form of sexual behavior. Exclusive preferences for young children are dysfunctions of sexual attraction mechanisms. Adults who are aroused by thoughts of having sex with prepubescent children but who are members of cultures that harshly sanction such behaviors are likely to have dysfunctions that stem from defective internal mechanisms that regulate appropriate objects of sexual attraction.[14]

Yet, many cultures have institutionalized sexual relationships between older men and prepubescent and adolescent boys. Most notably, the Classical Greeks esteemed erotic intergenerational ties, which were an integral part of their culture. They are only the best known of many groups that have valued such amatory unions. Numerous tribes in New Guinea and Melanesia feature regular sexual relationships between adolescent boys and older men. Such practices have also been found in North Africa, among Australian aborigines, and, most likely, in many Paleolithic groups, among others. For example, among the North African Siwans, "All men and boys engage in anal intercourse. Males are singled out as peculiar if they did not do so. Prominent Siwan men lend their sons to each other for this purpose."[15] These valued cultural practices, however, are never exclusive forms of sexuality but coexist with more traditional heterosexual relationships among adults. Involvement in culturally approved adult–child sex would not stem from defective sexual arousal mechanisms within individuals so that pederasty would not be a dysfunction in such groups. Similar modes of sexual attraction can thus be dysfunctions in some groups but not in others.

Mismatches

The HD analysis uses biological design to define the presence or absence of a dysfunction. However, it is often very difficult to define when some mechanism is or is not working as it was naturally designed to work. This is particularly so because natural design was established during the long period when the human genome was formed thousands of generations ago and only changes at a slow, glacial pace. Some biological, psychological, or behavioural trait might be performing its evolutionary function but be fundamentally out of step with contemporary circumstances. The question of whether a mechanism is currently maladaptive is distinct from whether it is performing in accordance withevolutionary design. Many harmful behaviors are not dysfunctions but result from disjunctions between natural design and modern ways of life.

Fear provides an example of how many conditions labeled as "disorders" in fact are evolutionary mismatches. Fears of objects such as animals, insects, or heights that were genuinely dangerous during prehistory but pose minimal threats at present nevertheless are vestiges of ancient predispositions to find certain stimuli frightening. Agoraphobia—the fear of being in crowds, public places, or far from home—also might have been adaptive under ancestral conditions when many dangers arose when people left their native territories. Agoraphobics in the modern world, however, can find it impossible to live normal lives. Fear of strangers can likewise reflect a mechanism that was adaptive when people lived in small groups of well-known others and rare encounters with outsiders generally represented real threats. Currently, when societies feature many short-term and changing relationships, high population densities, and frequent interactions with unfamiliar people, this fear might seem inexplicable and evidence of a disorder. However, it can actually indicate a mismatch between the way we are biologically designed and how our current environment has changed since we were evolutionarily shaped. The HD analysis implies that such mismatches are disorders only when they are failures of biological design; the fact that undesirable, impairing, and harmful mental conditions are maladaptive in our current environment does not make them disorders as long as they are part of our species-typical nature.[16]

Our food tastes reflect a similar mismatch between natural instincts and traits that are currently socially adaptive. Preferences for fat, sugar, and salt were selected in ancient environments when calories were scarce and adequate nutrition was difficult to obtain. Moreover, evolution did not equip humans with strong mechanisms that restricted caloric consumption; such limits were rarely necessary before plentiful and consistent food supplies became available. Ancestral preferences persist in our current calorie-rich environment, in which artificially engineered, processed foods capitalize on natural tastes for sweet, salty, and fatty foods. The widespread obesity that results is not a dysfunction, however harmful it might be, but a product of appetites that are working as evolution designed them to work. The biological basis of obesity under conditions of caloric abundance explains why dieting is so often doomed to failure and why changing environmental factors such as limiting portion sizes and facilitating physical activity should be more effective modes of weight control than restricting calories.

The pleasure that many people obtain from psychoactive drugs illustrates another trait that could have been adaptive under ancestral circumstances but that can entail serious negative consequences in the modern world. The brain developed receptors for substances including opiates, cannabis, nicotine, and ethanol because of their mood-enhancing, energizing, and consciousness-expanding qualities. Under ancestral conditions, substance use had few negative consequences because most drugs had low potencies and did not entail long-term consequences because of short life expectancies. Persistent drug use in the modern world, however, can entail severe costs that evolution never envisioned. It did not design the brain to cope with powerful synthetic drugs such as cocaine, heroin, or methamphetamine when they are used repeatedly for long periods of time. Substance abuse is less a failure of natural design than a mismatch between brains that evolution shaped to enjoy psychoactive chemicals and that possess few restraints against overuse of the powerful drugs that current environments feature.

Mismatches between natural design and modern life often make distinctions between natural and unnatural conditions especially difficult to specify. The importance of cultural evaluations of normality and abnormality adds another complicating layer to the process of answering the question of what is a disorder.

Cultural Evaluations of Dysfunctions

A dysfunction alone is not a sufficient criterion for the presence of a disorder, which also requires that a behavior is harmful in a particular cultural context. A host of relationships exist between biologically unnatural states and the values that different cultures attach to these conditions.

In some cases, cultural values reflect and buttress the harmful nature of biological dysfunctions. Incest provides an example of how cultural values reinforce natural instincts. Consider an episode of *Law and Order SUV* that features a man who did not acquire an aversion to incest because he neither lived with his half-sister from an early age nor even knew that she was genetically related to him. When told that he has unwittingly impregnated her and is the father of her baby, he immediately vomits. He states that if he had known the woman was his sister, he would have shot himself after having intercourse with her. Cultural transmission can lead people who did not naturally acquire the mechanism leading them to avoid incestuous relationships to develop intense disgust and shame over sexual contacts with genetic intimates.[17]

Conversely, in other cases, social values, public policies, and institutional arrangements can reduce or even eliminate the harmful consequences of dysfunctions. For example, the HD analysis views the inability to distinguish accurate from grossly disturbed perceptions of reality, bizarre and inappropriate behaviors, and paranoid delusions often found among persons with schizophrenia as serious malfunctions and not "gifts in need of cultivation and care." Yet, cultural evaluations do influence the harm that arises from this condition. Schizophrenics living in more tolerant and inclusive cultures have more benign and fewer enduring symptoms than those facing highly stigmatizing attitudes and much social exclusion. The degree of cultural acceptance or rejection toward persons with serious mental illnesses, as well as their inherent conditions, powerfully shapes the degree of harm that their dysfunction entails.[18]

Deafness provides another example of how cultural values and institutions can dramatically alter the impact of a dysfunction. Nature designed humans (and most other species) to hear; the inability to detect sounds restricts possibilities of communication, interaction, and responses to danger. Cultural beliefs traditionally stigmatized and isolated deaf people, which intensified the damage their condition created. The growth of deaf culture, however, shows how favorable social attitudes and welcoming environments create circumstances that minimize or remove the harmful aspect of a dysfunction. Deaf children who acquire sign language at an early age have the ability to communicate with other signing people. They can assimilate into a vibrant deaf community that features its own educational institutions, theaters, social clubs, and the like that positively value their conditions. Under these circumstances, deafness need not be harmful and so meets the criteria for a dysfunction but not those for a disorder.[19]

In other situations, cultural evaluations can be so strong that they overpower biological instincts. Consider the experience of Daniel Inouye (later a Senator from Hawaii) during World War II:

> On April 21, 1945, weeks before the end of the war in Europe, he led an assault near San Terenzo, Italy. His platoon was pinned down by three machine guns. Although shot in the stomach, he ran forward and destroyed one emplacement with a hand grenade and another with his submachine gun. He was crawling toward the third when enemy fire nearly severed his right arm, leaving a grenade, in his words, "clenched in a fist that suddenly didn't belong to me anymore." He pried it loose, threw it with his left hand and destroyed the bunker. Stumbling forward, he silenced resistance with gun bursts before being hit in the leg and collapsing unconscious.

From an evolutionary standpoint, Inouye's risk of his own life to save those of genetic strangers was inexplicable. Natural selection did not design people to willingly sacrifice themselves to save the lives of unrelated others. Conversely, cowards who flee from danger to save their own lives, an entirely natural response, are generally subject to scorn, ridicule, and disgrace. Cultural values define cowardice as a thoroughly degrading action that is one of the worst possible labels for a man to receive. Courage and cowardice provide the clearest cases in which social values transform an unnatural behavior into a highly cherished ideal while shaming a natural predisposition.[20]

People overcome their natural cowardice because cultural norms glorify individuals who sacrifice their own interests for the benefit of their comrades, communities, or nations. Courage in battle is perhaps the most esteemed cultural value. British Field Marshall Lord Slim asserted, "I don't believe there's any man who, in his heart of hearts, wouldn't rather be called brave than have any other virtue attributed to him." Likewise, the novelist William Thackeray emphasized how "men place military valor so far beyond every other quality for reward and worship." Cultural norms can be so significant that they override even the most deeply rooted natural instincts. However, because courage lacks any biological basis, it is often fragile and can easily crumble when danger arises. As a German officer notes in the movie *The Bridge*, "There is no need to drill retreat, they do that on their own." [21]

Norms about desirable and undesirable weight provide another instance in which cultural values transpose natural and unnatural conditions. Social evaluations stigmatize fatness that expectably results from our naturally insatiable appetites when they confront abundant and consistent supplies of calories. Cultural stereotypes associate fat people with laziness, lack of willpower, and greediness. At the same time, social labels glorify unnatural states of thinness and esteem slender bodies, especially slender female bodies. Most women, even those who are underweight according to body mass index, think that they are too heavy and want to lose weight. Indeed, some surveys indicate that women would rather lose weight than be successful in love or at work. One consequence is that dieting has become, in psychologist Judith Rodin's term, a "normative obsession."[22] Just as social norms promote unnatural courage over natural cowardice, judgments of thinness and fatness invert the relationship between the results of biologically natural appetites and cultural evaluations of appropriate body sizes. Like soldiers who do not need to be taught how to flee, people do not have to learn to indulge their appetites, which comes naturally to them. Evaluations of female thinness and fatness seem in certain respects to be gendered equivalents of assessments of male courage and cowardice.

Harm Without Dysfunction

Cultural evaluations and institutional arrangements can sometimes reinforce the impact of dysfunctions, sometimes minimize the harm they create, or sometimes even transpose their natural impacts. Yet, cultural values alone are never sufficient components for disorders, which also must involve breakdowns of natural functioning. Many maladaptive, impairing, and distressing conditions are not dysfunctions.[23]

Abnormal names provide an example of conditions that can be harmful but are not failures of natural design and so are not dysfunctions. Names are sounds that are constituted by culture without any biological basis; however, they can be very harmful. When Sue's father gave him a stereotypical female name, it was "the meanest thing he ever did." It led to extraordinary amounts of embarrassment, harassment, and bullying. Sue wanted to "kill that man who gave me that awful name." Despite Sue's distress and impairment, abnormal names are arbitrary culturally based sounds that cannot be dysfunctions.

Although it is implausible that anyone considers abnormal names to be failures of natural design, cultural values do mistakenly classify many natural phenomena as pathological. A particular strength of the HD concept lies in providing grounds for claims that cultural evaluations of natural functioning can simply be wrong when a dysfunction is not present. As Chapter 1 noted, left-handedness provides a model for a trait that historically was mistakenly considered to be defective. For centuries, left-handed people were stigmatized and subject to harsh routines that strove to make them right-handed. In fact, there was no justification for treating left-handedness as a defect in the first place: Judgments that this condition indicated a dysfunction were incorrect. Likewise, nineteenth-century psychiatrists, reflecting Victorian beliefs, believed that masturbation was a serious mental illness leading to impairments including sterility, a cornucopia of physical illnesses, and suicide. Because this behavior does not involve any dysfunction, their view was simply false. Masturbation was never a disease, regardless of what physicians and the general culture thought at the time. The harm that left-handed people or masturbators suffered did not result from any dysfunction but, rather, from erroneous cultural beliefs about their traits.[24]

The American Psychiatric Association's removal of the bereavement exclusion from the diagnostic criteria of depressive disorders in 2013 provides a recent instance of medical professionals mistakenly associating the harm that some condition creates with the issue of whether that condition is a dysfunction. Biology designed humans (among other species) to grieve after the death of an intimate. Before 2013, psychiatric criteria for depression recognized that intense sadness after the death of an intimate, however distressing it might be, was not disordered unless it was prolonged or involved an unusually serious symptom such as suicidal thoughts or hallucinations. The American Psychiatric Association, however, removed this exclusion on the grounds that the suffering accompanying grief warranted its classification as a mental disorder. This reasoning confuses the distress and impairment that some condition entails (in this case, pain that need only last for a 2-week period) with the presence of a dysfunction. The view of many current psychiatrists that bereavement is a dysfunction, like those of their nineteenth-century counterparts who thought the same about masturbation, is plainly false.[25]

Psychiatric definitions of a number of other conditions sometimes misclassify, for example, normal shyness as disordered social phobias, expectable responses to disadvantageous social circumstances as conduct disorders, or childish exuberance as attention deficit hyperactivity disorder. The television character Tony Soprano provides a compelling critique of such mistaken criteria. After a school psychologist tells him that his son displays many of the symptoms of attention deficit hyperactivity disorder, including fidgeting, he retorts,

> He fidgets? What constitutes a fidget? He's a 13 year old boy: He gets a hard-on every 10 minutes. He is not a case, he's a 13 year old boy. That's the trouble with you people, every time you see a problem you turn it into a disease.

The HD analysis provides support for Tony's claim that symptoms that do not stem from failures of natural functioning are not mental disorders, regardless of how psychiatric definitions classify them.[26]

Sometimes, the impact of cultural judgments goes beyond making mistaken claims that some harmful state is a disorder to actually creating much of the impairment that supposedly stems from the condition. The current response toward recreational psychoactive drug use provides an illustration. Former Drug Czar William Bennett claims, "The fact is that under the influence of drugs, normal people do not act normally and abnormal people behave in chilling and horrible ways." Yet, the natural properties of drugs that are classified as among the most dangerous, such as marijuana and heroin, lead to passivity. Whatever "chilling and horrible" acts are connected with their use are far more likely to result from their criminalized status and resultant extralegal drug trade than from their natural effects. Drug users are also at risk of losing their jobs, government benefits, and opportunities for loans, which in turn can make it more likely that they will engage in illegal drug activities. Cultural evaluations that marginalize and punish drug users can be responsible for more harm than the chemical impacts of many illicit substances.[27]

Social responses to devalued sexual behaviors also provide examples of how mistaken cultural definitions of natural design can create enormous amounts of suffering. Consider homosexuality. Pure Darwinian criteria view same-sex sexual activity that does not transmit genes to future generations as "almost certainly an evolutionary dysfunction in their gender modularity systems."[28] However, unlike incest, which also features atypical targets of sensual desirability, homosexuality is commonly found in other species, is widely accepted in many cultures, and does not harm participants. Moreover, homosexuals are distinct from people with sexual dysfunctions who wish to, but cannot, have orgasms. Their sexual organs perform perfectly well, but they are aroused by different erotic objects. Homosexuality better fits a model of human difference than of biological defect and so is neither a dysfunction nor a disorder. Nevertheless, the stigma attached to homosexuality historically led to extraordinary amounts of self-hatred, guilt, shame, and other psychological impairments as well as social discrimination and isolation.[29]

Even at present, infants who are born with well-functioning but unusual sex organs, such as very large clitorises or very small penises, are commonly subject to surgical interventions because of perceptions that their genitals will create social impairments as they grow older. Because these conditions do not involve failures of natural functioning, they are not disorders, however socially damaging they might be in particular contexts. Like homosexuality, whatever harm they entail results more from social responses than from a dysfunctional condition.[30]

Arguably, some cases of post-traumatic stress disorder (PTSD) also illustrate the iatrogenic impact of cultural values. Evolution seems to have designed traumatized people to develop persistent re-experiences of the initial shock, hyperarousal to stimuli reminiscent of the trauma, and emotional numbing, among other psychological consequences. These qualities presumably developed because they increased the likelihood that victims would avoid similar trauma-producing situations in the future. Natural design might also lead these disturbing symptoms to diminish or go away over time without outside intervention, although they might occasionally reappear. Especially since the 1990s, however, cultural representations emphasize how traumatic experiences invariably lead to lasting impairments in the absence of therapy. This framework can inadvertently exacerbate and prolong experiences of PTSD because it does not take into account the gradual natural improvement that many traumatized people experience over time. This cultural climate could be responsible for the explosion of PTSD cases in the twenty-first century among not just veterans who have experienced recent combat but also those who fought in earlier wars, whose symptoms should have declined with passing years. In some cases, a therapeutic cultural climate might produce the very conditions that it attempts to heal.[31]

Both biological failures and culturally defined harm are necessary components of disorders. Without the limits that the presence of a failure of designed functioning provides, labels of disorder could be applied to an endless array of undesirable behaviors, whether crime, ignorance, political dissent, or differences in sexual preferences. The HD concept both restricts the range of conditions that are considered to be disorders and recognizes the importance of cultural evaluations.

The Future of Normality

In coming years, biomedical technology might develop to the extent that it can detect and prevent many defects in natural design from ever arising. At the same time, increasing knowledge is likely to minimize or eliminate the impairments that dysfunctions involve. The potential ability to eradicate and control dysfunctions will raise basic questions about what are appropriate and inappropriate targets for biomedical and social interventions.

Procedures such as amniocentesis and ultrasound that identify chromosomal abnormalities and let parents decide whether to abort or give birth to fetuses with dysfunctions have been available for decades. An example is Down syndrome (DS), which involves an extra copy of chromosome 21, a condition that leads to a number of intellectual and developmental difficulties, problems with physical health, and atypical appearance, among others. About two-thirds of mothers who learn that their fetus has this condition choose to abort. However, the development of early intervention programs in recent decades has allowed people with DS the opportunity to engage in a range of social, educational, and occupational activities; many can now live relatively independently as adults. Their potential for a greatly enhanced quality of life illustrates the dilemma of whether their condition is a true defect or a different way of life. Andrew Solomon summarizes the quandary:

> Down syndrome may be an identity or a catastrophe or both; it may be something to cherish or something to eradicate; it may be rich and rewarding both for those whom it affects directly and for those who care for them; it may be a barren and exhausting enterprise; it may be a blend of all of these.

The prenatal identification and subsequent elimination of fetuses with DS raises questions about what conditions are defects in need of correction or differences that should be appreciated and supported.[32]

Down syndrome results from a genetic mutation that is not transmitted to future generations. Recently, scientists have acquired the ability to alter genetic material in ways that will be passed on. They can replace genes that they regard as defective with typical ones and so can potentially eradicate some genetic diseases from ever emerging. Mitochondrial replacement therapy (MRT) illustrates this possibility. Around 1 in every 4000 people have diseases related to mitochondrial mutations, which are associated with a variety of diseases, including deafness, blindness, cognitive impairments, and failures of heart, lung, and kidney functioning. MRT permanently places a third person's DNA in every cell of the child through inserting mitochondrial DNA from one woman into the fertilized eggs of another woman. The resulting embryo contains heritable genetic material of three different people. This technique does not just prevent diseases from arising in a child bearing the mother's own mitochondrial genes but also stops them from being transmitted to that child's children. Other, more sweeping, forms of genomic modification that take place in embryos are also rapidly developing. As with DS, questions will arise over which genetic traits are defects to be corrected and which are differences to be appreciated.[33]

Just as new genetic techniques have the promise of correcting heritable defects and preventing them from being conveyed to future generations, other procedures allow parents the ability to select highly valued traits for their children. In vitro fertilization procedures combine an egg and sperm outside the body to create an embryo that is then implanted in the womb. Women can choose what traits they desire in sperm donors; men can do the same with women who provide the eggs. Sperm banks, for example, exclude men with undesirable physical and mental attributes, such as shortness or depression. At the same time, they actively seek tall, intelligent, highly educated, and attractive donors. Many scientists and ethicists worry that in the future they "could be used to try to make so-called designer babies, kids who are more intelligent, who have other qualities that the parents find desirable." To the extent that these practices become widespread, they might fulfill eugenicist Francis Galton's dream of improving the gene pool of the human race through eliminating undesirable qualities. At the same time, they might increase inequalities between people who have the resources to take advantage of expensive techniques involving artificial selection and those who continue to reproduce in conventional ways.[34]

Other biomedical developments allow for the early correction of biological defects that become apparent in infancy. Cochlear implants (CIs) exemplify this technology. These electronic devices are placed under the skin of the ear to provide deaf or severely hearing-impaired individuals the ability to process sounds. Although these implants do not fully restore hearing, they allow recipients to engage in conversations, understand sounds, and detect auditory warning signals. Because CIs must be inserted at a very early age to be totally effective, parents must make decisions for their very young children. As CI technology continues to improve to the point that future devices will allow implanted individuals to have almost full hearing, it is likely that nearly all parents will choose to implant these devices in their children so that congenital deafness might be abolished. A technology that largely eliminates a dysfunction therefore also will entail the destruction of the deaf signing culture. Indeed, many deaf activists oppose CIs and consider them to be a form of genocide. Nevertheless, the availability of a normalizing procedure that can correct defective hearing will likely prevail.[35]

Biomedicine is also rapidly developing the ability to treat dysfunctions that arise later in life. The potential response to PTSD provides an example. Pharmacologists are developing drugs that might allow people who take them soon after a traumatic experience to reduce or eliminate the painful qualities of their memories of the event. Experiments with mice show how a class of drugs called histone deacetylase inhibitors can lead brains to separate memories of specific events from the associated agonizing emotions that they create. Because the drug would not allow the memory to consolidate in victims' brains, they should no longer have distressing and intrusive recollections of the trauma. Such drugs can potentially minimize the psychic pain and other impairing responses of traumatized people. It seems likely that most doctors will look favorably on these drugs and that most victims will readily take them. If these efforts are successful for humans, they will raise challenging questions about the boundaries between natural and pathological responses to trauma and the advisability of tampering with biologically designed mechanisms of memory and fear.[36]

At the same time as technological developments promise to eliminate many dysfunctions, changes in values are transforming the negative cultural evaluations that traditionally have been associated with many dysfunctions. Growing social movements regard many conditions that were previously considered as defects as diverse ways of living that should be celebrated. This combination of technological and cultural changes promises both to reduce the quantity of dysfunctions and to increase the range of culturally approved forms of behavior.

The sea change in responses to homosexuality exemplifies the rising approval of a multiplicity of behaviors and identities. Until recent years, most Western cultures considered homosexuality to be a sin, a perversion, and a mental illness. The deep stigma and exclusion that gay people faced led them to experience enormous psychic and social harm. Currently, however, values emphasizing the free choice of sexual partners and identities have grown. The sharply increased acceptance of gay people and of institutions such as gay marriage has largely eliminated the culture-based impairments associated with same-sex preferences. Homosexuality has become a widely established form of sexual expression that large segments of Western culture no longer stigmatize. Indeed, people and organizations that *disapprove* of same-sex relationships or institutions such as gay marriage can now be subject to more censure than people and organizations that support gay rights. Growing cultural acceptance also characterizes many other forms of previously devalued conditions, including transgender, many forms of mental illness, and physical disabilities.[37]

The rise of electronic communication will be another powerful force that will transform evaluations of normality and abnormality. Distance no longer presents a barrier to communication; regardless of space, any person can connect to anyone else. The ability to instantly contact millions of others who are not physically co-present allows new subcultures to form that are unconstrained by geography. This permits people with statistically rare proclivities to readily find others who share and reinforce these traits. Electronic communication can thus solve what sociologist Donald Black called "the problem of the Indonesian lesbian." In the 1970s, Black noted how a lesbian in Indonesia who was motivated to engage in same-sex behavior had never done so because she did not know of and had no way of finding other lesbians. In contrast to a time and place where such hidden desires remained unfulfilled, such a person could now instantly contact hundreds of other lesbians in Indonesia and millions worldwide. The likely result, as the title of a recent book—*You're Never Weird on the Internet*—indicates, will be to vastly enhance the ability of people with statistically rare traits to find communities that regard their conditions as reflecting diversities rather than defects. One person who identifies as asexual provides an example: "I spent hours scouring the website of the Asexual Visibility and Education Network, comparing others' experiences with my own. Asexuality began to make sense to me in a way that sexuality didn't." Virtual others can approve and reinforce behaviors that are devalued within one's spatial confines.[38]

Despite the cultural acceptance of growing numbers of behaviors that have previously been regarded as dysfunctions, the HD view should retain its ability to identify many clear cases of failures of natural design. For instance, the existence of many websites that promote and facilitate anorexia does not change the fact that voluntary extremes of thinness are unnatural. Nevertheless, in coming years, such virtual groups are likely to grow and expand as sources of social acceptance for people with dysfunctional conditions.

Conclusion

Future technologies will be able to eliminate many dysfunctions. At the same time, changes in cultural beliefs and the omnipresence of electronic communication can minimize the stigma of previously disvalued qualities and promote a far broader array of traits as valued ways of being human. Yet, the prospect of a world with fewer defects and more differences than has ever been possible before—which both Herodotus and Darwin probably would celebrate—might be impossible to fully realize.

Electronic communication, in particular, can be a force for promoting conformity as well as for accepting difference. The other side of the massively increased capacity to communicate with widely dispersed others is that disapproved activities become instantly available to millions of others. Facebook, Twitter, and Instagram can be tools to shame people who express objectionable sentiments or conduct themselves in offensive ways. Social norms can be rapidly transmitted and enforced, allowing for instant and worldwide outrage and condemnation of nonconformity. For example, comments or pictures that are perceived to be racist, homophobic, sexist, or unpatriotic can receive immediate global denigration. Those who are shamed might be forced to move residences, go underground, or change their names.[39]

Despite technological progress that prevents dysfunctions from occurring and that alleviates their impairing consequences when they do arise, it is unlikely that distinctions between normality and abnormality will disappear. As sociologist Emile Durkheim memorably proposed, even a society of saints will consider some of its members to be deviant. If current understandings of what are normal and abnormal behaviors change, it is perhaps inevitable that others will take their place. Ultimately, biological dysfunctions might be more susceptible to change than inescapable cultural value judgments that will always view some conditions as normal and others as pathological.[40]

NOTES

CHAPTER I

1. Herodotus, 1996, 3:38, p. 169; 4:26, p. 225; 1:140, p. 57; 3:16, p. 160, 1:198, p. 79.
2. Darwin, 1872/2007, p. 184, p. 176.
3. The Sophists encompassed fifth-century BCE philosophers Protagoras, Gorgias, and Antiphon, among others. See Long, 2005; Herodotus, 1996, 3:38, p. 169. For instance, Herodotus described the aftermath of a battle between two Greek tribes, where the Argives "who were previously compelled by custom to wear their hair long, began to cut it short," whereas the Spartans "also adopted a new custom, but in precisely the opposite sense: They used not to grow their hair long, but from that time they began to do so." Herodotus, 1996, 1:82, p. 34. Plato uses the character Callicles to criticize the Sophist view in the *Gorgias*. Internet Classics Library, http://classics.mit.edu/Plato/gorgias.html.
4. Herodotus, 1996, 3:38; Murray, 1986.
5. de Montesquieu, 1750/2011. See also Aron, 1968.
6. Locke, 1950, p. 42.
7. Zerubavel, 1985. The Romantic movement was another major source of the flourishing of cultural relativism and subsequent emergence of anthropological investigations in western Europe and Great Britain.
8. Mill, 1859/1991, pp. 21–22.
9. Quetelet, 1842/2015. Means were sums of many individuals and so were collective properties of groups, not aspects of particular individuals. Indeed, it was often the case that no individual could possibly be average. For example, an average woman might give birth to 2.3 children during her lifetime, a value no single person could ever have.
10. Quoted in Stigler, 1986, p. 171.
11. Boas, 1911/2007; Benedict, 1934/1959; Mead, 1928.
12. Benedict, 1959, p. 25; Benedict, 1934, p. 79; Mead, 1935/2001, p. 280.
13. Montagu, 1968, p. 9; Degler, 1991, p. 203.
14. Foucault, 1988. Foucault rejected the possibility of making any universal claims about human nature but developed a purely historical notion of individuals. See especially Foucault, 1984.

15. Watson, 1924, p. 104; Skinner, 1971.

16. https://www.goodreads.com/quotes/231590-i-am-different-not-less; Solomon, 2012, p. 28.

17. Canguilhem, 2000.

18. Darwin, 1879/2004, p. 86, p. 151.

19. Darwin, 1879/2004, p. 86, p. 676. The final sentence of *The Descent of Man* reads as follows: "Man still bears in his bodily frame the indelible stamp of his lowly origin" (p. 689).

20. Darwin, 1879/2004, pp. 22–23, p. 363, p. 207. As Chapter 8 explores, Darwin's emphasis on the unity of humankind did not extend to gender. He focused on the biologically grounded differences between men and women.

21. Darwin, 1872/2007, p. 259. See also Miller, 1997, pp. 1–4.

22. Darwin, 1872/2007, p. 354.

23. Darwin, 1859/2004, p. 250.

24. The term "social Darwinism" did not appear until 1900; Degler, 1991.

25. Lorenz, 1966; Goodall, 1969; Morris, 1967; Harlow, Harlow, & Suomi, 1971; Seligman, 1970, 1971.

26. For example, Kandel, 1998; Schildkraut, 1965; Schooler, 2007.

27. Wilson, 1998, p. 266.

28. Tooby & Cosmides, 1990; Pinker, 2002.

29. Cosmides & Tooby, 1999, p. 458. See also Buss, 1995. Quote from Tooby & Cosmides, 1990, p. 417.

30. Churchland, 2006, p. 3.

31. Many, or even most, sociologists retain the view of the discipline's founders, which sharply split social from biological forces. Indeed, sociologist Jeremy Freese and colleagues (2003, p. 234) observed that "few things provoke sociologists as easily or strongly as the perceivably improper invocation of 'biology' as an explanatory device." See also Ellis, 1996.

32. Segerstrale, 2000, p. 307. See also Guttmacher & Collins, 2003; Nature Editorial Group, 2012; Massey, 2002; Freese & Shostak, 2009; Schutt, Seidman, & Keshavan, 2015.

33. Caspi et al., 2003; Pescosolido et al., 2008; Freese & Shostak, 2009; Zhang & Meaney, 2010.

34. Ebrahim, 2012; Landecker & Panofsky, 2013; Meaney, 2010; Hijmans et al., 2008; Coyne, 2015; Schutt et al., 2015.

35. Gould, 1981; Rose, 2007.

36. It has become commonplace for scholars to emphasize the intrinsic connections of the genetic and social processes. Eisenberg, 1995, p. 1571; Griffiths, 1997, p. 138. Wakefield has published prolifically on the HD concept, but his initial statement (1992) remains the best overview.

37. Wakefield, 1999, p. 395.

38. Wakefield, 1999, p. 383.

39. Cosmides & Tooby (1999, p. 458) make this point in a different way.
40. Hertz, 1909.
41. For example, Horwitz & Wakefield, 2007, 2012.

CHAPTER 2

1. Mead, 1935/2001, pp. 67–68.
2. Bloom, 2011, p. 73; Haidt, 2012, p. 47. Only one of my students out of hundreds has found nothing wrong with this situation. She explained that her response did not stem from a specific endorsement of sibling incest but instead from her general libertarian belief that people should be able to have sex with anyone they want. Rutgers students seem to be more conservative than others. Haidt reports that 20 percent of his students found it acceptable for Julie and Mark to have sex. See Haidt, 2012, p. 45.
3. Levy-Bruhl, 1931/1972, p. 231; Herodotus, 1996, 3:31–38, pp. 167–169.
4. Long & Sedley, 1987, p. 67; Mandeville, 1714/1924, V. 1, p. 331.
5. Quoted in Fox, 1980, p. 16; Fox, 1980, p. 207.
6. Herodotus, 1996, 5:39, p. 293; Bittles, 2005, pp. 38–60, p. 38.
7. Freud, 1925/1958; Herman, 1981; Turner & Maryanski, 2005. See also Shepher, 1983, p. 127.
8. Murdock, 1949, pp. 284–285.
9. Malinowski, 1932, p. 519; Firth, 1936/1983, p. 180, p. 281.
10. Opler, 1941; Black, 2011, p. 79.
11. Plato, 1980, 838b; Arnhart, 2005, pp. 190–218, p. 193; https://www.youtube.com/watch?v=hPT174-fzQ;https://www.youtube.com/watch?v=jQp0KowG67A
12. Gates, 2005, p. 153.
13. Scheidel, 2004; among the Egyptians, one spouse commonly murdered the other. Schiff, 2010, p. 22; Hopkins, 1980; Gates, 2005, p. 153; Westermarck, 1891, p. 290.
14. Genesis 19:33; Genesis 19:31. The ancient Greek and Roman legend of Myrrha has many resemblances to Lot's situation. Myrrha disguises herself and has intercourse with her father, King Cinyras, resulting in the birth of the demigod Adonis. Like Lot, the King was unaware of his paramour's identity because their couplings took place in complete darkness. Myrrha also appears in Dante's *Inferno*, in which she is confined to the eighth circle of hell for her deceit and repugnant conduct.
15. 2 Samuel 13.
16. Murdock, 1949, p. 302, p. 286.
17. Long & Sedley, 1987, p. 430; Erickson, 2005, p. 162; Bateson, 2005, p. 25; Wolf, 2005, p. 4.
18. Fox, 1980, p. 98; Turner & Maryanski. 2005.
19. Quoted in Degler, 1991, p. 257; Fossey, 1983; Bagemihl, 1999, p. 73.
20. Pusey, 2005, p. 71.
21. Xenophon, *Memorabilia*, IV, 19–23. http://www.gutenberg.org/files/1177/1177-h/1177-h.htm; Durham, 2005, p. 131; Firth, 1936/1983, p. 289.

22. van den Berghe, 1983.
23. Pusey & Wolf, 1996; Pusey, 2005, p. 62.
24. Wilson, 1998, p. 174; Seemanova, 1971; Shepher, 1983, Table 7.2, p. 93.
25. The reproductive decline among inbred first cousins, although substantial, might not be large enough to offset corresponding benefits in enhancing social solidarity and so not have any selective effect. See Wolf, 2005, p. 3; Shepher, 1983, pp. 92–93.
26. Westermarck, 1891, p. 319; V. 2, p. 193; Westermarck, 1926, p. 80. Although little known at present, at the time Westermarck was a prominent sociologist whose reputation rivaled or exceeded such legendary figures as Emile Durkheim. Westermarck, however, did not establish any intellectual school, had no followers, and fell into obscurity until the emergence of sociobiology in the 1970s. See Roos, 2008.
27. Westermarck (1891, pp. 200–201) also explained that rare cases of incestuous relations develop because "sexual intercourse with a near relative may be resorted to when another, more suitable partner is out of reach."
28. Erickson, 2005, p. 177.
29. Pusey, 2005, p. 65; Penn & Potts, 1998.
30. Spiro, 1958, p. 34; Shepher, 1983, p. 59; Shepher, 1971, p. 296. One study claims that children raised together on kibbutzim did develop sexual attraction to each other when they reached sexual maturity. This study, however, relies on retrospective memories of 60 adults from as far back as 50 years. It presents no behavioral data to contradict the claim that there were no actual sexual relationships among people who grew up in such settings. Moreover, most of the participants did not share the intense early socialization experiences of those in the Manson and Shephard studies. Shor & Simchai, 2009. See also the critique in Maryanski, Sanderson, & Russell (2012).
31. Wolf, 1995; McCabe, 1983.
32. Harrison, 1997; Russell, 1999; Erickson, 2005, pp. 168–169; Wilson, 1988; Pinker, 1997, p. 45.
33. Russell, 1999, p. 276.
34. Lieberman, Tooby, & Cosmides, 2007.
35. Degler, 1991, p. 245. One of the founders of sociology, Emile Durkheim (1907), also wrote a long essay attempting to refute Westermarck. In fact, societies do prohibit behaviors to which people are naturally averse, such as suicide, cannibalism, or necrophilia.
36. Quoted in Degler, 1991, p. 250. Levi-Strauss, 1969; See also Parsons, 1954.
37. Freud, 1920/1953; Freud, 1930).
38. Freud, 1900/1965, p. 291.
39. Freud, 1900/1965; Freud, 1938/1989, pp. 192–193.
40. Note that the complete separation between Oedipus and his parents would mean that, according to the Westermarck effect, he would not naturally have developed an aversion to sex with his mother.

41. Freud, 1900/1965, pp. 296–297.
42. Sophocles, 1958, pp. 77–78.
43. Freud, 1925/1958, p. 34.
44. Herman, 1981, p. 9.
45. Freud, 1896/1958, p. 153.
46. Pinker, 1997, p. 456.
47. See especially Borch-Jacobsen & Shamdasani, 2012, especially pp. 126–159; quote from p. 156. See also McNally, 2003, pp. 111–112; pp. 162–168; Ofshe & Watters, 1994, p. 293. During the 1980s, the phenomenon of multiple personality disorder emerged in a similar way. Therapists who believed that their clients suffered from repressed memories of early child abuse used methods such as hypnosis and other suggestive techniques to convince their patients that forgotten traumas led to their current problems. See Hacking, 1995; Horwitz, 2002, pp. 120–124.
48. Herman, 1981, p. 7. Sociologists Jonathan Turner and Alexandra Maryanski (2005) suggest that incest aversion among fathers and daughters is weaker than that among other genetic intimates and is primarily regulated by cultural norms rather than biological avoidance.
49. Kinsey, Pomeroy, & Martin, 1948, p. 558; Shepher, 1983, p. 127; Herman, 1981, Table 1.1, p. 13.
50. Russell, 1999, p. 59; Russell, 1984.
51. Russell, 1999, p. 216; For brother–sister rate, see p. 271. For first cousin rate, see p. 346. Note that for brothers, uncles, and cousins, percentages are based on the number of females reporting incestuous relationships, not on the number of male relatives. The percentage of male relatives, other than fathers, who engaged in incestuous relationships would be much lower; Russell, 1999, table on p. 141; Russell, 1999, p. 104, p. 268. These findings probably understate rates of stepfather–daughter abuse because stepfathers were counted only if they raised the respondent up to age 14 years, not if respondents ever lived with a stepfather. See Russell, 1999, p. 233.
52. Russell, 1999, p. 149; Erickson, 2005, p. 167; Russell, 1999, p. 354; Herodotus, 1996, 2:131, p. 134.
53. Terance, 163 BC/2010.
54. Segerstrale, 2000, p. 369.

CHAPTER 3

1. Herodotus, 4:184, p. 274; Some scientists claim that dolphins have unique names for each other: See http://news.nationalgeographic.com/news/2013/07/130722-dolphins-whistle-names-identity-animals-science. However, others note that although dolphins might have their own signature whistles, they do not use the signature whistles of other dolphins, an essential aspects of names. See http://blog.oup.com/2013/07/do-dolphins-call-each-other-by-name.

2. Lieberson, 2000, p. 24, p. 98.

3. From a research standpoint, the study of names also can be more rigorous than investigations of most other social phenomena. Good data about names encompass entire populations because every child receives a name and all names are recorded. For example, the Social Security Administration operates a website that shows the 1000 most popular boys' and girls' name for each year since 1900 (https://www.ssa.gov/OACT/babynames). Issues of sampling, incompleteness, and nonresponse that plague much social scientific research do not pose problems for the study of names.

4. Gerhards & Hackenbroch, 2000.

5. http://www.lgpn.ox.ac.uk/names/practices.html; Salway, 1994.

6. Scott, 1998, pp. 64–71, p. 67. My discussion of surnames is heavily indebted to Scott's insightful analysis.

7. Smith-Bannister, 1997.

8. Smith-Bannister, 1997, p. 35, p. 135. A steep decline in the proportion of children receiving a godparent's name occurred during this period. Conversely, the number of sons who were named after their fathers increased from 15 to 31 percent, and the number of girls who were named after their mothers increased from 5 to 16 percent.

9. http://freepages.genealogy.rootsweb.ancestry.com/~clifflamere/Aid/AID-PuritanNaming.htm; Orenstein, 2003.

10. Smith-Bannister, 1997, p. 167, p. 169, p. 85. Religion still has a minor, if much diminished, role in naming practices. In 2011, Pope Benedict made a quixotic plea for parents "to give your children names that are in the Christian calendar." See https://uk.lifestyle.yahoo.com/blogs/yahoo-lifestyles/10-illegal-baby-names-194006397-3.htm.

11. Lieberson, 2000, p. 109. Nevertheless, as recently as 1961, 62 percent of children in one study in Chicago were named after a relative. Rossi, 1965, p. 503. The practice of naming children after deceased relatives also persists in the Jewish tradition, in which many children receive first or middle names held by dead family members.

12. Lieberson, 2000, p. 37; Rossi, 1965, p. 504; Taylor, 1984; Allen, Brown, Dickinson, & Pratt, 1941; Finch, Kilgren, & Pratt, 1944.

13. Wayne, 2013; Levitt & Dubner, 2005, p. 202.

14. Gerhards & Hackenbroch, 2000; Elchardus & Siongers, 2011, p. 405.

15. Kang, 2003.

16. Orenstein, 2003.

17. Orenstein, 2003. Lieberson (2000, pp. 159–161) asserts that names that go out of fashion rarely reappear and presents data that run up to 1989 that support his position. However, since this time, the revival of once-popular names seems to have soared. See also Levitt & Dubner, 2005, p. 206; Silver & McCann, 2014.

18. Curiously, the most eminent sociologist of naming patterns, Stanley Lieberson (2000, pp. xi–xii), also named his first child Rebecca, without knowing of its expanding popularity.

19. Levitt & Dubner, 2005, p. 203.
20. https://www.ssa.gov/oact/babynames/ Jessica might have succeeded in outwitting the cultural zeitgeist when she gave birth to her daughter, Georgia, in 2013. Georgia was ranked as the 252nd most popular name in that year.
21. Cf. Lieberson, 2000, p. 119.
22. Levitt & Dubner, 2005, p. 206.
23. Mann, 1930, p. 82.
24. Lieberson, 2000, p. 179, p. 180.
25. Lieberson, 2000, p. 182.
26. http://en.wikipedia.org/wiki/List_of_most_popular_given_names#Asia
27. Lieberson, 2000, p. 174; Hall, 2014. The author also reports that he added his wife's middle name "Nagayama" when he married in order to highlight his Asian ethnicity; Bahrampour, 2003. One Sikh cab driver in New York City changed his name to Michael Goldberg, assuming this was a normal name in New York City where large concentrations of Jews reside. Levitt & Dubner, 2005, p. 190.
28. Lieberson, 2000, p. 5. The poet Kenneth Goldsmith is an example of someone who transitioned from an Anglicized to a more ethnic name. Both of his grandfathers changed their names, in one case from Finkelstein to Field and in the other case from Goldsmith to Bromleigh. Goldsmith reclaimed his ethnic heritage, but it might be significant that he did not adopt the far more ethnically stereotypical name of "Finkelstein." Wilkinson, 2015, p. 29.
29. Glaberson, 2010.
30. Lieberson, 2000, pp. 182–183.
31. Lieberson, 2000, p. 76. Naming practices among blacks do not reflect income or educational differences but are *sui generis*.
32. Lieberson, 2000, p. 77; Levitt & Dubner, 2005, p. 186; Lieberson, 2000, p. 124; Lieberson & Bell, 1992.
33. Lieberson, 2000, p. 140. The study of naming practices in the German small town mentioned previously also indicates that two-thirds of names are class-specific and not shared with other classes. Elchardus & Siongers, 2010, p. 408; Gerhards & Hackenbroch, 2000.
34. Lieberson, 2000, p. 113; Orenstein, 2003; Lieberson & Bell, 1992, p. 542.
35. Lieberson & Bell, 1992, p. 537, p. 532; Orenstein, 2003.
36. Alford, 1988; Orenstein, 2003; https://www.ssa.gov/OACT/babynames.
37. Lieberson & Mikelson, 1995.
38. Smith-Bannister, 1997, pp. 102–103; Lieberson & Bell, 1992.
39. Lieberson, Dumais, & Baumann, 2000.
40. Lieberson et al., 2000.
41. Lieberson et al., 2000.
42. Lieberson & Mikelson, 1995, p. 940. In one Canadian case, a couple wanted to raise their child in as genderless a way as possible. They named the child "Storm," which could serve for either gender.

43. Lieberson, 2000, pp. 73–76.

44. Stone & Stone, 1984, pp. 126–127.

45. http://www.liftbump.com/2015/06/67627-top-baby-names-announced-and-its-clear-2015-is-the-year-of-parents-abandoning-major-tradition/?utm_source=facebook&utm_medium=Partners&utm_term=PRM17&ts_pid=2.

46. Lieberson, 2000, p. 131.

47. Lieberson, 2000, p. 174; Kolbert, 2015, p. 28. Mohamnod Youssef Abdulazeez, who murdered five military personnel in 2015, wrote in his Chattanooga high school yearbook page, "My name causes national security alerts. What does yours do?"

48. http://www.youtube.com/watch?v=nqWTJeW5o1c.

49. Erlanger, 2014.

50. Shatz, 2015, p. 61.

51. http://www.hrw.org/news/2011/09/13/netherlands-transgender-law-violates-rights; http://www.lgbt-ep.eu/wp-content/uploads/2010/07/NOTE-20100601-PE425.621-Transgender-Persons-Rights-in-the-EU-Member-States.pdf.

52. A rare exception occurred in 2013 when a Tennessee judge disallowed the use of the name "Messiah" and ordered it changed to "Martin." Oppenheimer, 2013; http://www.parentdish.co.uk/2012/03/20/banned-the-worlds-most-ridiculous-baby-names; https://uk.lifestyle.yahoo.com/blogs/yahoo-lifestyles/10-illegal-baby-names-194006397-3.html; http://www.youtube.com/watch?v=nqWTJeW5o1c.

53. Zweigenhaft, 1977, 1981.

54. Conley, 2010; Weller, 2013.

55. Tierney, 2008.

CHAPTER 4

1. Crane, 1895/2005, pp. 56–57; Herodotus, 1996, 7:229–231, pp. 446–447; Darwin, 1879/2004, p. 136.

2. Darwin, 1879/2004, p. 136; Herodotus, 1996, 7:104, p. 405; Herodotus, 1996, 7:232, p. 447; Darwin, 1879/2004, p. 142 (see also pp. 133–136).

3. Saul, 2001, pp. 41–42; Kandel, 1998. See Sapolsky (2004) for a comprehensive explanation of natural responses to danger. Crane (1895/2005)observes, "The squirrel, immediately upon recognizing danger, had taken to his legs without ado. He did not stand stolidly baring his furry belly to the missile, and die with an upward glance at the sympathetic heavens. On the contrary, he had fled as fast as his legs could carry him" (pp. 47–48).

4. Quoted in McPherson, 1997, p. 5; Swank & Marchand, 1946.

5. Marshall, 1947, p. 180; Darwin (1879/2004), too, noted how many men "disregarded the instinct of self-preservation, and plunged at once into a torrent to save a drowning man, though a stranger" (p. 134).

6. Hamilton, 1964; Haldane, 1955; Much earlier, Darwin (1879/2004, p. 129) indicated that natural selection was responsible for the development of parental and filial affects.

7. Segerstrale, 2000, p. 53; Trivers, 1971; Gouldner, 1960.

8. http://www.azquotes.com/author/10290-Baron_de_Montesquieu.

9. Quoted in Miller, 2000, pp. 77–78.

10. Darwin, 1879/2004, pp. 155–156. Indeed, sacrificing one's own life on behalf of groups that are weaker than their adversaries has no survival benefits for either the individual or the group. Darwin recognized that "in every country in which a large standing army is kept up, the finest young men are taken by the conscription or are enlisted. They are thus exposed to early death during war, are often tempted into vice, and are prevented from marrying during the prime of life. On the other hand the shorter and feebler men, with poor constitutions, are left at home, and consequently have a much better chance of marrying and propagating their kind" (p. 160). Darwin concluded this discussion by noting that the "problem . . . is at present much too difficult to solve" (p. 158). See also Williams, 1996.

11. Miller, 2000.

12. Aristotle, 1980, p. 49, p. 51, p. 54.

13. Miller, 2000, p. 233; Lendon, 2005, p. 49; Aristotle, 1980, p. 51. The words for "courage" are connected to words for "man" in many languages. For example, *Virtus* was the supreme Roman attribute, stemming from the word "manliness," and connoting valor, courage, and character.

14. Dodds, 1951; Finlay, 2002; Kagan, 2010. Aristotle (1980, p. 53) grouped fearless men, who rushed into the face of danger without regard to the consequences, with the cowardly and contrasted both groups to the courageous. Fearlessness was not a sign of courage but an inappropriate response to manifestly dangerous situations.

15. Homer, 1990, p. 51.

16. Alexander, 2009, pp. 97–98.

17. Homer, 1990, pp. 114–116.

18. Alexander, 2009, pp. 78–79.

19. Lendon, 2005, p. 94, p. 32. Such feelings persist. For example, "It would have been far worse," wrote US President Theodore Roosevelt about his son Quentin, who died in combat during World War I, "if he had lived at the cost of the slightest failure to perform his duty" (quoted in Salter, 2014, p. 6).

20. Aristotle, 1980, p. 24; Thucydides as quoted in Lendon, 2005, p. 110.

21. Aristotle, 1980, p. 53.

22. Aristotle, 1991, p. 159; Keegan, 1976, p. 53; Lendon, 2005, pp. 136–137. Darwin (1879/2004, p. 681) also emphasized how actions that benefited the group at the expense of the individual were not instinctive but were "much influenced by the praise or blame of his fellows."

23. Aristotle, 1980, p. 54.

24. "Courage and Cowardice," 1861.

25. Quotes from McPherson, 1997, p. 13, p. 61, p. 82.

26. McPherson, 1997, p. 59. This soldier was unwittingly echoing the words of George Washington, who had stated, "the Cowardice of a single Officer may prove the Destruction of the whole Army" (quoted in Walsh, 2014, p. 49).

27. Sylvanus Cadwallader as quoted in Wilson, 1962/1994, pp. 137–138.

28. McPherson, 1997, p. 77; quoted in Miller, 2000, p. 100.

29. McPherson, 1997, p. 78, p. 80, p. 163.

30. Crane, 1895/2005, p. 12, p. 13, p. 57.

31. Crane, 1895/2005, p. 93, p. 145, p. 186.

32. Remarque, 1929/1961, p. 11, p. 12, p. 84.

33. Keegan, 1976, p. 272; Brooke, 1915/1986, p. 1893; Fussell, 1975, p. 19; Remarque, 1929/1961, p. 11.

34. Fussell, 1975, pp. 27–28, p. 17.

35. Quoted in Miller, 2000, p. 56. Although the passage refers to World War II, it is equally appropriate for World War I. Madigan, 2013, p. 87.

36. Remarque, 1929/1961, p. 20, p. 129, p. 130, p. 164.

37. Shephard, 2000, pp. 39–72; Fassin & Rechtman, 2009, p. 41.

38. Miller, 2000, p. 45; Shephard, 2000, p. 71.

39. Moran, 1945/2007, pp. 25–26, p. 13.

40. Young, 1995, p. 57; Shephard, 2000, p. 167; Shephard, 2004.

41. Smith & Pear, 1918. The conflict between Rivers and his antagonist, psychiatrist Lewis Yealland, is a major theme of Pat Barker's popular novel, *Regeneration* (1991). See also Young, 1995, pp. 43–85.

42. Cox, 2002.

43. Hemingway, 1929, p. 191; Hemingway, 1942/1982, p. xiii.

44. Quoted in Fussell, 1990, p. 79. Note that Corsellis was British.

45. Jones & Wessely, 2007, p. 169; Shephard, 2000, p. 218, p. 202, p. 234; Menninger, 1948, p. 22.

46. Shephard, 2000, p. 326; Fussell, 1990, pp. 277–278. The transformation in conceptions of wartime behavior during World War II was culture-bound. Japanese soldiers faced total disgrace if they were captured, regardless of their behavior in combat. It was assumed that an honorable soldier would be killed before he would surrender. Japanese prisoners "asked to be shot or to be allowed to shoot themselves. They could never return to Japan." Moran, 1945/2007, p. 17.

47. Moran, 1945/2007, p. xxii.

48. Appel & Beebe, 1946; Menninger, 1948, p. 12; Shephard, 2000, p. 121.

49. Swank & Marchand, 1946, p. 236, pp. 243–244.

50. Walsh, 2014, p. 79.

51. Although the military commissioned Huston's documentary, it feared that it could harm recruitment efforts and so would not allow the film to be released. The film did not become available for public viewing until the 1980s. Heller, 1961, p. 56. Although most popular films presented a romanticized view of courageous behavior in combat, the most acclaimed literary portrayals emphasized the futility, blunders, and errors that the war featured.

52. American Psychiatric Association, 1952, p. 40, p. 49.

53. American Psychiatric Association, 1980, p. 238; Fassin & Rechtman, 2009, p. 77; Andreasen, 1995, p. 964.

54. Lee, Vaillant, Torrey, & Elder, 1995; Schnurr, Spiro, Vielhaer, Findler, & Hamblen, 2002; http://center4research.org/medical-care-for-adults/depression-stress-and-mental-health/traumatic-brain-injury-and-post-traumatic-stress-disorder-in-military-veterans-when-two-problems-collide/ The Google NGram viewer indicates that after PTSD became a psychiatric diagnosis in 1980, the use of this term rocketed by 400 percent in the following 10 years; between 1990 and 2008, it increased by another 400 percent. Conversely, the use of the words "courage" and "cowardice" tumbled by approximately 400 percent between 1800 and 2000. See also Walsh, 2014, p. 8.

55. Herodotus, 1996, 9:21, p. 506; Walsh, 2014, p. 61; Pinker, 2011, p. 686; Bourke, 2005, p. 379. Relatedly, growing acceptance of homosexuality has led to less tolerance of traditionally male aggression toward "sissies," as the anti-bullying movement shows.

56. Conrad, 2007.

57. http://usatoday30.usatoday.com/news/military/story/2012-06-29/military-purple-heart/55923610/1.

CHAPTER 5

1. Gilman, 2008, p. 165.
2. Arcelus, Mitchell, Wales, & Nielsen, 2011; Currin, Schmidt, Treasure, & Jick, 2005.
3. Kelly, 2011; Curtis, 2007, p. 661; Oaten, Stevenson, & Case, 2009, p. 316.
4. Curtis, de Barra, & Aunger, 2011; Curtis, 2007; Herz, 2012, p. 221; Darwin, 1872/2007; Kelly, 2011, p. 54.
5. Quoted in Miller, 1997, p. 13.
6. Oaten et al., 2009; Rozin, Millman, & Nemeroff, 1986; Herz, 2012, p. 3; Rozin, Nemeroff, Horowitz, Gordon, & Voet, 1995.
7. Herodotus, 1996, 3: 25–26, pp. 163–164; Fussell, 1989, p. 273. A famous example stems from the circumstances of the survivors of a plane crash in a remote area of the Andes Mountains in Chile in 1972, recounted in the best-selling novel and movie *Alive* (Read, 1974).
8. Seligman & Hager, 1972.
9. Bloom, 2010, p. 29; Herodotus, 1996, 3: 99, p. 194; 2: 38, p. 100; Darwin, 1872/2007, p. 260.
10. Miller, 1997, pp. 46–47; Murphy & Medin, 1985, p. 289; Lauden, 2014; Bagri, 2015.
11. Herz, 2012, p. 2.
12. Goodyear, 2013, pp. 72–81.
13. Shrestha et al., 1998, p. 445; Herz, 2012, p. 57.
14. Power & Schulkin, 2009.
15. Diamond, 2012, p. 299; Eaton, Shostak, & Konner, 1988, p. 26.
16. Kessler, 2009, p. 54. For example, consider the ingredients in one of my favorite treats, Skinny Cow Chocolate with Fudge ice cream cones: skim milk, cone (wheat flour, sugar, palm oil, soy lecithin, caramel color, salt), sugar, corn syrup,

cone coating (sugar, coconut oil, salatrim, cocoa powder, soy lecithin, artificial flavor), fudge topping (high-fructose corn syrup, corn syrup, water, cocoa processed with alkali, sugar, modified corn starch, salt, mono and diglycerides, vanilla, natural flavor, artificial flavor), polydextrose, cocoa processed with alkali, whey protein, calcium carbonate, cream, inulin (dietary fiber), natural flavor, propylene glycol monostearate, microcrystalline cellulose, sodium carboxymethylcellulose, guar gum, monoglycerides, carob bean gum, sorbitol, vitamin A palmitate, carrageenan, and salt.

17. Kessler, 2009, p. 84; Tannahill, 1988, p. 357; Power & Schulkin, 2009, p. 155, p. 5.
18. Neel, 1962.
19. Eaton et al., 1988, p. 7. See also Kolbert, 2014.
20. Despite these developments, widespread malnutrition persisted. For example, during World War I, approximately 40 percent of British men were rejected from military service; the most common cause was undernourishment. Tannahill, 1988, p. 334.
21. Kessler, 2009; Clifford, 2013; Herszenhorn, 2014, p. A4.
22. Jacobs & Shipp, 1990; Power & Schulkin, 2009, p. 42; http://today.msnbc.msn.com/id/38959769/ns/today-today_health/t/stuffed-weighty-truth-behind-restaurant-portion-sizes/#.TuoRTVZ-fJY; US Department of Agriculture, 2002, p. 14. A Cochrane review of 72 randomized controlled trials found a very strong relationship between large portion sizes and the amount of food consumed. http://www.cochrane.org/CD011045/PUBHLTH_portion-package-or-tableware-size-changing-selection-and-consumption-food-alcohol-and-tobacco.
23. Levenstein, 2012.
24. http://blogs.bmj.com/bjsm/2015/01/21/sitting-ducks-sedentary-behaviour-and-its-health-risks-part-one-of-a-two-part-series; http://annals.org/article.aspx?articleid=2091327.
25. Power & Schulkin, 2009, p. 38.
26. http://www.cdc.gov/healthyweight/assessing/bmi/adult_bmi.
27. http://www.rwjf.org/en/library/articles-and-news/2012/09/adult-obesity-rates-could-exceed-60-percent-in-13-states-by-2030.html
28. Ogden, Fryar, Carroll, & Flegal, 2004, p. 347; http://www.cdc.gov/nchs/fastats/obesity-overweight.htm; http://www.healthyamericans.org; https://www.google.com/search?q=department+of+agriculture+per-capita+calorie+consumption&ie=utf-8&oe=utf-8.
29. Gilman, 2008, p. 148; Tavernise, 2015a; Gilman, 2008, p. 164.
30. Boyd et al., 1988, pp. 44–45; Diamond, 2012, p. 410, p. 412.
31. Diamond, 2012, p. 425.
32. Diamond, 2012, p. 428, p. 443. It is possible that the steady upsurge in diabetes during recent decades is starting to decline. See Tavernise, 2015b.
33. Quoted in Vigarello, 2013, p. 4; Gilman, 2008, pp. 129–130.
34. Vigarello, 2013, p. 198; Quoted in Gilman, 2008, p. 45; Gilman, 2008, p. 81.

35. Vigarello, 2013, p. 145.

36. Power & Schulkin, 2009, pp. 265–291; Pratt & Brody, 2014; Wadsworth & Pendergast, 2014. Although the stigma of fatness is particularly acute for women, it is not limited to them. For example, the corpulent governor of New Jersey, Chris Christy, was mercilessly derided in the media for being obese. In 2013, he underwent gastric surgery to control his weight.

37. Saguy, 2013, p. 13.

38. For example, Brody, 2013.

39. Campos, Saguy, Ernsberger, Oliver, & Gaesser, 2006; Flegal, Graubard, Williamson, & Gail, 2007; Roth, Qiang, Marban, Redelt, & Lowell, 2004.

40. Flegal, Graubard, Williamson, & Gail, 2005; http://www.prb.org/pdf11/ TodaysResearchAging22.pdf.

41. http://care.diabetesjournals.org/content/26/suppl_1/s5.full See Greene (2007) for a discussion about how changing definitions of risk factors can create disease epidemics.

42. Gilman, 2008, pp. 33–34; Levenstein, 2012, p. 143; Siri-Tarino, Sun, Hu, & Krauss, 2010.

43. Tannahill, 1988, p. 355; Oparil, 2014.

44. For example, the H. J. Heinz Company owned Weight Watchers for more than 20 years before selling it to a Belgium-based food conglomerate, and Jenny Craig has been part of the Nestlé food empire since 2006.

45. Brumberg, 1988, p. 251; Dallman, Pecoraro, & la Fleur, 2005.

46. Specter, 2015, p. 59; Markey, 2014.

47. Gilman, 2008, pp. 14–15; Kessler, 2009, p. 142, p. 143.

48. Pollak, 2013.

49. Levenstein, 2012, p. 161. Opposition to genetically modified foods is especially intense. Despite increasing concerns about these products, to date, they have not been linked to a single case of illness, much less death. See Specter, 2014. A conflicting array of diets contributes to the confusion surrounding weight-loss techniques. Some popular diets, such as the Atkins or South Beach diets, promote the consumption of high amounts of fat and low amounts of carbohydrates; others, such as that of the American Heart Association, encourage eating low-fat, high-carbohydrate diets. Other regimes tout styles of eating presumably common in the Paleolithic period or in Mediterranean countries. Fashionable diets come and go, but none have proven to be effective in the long term.

50. In addition, rates of presumed allergies to food products such as nuts, soy, lactate, and gluten have soared.

CHAPTER 6

1. Quoted in Fisher, 2002, p. 116; Pinker, 2011.

2. Curtis, Magee, Eaton, Wittchen, & Kessler, 1998, p. 213; Ruscio, Brown, Chiu, Sareen, Stein, & Kessler, 2008.

3. Darwin, 1872/2007, p. 77; Cannon, 1915/1963; Sapolsky, 2004.

4. Aristotle, 1980, p. 153. Aristotle (1991, p. 49) also tellingly noted that people who *do not* become afraid in dangerous situations can be the disordered ones, observing, "Of those who go to excess he who exceeds in fearlessness has no name . . ., but he would be sort of a madman or insensitive to pain if he feared nothing, neither earthquakes nor the waves, as they say the Celts do not." The Celts were "mad" because they did not fear things that any reasonable person ought to fear.

5. For example, Breslau, 1985; Grinker & Spiegel, 1945; Radloff, 1977.

6. Lewis, 1970, p. 77; Spinoza quoted in May, 1977, p. 24.

7. Watson & Rayner, 1920. Contrary to Watson's assertion that Albert was a normal child, in fact he suffered from severe neurological impairments that likely stemmed from congenital hydrocephalus and mental retardation. See Fridlund, Beck, Goldie, & Irons, 2012.

8. Watson & Rayner, 1920, p. 14.

9. Bourke, 2005, p. 36.

10. Benedict, 1934/1959; Nance, 1976.

11. Scott, 2007.

12. See especially Shorter, 1994; Kleinman, 1988.

13. Darwin, 1872/2007, p. 43.

14. Tooby & Cosmides, 1990.

15. For example, Mineka, Davidson, Cook, & Keir, 1984.

16. Seligman, 1971.

17. Epictetus quoted in Graver, 2007, p. 87.

18. Gendler, 2008, 2009.

19. LeDoux, 1996; Nesse, 2005; Mineka & Ohman, 2002; Ohman & Mineka, 2001.

20. Wilford, 2013; Kramer, 1959, p. 224.

21. Montaigne, 1958, p. 53. One of the world's leading experts on the treatment of anxiety disorders, psychologist David Barlow, likewise has an intense fear of heights of which he cannot cure himself. See Stossel, 2014, p. 69.

22. http://en.wikipedia.org/wiki/List_of_motor_vehicle_deaths_in_U.S._by_year.

23. Hall quoted in Bourke, 2005, p. 116; Rush quoted in Treffers & Silverman, 2001, p. 5; Freud, 1936/1963, p. 117.

24. Marks, 1987, p. 52; Ohman & Mineka, 2001.

25. For example, Tooby & Cosmides, 1990; Massey, 2005, p. 3.

26. Ruprecht, 2010, p. 50.

27. Halttunen, 1982. Indeed, the *DSM-5* includes the condition of disinhibited social engagement disorder, "a pattern of behavior in which a child actively approaches and interacts with unfamiliar adults." American Psychiatric Association, 2013, pp. 268–269.

28. Ruscio et al., 2008; Darwin, 1872/2007, p. 334; Seneca quoted in Graver, 2007, p. 96; Wise, 2009, p. 91.

29. Darwin, 1879/2004, p. 90; Darwin, 1872/2007, p. 365; Cook & Mineka, 1989; Mineka et al., 1984; Ohman & Mineka, 2001.

30. Gibson & Walk, 1960; Walk & Gibson, 1961.
31. Menzies & Clarke, 1995, p. 41.
32. Darwin, 1877/1971, p. 5.
33. Marks, 1987, p. 150, p. 40.
34. Ohman & Mineka, 2001; Valentine, 1930; Seligman, 1971; Gibson & Walk, 1960; Walk & Gibson, 1961.
35. Kelly et al., 2005; Tien, 1979, p. 213.
36. Super & Harkness, 2010.
37. LeDoux, 1996, p. 224.
38. Sapolsky, 2004.
39. Jerome Wakefield developed this analogy.
40. Aldrich et al., 2010, p. 1272.
41. Wakefield, 1992.
42. Oppenheim, 1991, p. 315.

CHAPTER 7

1. Darwin, 1872/2007, pp. 258–263.
2. Darwin, 1872/2007, p. 173, p. 190; Bonanno, 2009, p. 32; American Psychiatric Association, 2013, p. 20.
3. Herodotus, 1996, 2:85, p. 114; 2:36, p. 99; IX:24.
4. Herodotus, 1996, 5:4, p. 282; 6:58, p. 342.
5. Benedict, 1934/1959, p. 257; Stone, 1977.
6. For example, Kleinman & Good, 1985; Harre & Parrott, 1996.
7. Archer, 1999, p. 52. Darwin (1872/2007) also recognized this, using gendered norms as an example: "With adults, especially of the male sex, weeping soon ceases to be caused by, or to express, bodily pain. This may be accounted for by its being thought weak and unmanly by men, both of civilized and barbarous races, to exhibit bodily pain by any outward sign" (p. 151). American Psychiatric Association, 2013, p. 20.
8. Portions of this section are adapted from Horwitz & Wakefield, 2007.
9. Carroll, 2008, p. 27.
10. Kovacks, 1989, pp. 70–71, pp. 84–85.
11. Homer, 1990, p. 468.
12. Hippocrates, 1923–1931, p. 185.
13. Burton, 1621/2001, pp. 143–144.
14. Didion, 2006, p. 27; Kleinman, 2012, p. 608; Oates, 2011.
15. Bonanno, 2009, p. 26; Burton, 1621/2001, p. 259.
16. For example, Clayton, 1982, 1998.
17. Kagan, 2012, p. 153; Didion, 2006, p. 4; Clayton & Darvish, 1979; Hays, Kasl, & Jacobs, 1994.
18. Hippocrates, 1923–1931, p. 263; Freud, 1917/1957, p. 165.

19. Clayton, 1982; Archer, 1999, pp. 98–100; Clayton, 1982; Bonanno, 2009.
20. For example, Carr, 2004; Wortman & Silver, 1989; Umberson, Wortman, & Kessler, 1992.
21. Kleinman, 2012, p. 608.
22. Jackson, 1986, p. 39; Burton, 1621/2001, p. 331.
23. American Psychiatric Association, 1968, p. 40.
24. Deraniyagala, 2013.
25. Bonanno et al., 2002; Bonanno, 2009.
26. American Psychiatric Association, 2013, pp. 160–161.
27. Darwin, 1872/2007, p. 181; Darwin, 1879/2004, p. 91, p. 177; Harlow & Suomi, 1974; Gilmer & McKinney, 2003. See also Archer, 1999, pp. 54–57; Rottenberg, 2014, pp. 39–56; Worden, 2009.
28. Sapolsky, 2004, p. 256; Harlow & Suomi, 1974; Suomi, 1991; Sloman, Gilbert, & Hasey, 2003.
29. Darwin, 1872/2007, pp. 143–174; Bowlby, 1980.
30. Darwin, 1872/2007, p. 185, p. 176.
31. Ekman & Friesen, 1971.
32. Ekman, 1973; Ekman et al., 1987.
33. Ekman & Friesen, 1971. Psychologist Lisa Barrett and colleagues have disputed Ekman's (and Darwin's) contention that the expressions of emotions have a universal element because their studies of the response to presentations of emotional expressions among the isolated Himba ethnic group in Namibia diverged from those among Americans. Their work, however, failed to provide any context for facial expressions and so did not test the most critical aspect of Darwinian theory: Contexts provide the essential cues for the emergence and recognition of each emotion. Barrett, 2013; Gendron, Roberson, van der Vyver, & Barrett, 2014.
34. Massey, 2005, p. 54.
35. Lewis, 1934; Bonanno & Kaltman, 2001. Riley, in the popular movie *Inside Out*, realizes the positive value of sadness after she causes her team to lose a hockey game and finds that others respond to her distress with comfort, reassurance, and help.
36. Bowlby, 1980.
37. Bonanno, 2009, p. 75; Carr, 2004.
38. Turner, 2000.
39. Broadhead & Abas, 1998; Desjarlais, Eisenberg, Good, & Kleinman, 1995.
40. Hochschild, 1983.
41. Schieffelin, 1985; Darwin, 1872/2007, p. 151.
42. Kleinman, 1986; Cheung, 1982.
43. Miller & Schoenfeld, 1973; Archer, 1999.
44. Good, Cood, & Moradi, 1985, p. 386; Wikann, 1990.
45. American Psychiatric Association, 2013, pp. 160–161.
46. For example, Wakefield, 2013.

CHAPTER 8

1. Buss, 2003.
2. Mead, 1928/1971; for a refutation of Mead's contentions, see Freeman, 1996; Bagemihl, 1999.
3. Hills, 2015.
4. For example, Tannahill, 1982; Genesis 3:7.
5. Greenberg, 1988; Levitacus 20:13.
6. Examples include the wild popularity of the erotic *Fifty Shades* novels and movie, the success of TV series such as *Sex in the City* and *Girls*, and the many gay characters in shows ranging from Ellen DeGeneres to those in *Modern Family* and *Glee*. Hills, 2015, p. 8; de Beauvoir, 1953, p. 267; Fausto-Sterling, 2000.
7. http://abcnews.go.com/blogs/headlines/2014/02/heres-a-list-of-58-gender-options-for-facebook-users; Google Ngram indicates that use of the term "gender," which barely existed in 1980, has increased by 700 percent since that year.
8. In 2013, American women bore an average of 1.9 children during their lifetime, well below the rate required to maintain a stable population. A number of factors, including women's entry into the workforce, the increasing cost of raising children, and rising age at marriage, account for declining fertility rates.
9. Allen, 1931/1959; accurate information on sexual orientation remains notoriously difficult to obtain. A good example stems from what is perhaps the best study of sexual behavior among adolescents, the Add Health Study. Investigators were shocked to find that between 5 and 7 percent of adolescents reported they were homosexual or bisexual when they were studied in the mid-1990s. However, later waves of data collected from the same individuals found that greater than 70 percent of this group reported that they were heterosexual. The researchers believe that most of the initial non-heterosexual respondents were joking or misunderstood the questions about sexual orientation. Savin-Williams & Joyner, 2014.
10. D'Emilio & Freedman, 1988, p. 285; *Time*, August 24, 1953.
11. Trilling, 1948, p. 135;
12. Kinsey, Pomeroy, & Martin, 1948, p. 199, p. 224.
13. D'Emilio & Freedman, 1988, p. 286.
14. Trilling, 1948, p. 217; Boyle, 2005, p. 170; Mead, 1948, p. 67.
15. Kinsey, Pomeroy, Martin, & Gebhard, 1953, p. 121; Jones, 1997, p. 512.
16. Quoted in Igo, 2007, p. 263, p. 234.
17. Igo, 2007, p. 260, p. 258; Deutsch, 1947, p. 490.
18. Tannahill, 1992, p. 425.
19. Quoted in Igo, 2007, p. 223.
20. Cochran, Mosteller, & Tukey, 1953; Kinsey et. al., 1948, p. 53; Pomeroy, 1972, p. 113.
21. Kinsey et al., 1948, p. 281, p. 588.
22. Their idiosyncratic samples led some well-known and widely cited studies to be all but useless. The *Hite Report* (Hite, 1976), for example, used 3000 questionnaires

out of the 100,000 that Hite distributed. As late as 1989, a leading student of sex research stated that the Kinsey volumes "remain the most reliable sources of information about American sexual behavior" (Robinson, 1989, p. 43).

23. Michael, Gagnon, Laumann, & Kolata, 1994, p. 132, p. 114.

24. Michael et al., 1994, p. 101, p. 79, p. 89, p. 101, p. 105, p. 91, p. 97, p. 124, p. 36.

25. Santelli, Lindberg, Abma, McNeely, & Resnick, 2000; Regnerus & Uecker, 2009, p. 25; Parry, 2013; Parker-Pope, 2014.

26. Darwin, 1879/2004, p. 658; Toohey, 2014, p. 28.

27. Trivers, 1972; According to Darwin (1879/2004, p. 246), "It is certain that amongst almost all animals there is a struggle between the males for the possession of the female. This fact is so notorious that it would be superfluous to give instances." Promiscuity and selectivity are not inherent aspects of maleness and femaleness, respectively. Not sex per se but the degree of investment that each sex must make in reproduction determines the optimal reproductive strategy. The theory of parental investment implies that when males have greater investment in their offspring than females, they will behave in ways typically associated with females and vice versa. Seahorses provide a test of differential mating strategies. Female seahorses are not inseminated by males but transfer their eggs to the brood pouch in the males, where they develop. Therefore, males have a much higher investment than females in their offspring. As the theory of sexual selection predicts, female seahorses display aggressiveness in courtship and copulation, whereas the males show cautious and discriminatory sexual behavior. Likewise, in bird species in which males incubate eggs and feed the young, the females are the sexual aggressors. Cautious discrimination will mark whatever sex has to make the most sustained efforts to produce offspring.

28. Circumstances in which their children have a greater chance of survival when men bond with one woman than when they father many offspring with different women are likely to lead to male monogamy. See Hrdy, 2011.

29. Darwin, 1879/2004, p. 668, p. 257. Sexual strategies change, however, in response to existing sex ratios. When large numbers of females compete for fewer males, they increase their competitive behavior with other women and are less intent on obtaining long-term commitments from men. Conversely, when men face a shortage of women, they increase their competitive behaviors with other males and their promises of long-term commitments to women. Buss, 2003, pp. 204–205.

30. Herodotus, 1996, 4:177, p. 271; 4:111–115, pp. 250–251; 5:6, p. 282; 1:216, p. 85; 4:104, p. 248; 4:172, p. 270; 1:199, p. 79.

31. Kinsey et al., 1953, pp. 142, 196, 233, 286, 416, 454, 473, 505, 716–717; Kinsey et al., 1948, p. 589.

32. Quoted in D'Emilio & Freedman, 1988, p. 304.

33. Michael et al., 1994, p. 102.

34. Michael et al., 1994, p. 35, p. 102, p. 136.

35. Poovey, 1998, p. 374; Santelli et al., 2000; Regnerus & Uecker, 2011, p. 60, p. 67.

36. Birger, 2015; Regnerus & Uecker, 2011, p. 123. See also http://www.nytimes.com/2013/07/14/fashion/sex-on-campus-she-can-play-that-game-too.html?emc=eta1.

37. The strong opposition to homosexuality in Victorian England could also explain Darwin's inattention to this behavior; Grant, 1987, p. 32; Herodotus, 1996, 1:135, p. 56.

38. Jones, 1997.

39. Robinson, 1989, p. 73; Kinsey quoted in Jones, 1997, p. 384.

40. American Psychiatric Association, 1952, pp. 38–39.

41. Kinsey et al., 1948, p. 638.

42. Kinsey et al., 1948, p. 656.

43. Kinsey et al., 1948, p. 660.

44. Humphreys, 1975; D'Emilio & Freedman, 1988, pp. 288–300, p. 340; Bayer, 1981, p. 8.

45. Michael et al., 1994, p. 177; Quote from D'Emilio & Freedman, 1988, p. 317; Warner, 1999.

46. American Psychiatric Association, 1968, p. 44; Bayer, 1981, p. 137.

47. D'Emilio, 2002; Warner, 1999.

48. Some Darwinian theorists assert that the relatively promiscuous sexual behaviors among gay men reflect natural male desires that are unconstrained by female monogamous sexual preferences (see Buss, 2003, p. 84). In fact, once social norms came to accept open, long-term partnerships, the sexual behavior of homosexual men changed radically.

49. Opposition to homosexuality remains fierce in other areas of the world, especially Africa, Russia, and many Muslim nations.

50. Bagemihl, 1999, p. 9.

51. Michael et al., 1994, p. 175, p. 176; Ward, Dahlhamer, Galinsky, & Joestl, 2014; Gates, 2011; See also Regnerus & Uecker, 2009, p. 8.

52. LeVay, 1991; Hamer, Hu, Magnuson, Hu, & Pattatucci, 1993, p. 325; LeVay & Hamer, 1994, p. 49.

53. Terry, 1999, pp. 397–398; D'Emilio, 2002; Brookey, 2002; Conrad, 2007, p. 110.

54. See Ellis & Ames (1987) for an early statement of this theory. More recent research is discussed in Bao and Swaab (2011) and Hines (2011).

55. Hamer & Copeland, 1994, pp. 180–186; See also Buss, 2003, pp. 250–256.

56. Robinson, 1989.

57. Although even less is known about the number of transsexuals, the best guesses are approximately 0.3 percent (Gates, 2011). Most people are born as either males or females. One or two in every 1000 births are ambiguous enough to become the subject of specialist medical attention. When intersexuals are limited to people whose chromosomal sex is inconsistent with their phenotypic sex or is unclassifiable as either male or female, then the best estimate of the number of people who are not biological males or females is aabout 0.018 percent (Sax, 2002).

CHAPTER 9

1. Benedict, 1934, p. 80; Brody, 2015.
2. Ibid.
3. See especially Solomon, 2012; Quotes from p. 337, p. 284.
4. One difference between Herodotus and current cultural theory, however, is that Herodotus usually celebrated the variety of norms that he observed, whereas social constructionists are often critical of the norms of their societies. See Hacking, 1999, p. 6.
5. Wilson, 1998, p. 250, p. 253; Churchland, 2006, p. 3.
6. Westermarck, 1891.
7. Wakefield, 1992.
8. Males who display promiscuous sexual desires or violent sexual jealousy might be acting naturally but not desirably. Conversely, parents who adopt and care for other people's children or provide resources to strangers that they might otherwise use for their own children are not acting naturally but are engaged in highly esteemed activities. Cosmides & Tooby, 1999, p. 458; Camus, 1960, p. 198.
9. Benedict, 1934, p. 60. There are indications in Benedict's own writing that the shamans she described were not as normal as she claimed. For example, she notes that some Siberian shamans "are violently insane for several years, others irresponsible to the point where they have to be watched constantly lest they wander off in the snow and freeze to death, others ill and emaciated to the point of death, sometimes with bloody sweat" (p. 62).
10. Luhrmann, 2015, p. SR5.
11. Wakefield, 1999, p. 383, p. 395. Social and psychological, as much as biological or genetic, factors can cause dysfunctions.
12. For a contrasting view, see Bell, 1985.
13. Horwitz & Wakefield, 2007.
14. Spitzer & Wakefield, 2002.
15. Finley, 2002, p. 131; Biologist Bruce Bagemihl, 1999, p. 9 proclaims, "The world is, indeed, teeming with homosexual, bisexual, and transgendered creatures of every stripe and feather." Many types of primates of both sexes engage in sexual activities between adults and children. For example, adult male and female bonobos have sexual relations with adolescents and juveniles. Bagemihl, 1999, p. 274. For a summary of the cross-cultural prevalence of such relationships, see Greenberg, 1988, pp. 26–40. Quote from Green, 2002, pp. 467–468. Across cultures and history, the average age of marriage for females—who typically married during their young and mid-teenage years—would qualify as pederasty under modern American laws.
16. Horwitz & Wakefield, 2011; Marks & Nesse, 1994.
17. http://lawandorder.wikia.com/wiki/Families.
18. Sartorius, Jablensky, & Shapiro, 1978; Hopper, 1992.
19. See, especially, Solomon, 2012, Chap. 2.
20. McFadden, 2012, p. A33. A recent example of cowardice is an Italian ship captain who deserted his sinking cruise ship, the Costa Concordia, in 2012. He was viewed

as "a man hopelessly lost, a coward who shirks his responsibility as a man and an officer, indelibly stained." http://en.wikipedia.org/wiki/Costa_Concordia_disaster.

21. Slim, 2004, p. 5; quote from Miller, 2000, p. 128. Even today, when a small minority of people enter military service, courage in combat is so highly valued that men commonly exaggerate their proximity to danger. The cases of NBC anchorman Brian Williams, who falsely claimed that his helicopter was shot down while he was on assignment in Iraq, or Fox News commentator Bill O'Reilly, who embellished his experiences in a reputed combat zone in Argentina, indicate the extent to which males still desire to show how courageous they have been. Such exaggerations are typically, but not completely, confined to men. Hillary Clinton, for example, falsely claimed to have come under sniper fire during a visit to Bosnia. http://www.cnn.com/2008/POLITICS/03/25/campaign.wrap/index.html?iref=hpmostpop.

22. Wolf, 2002, pp. 185–187.

23. Wakefield, 1992.

24. Murphy, 2006, pp. 27–28.

25. See Wakefield & First, 2012.

26. See, for example, Lane, 2007; Diller, 2006; Wakefield, Pottick, & Kirk, 2002; *Sopranos*, Season One, Episode Seven.

27. Husak, 2002, p. 88, pp. 82–93.

28. Cosmides & Tooby, 1999, p. 458. Cosmides and Tooby clearly indicate that the dysfunctional aspect of homosexuality in no way implies that it should be subject to moral disapproval.

29. Bagemihl, 1999; Greenberg, 1988.

30. Dreger, 2015.

31. Horwitz & Wakefield, 2011, Chap. 7; Fassin & Rechtman, 2009; Zarembo, 2014.

32. Solomon, 2012, p. 198, p. 190.

33. Baltimore et al., 2015; Tingley, 2014, p. MM26. Unlike other forms of DNA, mitochondrial DNA does not result from combining sperm and eggs but passes solely through maternal inheritance.

34. John LaPook quoted in Tingley, 2014, p. 26.

35. Solomon, 2012, p. 103. Similarly, ophthalmologists are developing surgical procedures that implant retinal prosthesis devices that allow formerly blind people to have some ability to see.

36. Reardon, 2014.

37. Liptak, 2015. Homosexuality is still fiercely resisted in Russia, Africa, and many areas of the United States.

38. Massey, 2005, p. 237; Black used this example in a class he taught to Yale undergraduates in the 1970s; Kaletsky, 2015, p. 5; Day, 2015.

39. Ransom, 2015. For an example, see Capecchi & Rogers, 2015.

40. Durkheim, 1895/1982.

REFERENCES

Aldrich, T. K., Jackson, G., Hall, C. B., Cohen, H. W., Mayris, P. H., Webber, P., et al. (2010, April 8). Lung function in rescue workers at the World Trade Center after 7 years. *New England Journal of Medicine, 362*, 1263–1272.

Alexander, C. (2009). *The war that killed Achilles.* New York, NY: Viking.

Alford, R. D. (1988). *Naming and identity: A cross-cultural study of personal naming practices.* New Haven, CT: HRAF Press.

Allen, F. L. (1959). *Only yesterday: An informal history of the nineteen-twenties.* New York, NY: Harper & Brothers. (Original work published 1931.)

Allen, L., Brown, V., Dickinson, L., & Pratt, K. C. (1941). The relation of first name preferences to their frequency in the culture. *Journal of Social Psychology, 14*, 279–293.

American Psychiatric Association. (1952). *Diagnostic and statistical manual of mental disorders.* Washington, DC: Author.

American Psychiatric Association. (1968). *Diagnostic and statistical manual of mental disorders* (2nd ed.). Washington, DC: Author.

American Psychiatric Association (1980). *Diagnostic and statistical manual of mental disorders* (3rd ed.). Washington, DC: Author.

American Psychiatric Association. (2013). *Diagnostic and statistical manual of mental disorders* (5th ed.). Washington, DC: American Psychiatric Publishing.

Andreasen, N. (1995). Posttraumatic stress disorder: Psychology, biology, and the Manichaean warfare between false dichotomies. *American Journal of Psychiatry, 152*, 964.

Appel, J., & Beebe, G. H. (1946). Preventive psychiatry: An epidemiologic approach. *Journal of the American Medical Association, 131*, 1469–1475.

Arcelus, J., Mitchell, A. J., Wales, J., & Nielsen, S. (2011). Mortality rates in patients with anorexia nervosa and other eating disorders. *Archives of General Psychiatry, 68*, 724–731.

Archer, J. (1999). *The nature of grief: The evolution and psychology of reactions to loss.* New York, NY: Routledge.

Aristotle. (1980). *The Nichomachean ethics* (D. Ross, Trans.). New York, NY: Oxford World Classics.

Aristotle. (1991). *The art of rhetoric* (H. C. Lawson-Tancred, Trans.). New York, NY: Penguin.

Arnhart, L. (2005). The incest taboo as Darwinian natural right. In A. P. Wolf & W. H. Durham (Eds.), *Inbreeding, incest, and the incest taboo* (pp. 190–218). Stanford, CA: Stanford University Press.

Aron, R. (1968). *Main currents in sociological thought 1* (pp. 17–62). New York, NY: Pelican.

Bagemihl, B. (1999). *Biological exuberance: Animal homosexuality and natural diversity.* New York, NY: St. Martin's.

Bagri, N. (2015, March 3). Indian state bans possession and sale of beef. *The New York Times*, p. A8.

Bahrampour, T. (2003, September 25). A boy named Yo, Etc.; Name changes, both practical and fanciful, are on the rise. *The New York Times*.

Baltimore, D., Berg, P., Botchan, M., Carroll, D., Charo R. A., Church, G., et al. (2015, April 3). A prudent path forward for genomic engineering and germline gene modification. *Science, 348*, 36–38.

Bao, A.-M., & Swaab, D. F. (2011). Sexual differentiation of the human brain: Relation to gender identity, sexual orientation and neuropsychiatric disorders. *Frontiers in Neuroendocrinology, 32*, 214–226.

Barker, P. (1991). *Regeneration.* London, England: Penguin.

Barrett, L. F. (2013). Psychological construction: The Darwinian approach to the science of emotion. *Emotion Review, 5*, 379–389.

Bateson, P. (2005). Inbreeding avoidance and incest taboos. In A. P. Wolf & W. H. Durham (Eds.), *Inbreeding, incest, and the incest taboo* (pp. 24–37). Stanford, CT: Stanford University Press.

Bayer, R. (1981). *Homosexuality and American psychiatry.* Princeton, NH: Princeton University Press.

Bell, R. (1985). *Holy anorexia.* Chicago, IL: University of Chicago Press.

Benedict, R. (1934). Anthropology and the abnormal. *Journal of General Psychology, 10*, 59–80.

Benedict, R. (1959). *Patterns of culture.* New York, NY: Houghton Mifflin. (Original work published 1934.)

Birger, J. (2015). *Date-onomics: How dating became a lopsided numbers game.* New York, NY: Workman.

Bittles, A. H. (2005). Genetic aspects of inbreeding and incest. In A. P. Wolf & W. H. Durham (Eds.), *Inbreeding, incest, and the incest taboo* (pp. 38–60). Stanford, CT: Stanford University Press.

Black, D. (2011). *Moral time.* New York, NY: Oxford University Press.

Bloom, P. (2010). *How pleasure works: The new science of why we like what we like.* New York, NY: Norton.

Boas, F. (2007). *The mind of primitive man.* Whitefish, MT: Kessinger. (Original work published 1911.)

Bonanno, G. (2009). *The other side of sadness.* New York, NY: Basic Books.

Bonanno, G. A., & Kaltman, S. (2001). The varieties of grief experience. *Clinical Psychology Review, 21,* 705–734.

Bonanno, G. A., Wortman, C. B., Lehman, D. R., Tweed, R. G., Haring, M., Sonnega, J., et al. (2002). Resilience to loss and chronic grief: A prospective study from preloss to 18 months postloss. *Journal of Personality and Social Psychology, 83,* 1150–1164.

Borch-Jacobsen, M., & Shamdasani, S. (2012). *The Freud files: An inquiry into the history of psychoanalysis.* Cambridge, England: Cambridge University Press.

Bourke, J. (2005). *Fear: A cultural history.* Emoryville, CA: Shoemaker & Hoard.

Bowlby, J. (1980). *Attachment and loss: Vol. 3. Loss: Sadness and depression.* London, England: Hogarth.

Boyle, T. C. (2005). *The inner circle.* New York, NY: Penguin.

Breslau, N. (1985). Depressive symptoms, major depression, and generalized anxiety: A comparison of self-reports on CES-D and results from diagnostic interviews. *Psychiatry Research, 15,* 219–229.

Broadhead, J., & Abas, M. (1998). Life events, difficulties, and depression amongst women in an urban setting in Zimbabwe. *Psychological Medicine, 28,* 39–50.

Brody, J. E. (2013, July 2). A label calls attention to obesity. *The New York Times,* p. D7.

Brody, R. (2015, August 17). Buckley, Vidal, and the birth of buzz. *The New Yorker* http://www.newyorker.com/culture/richard-brody/buckley-vidal-and-the-birth-of-buzz

Brooke, R. (1986). The soldier. In *Norton anthology of English literature* (5th ed., Vol. 2). New York, NY: Norton. (Original work published 1915.)

Brookey, R. A. (2002). *Reinventing the male homosexual: The rhetoric and power of the gay gene.* Bloomington, IN: University of Indiana Press.

Brumberg, J. J. (1988). *Fasting girls: The history of anorexia nervosa.* Cambridge, MA: Harvard University Press.

Burton, R. (2001). *The anatomy of melancholy.* New York, NY: New York Review Books. (Original work published 1621.)

Buss, D. M. (1995). Evolutionary psychology: A new paradigm for psychological science. *Psychological Inquiry, 6,* 1–10.

Buss, D. M. (2003). *The evolution of desire: Strategies of human mating.* New York, NY: Basic Books.

Campos, P., Saguy, A., Ernsberger, P., Oliver, E., & Gaesser, G. (2006). The epidemiology of overweight and obesity: Public health crisis or moral panic? *International Journal of Epidemiology, 35,* 55–60.

Camus, A. (1989). *The stranger.* New York, NY: Vintage.

Camus, A. (1960). *Resistance, rebellion, and death.* New York, NY: Knopf.

Canguilhem, G. (2000). *A vital rationalist: Selected writings from Georges Canguilhem.* New York, NY: Zone Books.

Cannon, W. (1963). *Bodily changes in pain, hunger, fear and rage.* New York, NY: Harper Torchbooks. (Original work published 1915.)

Capecchi, C., & Rogers, K. (2015, July 30). Killer of Cecil the Lion finds out that he is a target now, of Internet vigilantism. *The New York Times*, p. A11.

Carnegie, D. (2009). *How to win friends and influence people.* New York, NY: Simon & Schuster. (Original work published 1936.)

Carr, D. S. (2004). Gender, pre-loss marital dependence and older adults' adjustment to widowhood. *Journal of Marriage and the Family, 66,* 220–235.

Carroll, D. (2008). *Albert Camus the Algerian: Colonialism, terrorism, justice.* New York, NY: Columbia University Press.

Caspi, A., Sugden, K., Moffitt, T. E., Taylor, A., Craig, I. W., Harrington, H., et al. (2003). Influence of life stress on depression: Moderation by a polymorphism in the 5-HTT gene. *Science, 301,* 386–389.

Cheung, F. M. (1982). Psychological symptoms among Chinese in urban Hong Kong. *Social Science and Medicine, 16,* 1339–1344.

Churchland, P. S. (2006). Moral decision-making and the brain. In J. Illes (Ed.), *Neuroethics in the twenty-first century.* New York, NY: Oxford University Press.

Clayton, P. J. (1982). Bereavement. In E. S. Paykel (Ed.), *Handbook of affective disorders* (pp. 15–46). London, England: Churchill Livingstone.

Clayton, P. J. (1998). The model of stress: The bereavement reaction. In B. P. Dohrenwend (Ed.), *Adversity, stress, and psychopathology* (pp. 96–110). New York, NY: Oxford University Press.

Clayton, P. J., & Darvish, H. S. (1979). Course of depressive symptoms following the stress of bereavement. In J. E. Barrett, R. M. Rose, & G. Klerman (Eds.), *Stress and mental disorder* (pp. 121–136). New York, NY: Raven Press.

Clifford, S. (2013, June 30). Why healthy eaters fall for fries. *The New York Times,* Sunday Review, p. 5.

Cochran, W. G., Mosteller, F., & Tukey, J. W. (1953). Statistical problems of the Kinsey Report. *Journal of the American Statistical Association, 48,* 673–716.

Conley, D. (2010, March 1). Raising E and Yo: A sociologist reconsiders his kids' outrageous names—and mines the data for clues to the consequences. *Psychology Today.* Retrieved from https://www.psychologytoday.com/articles/201003/raising-e-and-yo

Conrad, P. (2007). *The medicalization of society: The transformation of human conditions into treatable disorders.* Baltimore, MD: Johns Hopkins University Press.

Cook, M., & Mineka, S. (1989). Observational conditioning of fear to fear-relevant versus fear-irrelevant stimuli in rhesus monkeys. *Journal of Abnormal Psychology, 98,* 448–459.

Cosmides, L., & Tooby, J. (1999). Toward an evolutionary taxonomy of treatable conditions. *Journal of Abnormal Psychology, 108,* 453–464.

Courage and cowardice. (1861, August 14). *The New York Times.*

Cox, C. (2002). Invisible wounds: The American Legion, shell-shocked veterans, and American society, 1919-1924. In M. Micale & P. Lerner (Eds.), *Traumatic pasts* (pp. 280–305). New York, NY: Cambridge University Press.

Coyne, J. (2015). Holocaust trauma: Is it epigenetically inherited? Retrieved from https://whyevolutionistrue.wordpress.com/2015/08/24/holocaust-trauma-is-it-epigenetically-inherited

Crane, S. (2005). *The red badge of courage*. New York, NY: Simon & Schuster. (Original work published 1895.)

Currin, L., Schmidt, U., Treasure, J., & Jick, H. (2005). Time trends in eating disorder incidence. *British Journal of Psychiatry, 186*, 132–135.

Curtis, G. C., Magee, W. J., Eaton, W. W., Wittchen, H.-U., & Kessler, R. C. (1998). Specific fears and phobias: Epidemiology and classification. *British Journal of Psychiatry, 173*, 212–217.

Curtis, V., de Barra, M., & Aunger, R. (2011). Disgust as an adaptive system for disease avoidance behavior. *Philosophical Transactions of the Royal Society B, 366*, 389–401.

Curtis, V. A. (2007). Dirt, disgust and disease: A natural history of hygiene. *Journal of Epidemiology and Community Health, 61*, 660–664.

Dallman, M. F., Pecoraro, N. C., & la Fleur, S. E. (2005). Chronic stress and comfort foods: Self-medication and abdominal obesity. *Brain, Behavior, and Immunity, 19*, 275–280.

Darwin, C. (1971). A biographical sketch of an infant. *Developmental Medicine and Child Neurology, 13*(Suppl. 24), 3–8 (originally in *Mind, 7*, 285–294, 1877). (Original work published 1877)

Darwin, C. (2004). *On the origin of species by means of natural selection*. Edison, NJ: Castle Books. (Original work published 1859)

Darwin, C. (2004). *The descent of man, and selection in relation to sex*. New York, NY: Penguin. (Original work published 1879)

Darwin, C. (2007). *The expression of emotions in man and animals*. Minneapolis, MN: Filiquarian. (Original work published 1872)

Day, F. (2015). *You're never weird on the Internet (almost): A memoir*. New York, NY: Touchstone.

de Beauvoir, S. (1953). *The second sex*. New York, NY: Knopf.

de Montesquieu, C. (2011). *The spirit of the laws*. New York, NY: Cosimo Classics. (Original work published 1750)

Degler, C. N. (1991). *In search of human nature: The decline and revival of Darwinism in American social thought*. New York, NY: Oxford University Press.

D'Emilio, J. (2002). *The world turned: Essays on gay history, politics, and culture*. Durham, NC: Duke University Press.

D'Emilio, J., & Freedman, E. (1988). *Intimate matters: A history of sexuality in America*. New York, NY: Harper & Row.

Deraniyagala, S. (2013). *Wave: A memoir of life after the tsunami*. New York, NY: Knopf.

Desjarlais, R., Eisenberg, L., Good, B., & Kleinman, A. (1995). *World mental health: Problems and priorities in low-income countries*. New York, NY: Oxford University Press.

Deutsch, A. (1947, December). The sex habits of American men. *Harpers*, 490–497.

Diamond, J. (2012). *The world until yesterday: What can we learn from traditional societies?* New York, NY: Viking.

Didion, J. (2006). *The year of magical thinking.* New York, NY: Knopf.

Diller, L. (2006). *The last normal child.* New York, NY: Praeger.

Dodds, E. R. (1951). *The Greeks and the irrational.* Berkeley, CA: University of California Press.

Dreger, A. (2015). *Galileo's middle finger: Heretics, activists, and the search for justice in science.* New York, NY: Penguin.

Durham, W. H. (2005). Assessing the gaps in Westermarck's theory. In A. P. Wolf & W. H. Durham (Eds.), *Inbreeding, incest, and the incest taboo* (pp. 121–138). Stanford, CT: Stanford University Press.

Durkheim, E. (1907). Sur l'evolution generale des idees morales (Revue de Westermarck, *The origin and development of the moral ideas,* Vol. I). *L'Annee sociologique, 10,* 383–395.

Durkheim, E. (1982). *The rules of sociological method.* New York, NY: Free Press. (Original work published 1895)

Eaton, B., Shostak, M., & Konner, M. (1988). *The Paleolithic prescription: A program of diet & exercise and a design for living.* New York: Harper & Row.

Ebrahim, S. (2012). Epigenetics: The next big thing. *International Journal of Epidemiology, 41,* 1–3.

Eisenberg, L. (1995). The social construction of the human brain. *American Journal of Psychiatry, 152,* 1563–1575.

Ekman, P. (1973). *Darwin and facial expression: A century of research.* San Diego, CA: Academic Press.

Ekman, P., & Friesen, W. V. (1971). Constants across cultures in the face and emotion. *Journal of Personality and Social Psychology, 17,* 124–129.

Ekman, P., Friesen, W. V., O'Sullivan, M., Chan, A., Diacoyanni-Tarlatzis, I., Heider, K., et al. (1987). Universals and cultural differences in the judgments of facial expressions of emotion. *Journal of Personality and Social Psychology, 53,* 712–717.

Elchardus, M., & Siongers, J. (2011). First names as collective identifiers: An empirical analysis of the social meanings of first names. *Cultural Sociology, 5,* 403–422.

Ellis, L. (1996). A discipline in peril: Sociology's future hinges on curing its biophobia. *American Sociologist, 27,* 21–41.

Ellis, L., & Ames, M. A. (1987). Neurohormonal functioning and sexual orientation: A theory of homosexuality–heterosexuality. *Psychological Review, 101,* 233–258.

Erickson, M. T. (2005). Evolutionary thought and the current clinical understanding of incest. In A. P. Wolf & W. H. Durham (Eds.), *Inbreeding, incest, and the incest taboo* (pp. 161–189). Stanford, CA: Stanford University Press.

Erlanger, S. (2014). A writer whose pen never rests, even facing death. *The New York Times,* November 1, p. A6.

Fassin, D., & Rechtman, R. (2009). *The empire of trauma: An inquiry into the condition of victimhood.* Princeton, NJ: Princeton University Press.

Fausto-Sterling, A. (2000). *Sexing the body: Gender politics and the construction of sexuality*. New York, NY: Basic Books.

Finch, M., Kilgren, H., & Pratt, K. C. (1944). The relation of first name preferences to age of judges or to different although overlapping generations. *Journal of Social Psychology, 20,* 249–264.

Finley, M. I. (2002). *The world of Odysseus*. New York, NY: New York Review of Books Classics.

Firth, R. (1983). *We the Tikopia: A sociological study of kinship in primitive Polynesia*. Stanford, CA: Stanford University Press. (Original work published 1936)

Fisher, P. (2002). *The vehement passions*. Princeton, NJ: Princeton University Press.

Flegal, K. M., Graubard, B. I., Williamson, D. F., & Gail, M. H. (2005). Excess deaths associated with underweight, overweight, and obesity. *JAMA, 293,* 1861–1867.

Flegal, K. M., Graubard, B. I., Williamson, D. F., & Gail, M. H. (2007). Cause-specific excess deaths associated with underweight, overweight, and obesity. *JAMA, 298,* 2028–2037.

Fossey, D. (1983). *Gorillas in the mist*. Boston, MA: Houghton-Mifflin.

Foucault, M. (1984). What is enlightenment? In P. Rabinow (Ed.), *The Foucault reader* (pp. 32–50). New York, NY: Pantheon.

Foucault, M. (1988). *Madness and civilization: A history of insanity in the Age of Reason*. New York, NY: Vintage.

Fox, R. (1980). *The red lamp of incest*. Notre Dame, IN: University of Notre Dame Press.

Freeman, D. (1996). *Margaret Mead and the heretic*. New York, NY: Penguin.

Freese, J., Li, J. C., & Wade, L. D. (2003). The potential relevances of biology to social inquiry. *Annual Review of Sociology, 29,* 233–256.

Freese, J., & Shostak, S. (2009). Genetics and social inquiry. *Annual Review of Sociology, 35,* 107–128.

Freud, S. (1930). *Civilization and its discontents*. New York, NY: Norton.

Freud, S. (1953). *A general introduction to psychoanalysis* (J. Riviere, Trans.). New York, NY: Pocket Books. (Original work published 1920)

Freud, S. (1957). Mourning and melancholia. In J. Strachey (Ed. & Trans.), *Standard edition of the complete works of Sigmund Freud* (Vol. 14, pp. 237–258). London, England: Hogarth. (Original work published 1917)

Freud, S. (1958). Heredity and the aetiology of the neuroses. In J. Strachey (Ed. & Trans.), *Standard edition of the complete works of Sigmund Freud* (Vol. 3, pp. 141–156). London, England: Hogarth. (Original work published 1896)

Freud, S. (1958). *An autobiographical study*. In J. Strachey (Ed. & Trans.), *Standard edition of the complete works of Sigmund Freud* (Vol. 20, p. 34). London, England: Hogarth. (Original work published 1925)

Freud, S. (1963). *The problem of anxiety*. New York, NY: Norton. (Original work published 1936)

Freud, S. (1965). *The interpretation of dreams*. New York, NY: Avon. (Original work published 1900)

Freud, S. (1989). *An outline of psychoanalysis.* New York, NY: Norton. (Original work published 1938)

Fridlund, A. J., Beck, H. P., Goldie, W. D., & Irons, G. (2012). Little Albert: A neurologically impaired child. *History of Psychology, 15*(4), 302–327

Fussell, P. (1975). *The great war and modern memory.* New York, NY: Oxford University Press.

Fussell, P. (1989). *Wartime: Understanding and behavior in the Second World War.* New York, NY: Oxford University Press.

Gates, G. J. (2011). *How many people are lesbian, gay, bisexual, and transgender?* Los Angeles: Williams Institute.

Gates, H. (2005). Refining the incest taboo: With considerable help from Bronislaw Malinowski. In A. P. Wolf & W. H. Durham (Eds.), *Inbreeding, incest, and the incest taboo* (pp. 139–160). Stanford, CA: Stanford University Press.

Gendler, T. S. (2008). Alief in action (in reaction). *Mind and Language, 23,* 552–585.

Gendler, T. S. (2009). Alief and belief. *Journal of Philosophy, 105,* 634–663.

Gendron, M., Roberson, D., van der Vyver, J., & Barrett, L. F. (2014). Perceptions of emotion from facial expressions are not culturally universal: Evidence for a remote culture. *Emotion, 14,* 251–262.

Gerhards, J., & Hackenbroch, R. (2000). Trends and causes of cultural modernization: An empirical study of first names. *International Sociology, 15,* 501–531.

Gibson, E. J., & Walk, R. D. (1960). The "visual cliff." *Scientific American, 202,* 67–71.

Gilman, S. L. (2008). *Fat: A cultural history of obesity.* Malden, MA: Polity.

Gilmer, W. S., & McKinney, W. T. (2003). Early experience and depressive disorder: Human and non-human primate studies. *Journal of Affective Disorders, 7,* 97–113.

Glaberson, W. (2010, January 25). For transgender people, name is a message. *The New York Times.*

Good, B., Cood, M. J., & Moradi, R. (1985). The interpretation of Iranian depressive illness. In A. Kleinman & B. Good (Eds.), *Culture and depression* (pp. 369–428). Berkeley, CA: University of California Press.

Goodall, J. (1969). *My friends, the wild chimpanzees.* Washington, DC: National Geographic Society.

Goodyear, D. (2013, November 4). Beastly appetites. *The New Yorker,* pp. 72–81.

Gould, S. J. (1981). *The mismeasure of man.* New York, NY: Norton.

Gouldner, A. W. (1960). The norm of reciprocity: A preliminary statement. *American Sociological Review, 25,* 161–170.

Grant, M. (1987). *The rise of the Greeks.* New York, NY: Scribners.

Graver, M. R. (2007). *Stoicism and emotion.* Chicago, IL: University of Chicago Press.

Green, R. (2002). Is pedophilia a mental disorder? *Archives of Sexual Behavior, 31,* 467–471

Greenberg, D. (1988). *The construction of homosexuality.* Chicago, IL: University of Chicago Press.

Greene, J. (2007). *Prescribing by numbers: Drugs and the definition of disease*. Baltimore, MD: Johns Hopkins University Press.

Griffiths, P. E. (1997). *What emotions really are: The problem of psychological categories*. Chicago, IL: University of Chicago Press.

Grinker, R. R., & Spiegel, J. P. (1945). *Men under stress*. Philadelphia, PA: Blakiston.

Guttmacher, A. E., & Collins, F. S. (2003). Welcome to the genomic era. *New England Journal of Medicine, 349,* 996–998.

Hacking, I. (1995). *Rewriting the soul: Multiple personality and the sciences of memory*. Princeton, NJ: Princeton University Press.

Hacking, I. (1999). *The social construction of what?* Cambridge, MA: Harvard University Press.

Haidt, J. (2012). *The righteous mind: Why good people are divided by politics and religion*. New York, NY: Vintage.

Haldane, J. B. S. (1955). Population genetics. *New Biology, 18,* 34–51.

Hall, G. C. N. (2014, May 27). Becoming white in service of diversity. *Chronicle of Higher Education*.

Halttunen, K. (1982). *Confidence men and painted women: A study of middle-class culture in America, 1830–1870*. New Haven, CT: Yale University Press.

Hamer, D., & Copeland, P. (1994). *The science of desire: The search for the gay gene and the biology of behavior*. New York, NY: Simon & Schuster.

Hamer, D., Hu, S., Magnuson, V. L., Hu, N., & Pattatucci, A. M. L. (1993). A linkage between DNA markers on the X chromosome and male sexual orientation. *Science, 261,* 321–327.

Hamilton, W. D. (1964). The genetical evolution of social behaviour I and II. *Journal of Theoretical Biology, 7,* 1–16, 17–52.

Harlow, H. F., Harlow, M. K., & Suomi, S. J. (1971). From thought to therapy: Lessons from a primate laboratory. *American Scientist, 59,* 538–549.

Harlow, H. F., & Suomi, S. (1974). Induced depression in monkeys. *Behavioral Biology, 12,* 273–296.

Harre, R., & Parrott, W. G. (1996). *The emotions: Social, cultural, and biological dimensions*. Beverly Hills, CA: Sage.

Harrison, K. (1997). *The kiss: A memoir*. New York, NY: Avon.

Hays, J. C., Kasl, S. V., & Jacobs, S. C. (1994). The course of psychological distress following threatened and actual conjugal bereavement. *Psychological Medicine, 24,* 917–927.

Heller, J. (1961). *Catch-22*. New York, NY: Simon & Schuster.

Hemingway, E. (1929). *A farewell to arms*. New York, NY: Scribner.

Hemingway, E. (1982). *Men at war*. New York, NY: Random House. (Original work published 1942)

Herman, J. (1981). *Father–daughter incest*. Cambridge, MA: Harvard University Press.

Herodotus. (1996). *The histories, revised* (J. M. Marincola, Ed.). New York, NY: Penguin.

Herszenhorn, D. M. (2014, August 21). A fast-food symbol of America falls in Moscow. *The New York Times*, p. A4.

Hertz, R. (1909). The pre-eminence of the right hand: A study of religious polarity. *Revue Philosophique, 68,* 553–580.

Herz, R. (2012). *That's disgusting.* New York, NY: Norton.

Hijmans, B. T., Tobi, E. W., Stein, A. D., Putter, H., Blauw, G. J., Susser, E. S., et al. (2008). Persistent epigenetic differences associated with prenatal exposure to famine in humans. *Proceedings of the National Academy of Sciences of the United States of America, 105,* 17046–17049.

Hills, R. (2015). *The sex myth: The gap between our fantasies and reality.* New York, NY: Simon & Schuster.

Hines, M. (2011). Prenatal endocrine influences on sexual orientation and on sexually differentiated childhood behavior. *Frontiers in Neuroendocrinology, 32,* 170–182.

Hippocrates. (1923–1931). *Works of Hippocrates* (Vols. 1–4; W. H. S. Jones & E. T. Withington, Eds. & Trans.). Cambridge, MA: Harvard University Press.

Hite, S. (1976). *The Hite report.* New York, NY: Dell.

Hochschild, A. (1983). *The managed heart: The commercialization of human feeling.* Berkeley, CA: University of California Press.

Homer. (1990). *The iliad* (R. Fagles, Trans.). New York, NY: Viking.

Hopkins, K. (1980). Brother–sister marriage in Roman Egypt. *Comparative Studies in Society and History, 22,* 303–354.

Hopper, K. (1992). Some old questions for the new cross-cultural psychiatry. *Medical Anthropology Quarterly, 7,* 299–330.

Horwitz, A. V. (2002). *Creating mental illness.* Chicago, IL: University of Chicago Press.

Horwitz, A. V. (2013). *Anxiety: A short history.* Baltimore, MD: Johns Hopkins University Press.

Horwitz, A. V., & Wakefield, J. C. (2007). *The loss of sadness.* New York, NY: Oxford University Press.

Horwitz, A. V., & Wakefield, J. C. (2012). *All we have to fear.* New York, NY: Oxford University Press.

Hrdy, S. (2011). *Mothers and others: The evolutionary origins of mutual understanding.* Cambridge, MA: Belknap.

Humphreys, L. (1975). *Tearoom trade.* Chicago, IL: Aldine.

Husak, D. N. (2002). *Legalize this? The case for decriminalizing drugs.* New York, NY: Verso.

Igo, S. (2007). *The averaged American: Surveys, citizens, and the making of a mass public.* Cambridge, MA: Harvard University Press.

Jackson, S. W. (1986). *Melancholia and depression: From Hippocratic times to modern times.* New Haven, CT: Yale University Press.

Jacobs, E., & Shipp, S. (1990, March). How family spending has changed in the U.S. *Monthly Labor Review,* 20–27.

Jones, E., & Wessely, S. (2007). A paradigm shift in the conceptualization of psychological trauma in the 20th century. *Journal of Anxiety Disorders, 21,* 164–175.

Jones, J. (1997). *Alfred Kinsey: A public/private life*. New York, NY: Knopf.

Kagan, D. (2010). *Thucydides: The reinvention of history*. New York, NY: Penguin.

Kagan, J. (2012). *Psychology's ghosts: The crisis in the profession and the way back*. New Haven, CT: Yale University Press.

Kaletsky, K. (2015, July 5). Falling into bad and holding hands. *The New York Times*, Sunday Styles, p. 5.

Kandel, E. R. (1998). A new intellectual framework for psychiatry. *American Journal of Psychiatry, 155*, 457–469.

Kang, S. (2003, December 26). Naming the baby: Parents brand their tot with what's hot. *Wall Street Journal*.

Keegan, J. (1976). *The face of battle*. New York, NY: Penguin.

Kelly, D. (2011). *Yuck! The nature and moral significance of disgust*. Cambridge, MA: MIT Press.

Kelly, D. J., Quinn, P. C., Slater, A. M., Lee, K., Gibson, A., Smith, M., et al. (2005). Three-month-olds, but not newborns, prefer own-race faces. *Developmental Science, 8*, F31–F36.

Kessler, D. (2009). *The end of overeating: Taking control of the American appetite*. New York, NY: Rodale.

Kinsey, A. C., Pomeroy, W. B., & Martin, C. E. (1948). *Sexual behavior in the human male*. Philadelphia, PA: Saunders.

Kinsey, A. C., Pomeroy, W. B., Martin, C. E., & Gebhard, P. H. (1953). *Sexual behavior in the human female*. Philadelphia, PA: Saunders.

Kleinman, A. (1986). *Social origins of distress and disease: Depression, neurasthenia and pain in modern China*. New Haven, CT: Yale University Press.

Kleinman, A. (1988). *Rethinking psychiatry: From cultural category to personal experience*. New York, NY: Free Press.

Kleinman, A. (2012). Culture, bereavement, and psychiatry. *Lancet, 379*, 608.

Kleinman, A., & Good, B. (Eds.). (1985). *Culture and depression*. Berkeley, CA: University of California Press.

Kolbert, E. (2014, July 28). Stone soup. *The New Yorker*, 26–29.

Kolbert, E. (2015, February 16). The last trial. *The New Yorker*, 28.

Kovacks, M. G. (Trans.). (1989). *The epic of Gilgamesh*. Stanford, CA: Stanford University Press.

Kramer, S. N. (1959). *History begins at Sumer: Thirty nine firsts in recorded history*. Philadelphia, PA: University of Pennsylvania Press.

Landecker, H., & Panofsky, A. (2013). From social structure to gene regulation, and back: A critical introduction to environmental epigenetics for sociology. *Annual Review of Sociology, 39*, 333–357.

Lane, C. (2007). *Shyness: How a normal behavior became a sickness*. New Haven, CT: Yale University Press.

Lauden, R. (2014). *Cuisine and empire: Cooking in world history*. Berkeley, CA: University of California Press.

LeDoux, J. (1996). *The emotional brain: The mysterious underpinnings of emotional life.* New York, NY: Simon & Schuster.

Lee, K. A., Vaillant, G. E., Torrey, W. C., & Elder, G. H. (1995). A 50-year prospective study of the psychological sequelae of World War II combat. *American Journal of Psychiatry, 152,* 516–522.

Lendon, J. E. (2005). *Soldiers and ghosts: A history of battle in classical antiquity.* New Haven, CT: Yale University Press.

LeVay, S. (1991). A difference in the hypothalmic structure between heterosexual and homosexual men. *Science, 253,* 1034–1037.

LeVay, S., & Hamer, D. H. (1994, May). Evidence for a biological influence in male homosexuality. *Scientific American,* 45–50.

Levenstein, H. (2012). *Fear of food: A history of why we worry about what we eat.* Chicago, IL: University of Chicago Press.

Levi-Strauss, C. (1969). *The elementary structures of kinship.* Boston, MA: Beacon.

Levitt, S. D., & Dubner, S. J. (2005). *Freakonomics.* New York, NY: Harper.

Levy-Bruhl, L. (1972). *Primitives and the supernatural.* New York, NY: Haskell House. (Original work published 1931)

Lewis, A. J. (1934). Melancholia: A clinical survey of depressive states. *Journal of Mental Science, 80,* 1–43.

Lewis, A. J. (1970). The ambiguous word "anxiety." *International Journal of Psychiatry, 9,* 62–79.

Lieberman, D., Tooby, J., & Cosmides, L. (2007). The architecture of human kin detection. *Nature, 445,* 727–731.

Lieberson, S. (2000). *A matter of taste: How names, fashions, and culture change.* New Haven, CT: Yale University Press.

Lieberson, S., & Bell, E. O. (1992). Children's first names: An empirical study of social taste. *American Journal of Sociology, 9,* 511–554.

Lieberson, S., Dumais, S., & Baumann, S. (2000). The instability of androgynous names: The symbolic maintenance of gender boundaries. *American Journal of Sociology, 105,* 1249–1287.

Lieberson, S., & Mikelson, K. S. (1995). Distinctive African American names: An experimental, historical, and linguistic analysis of innovation. *American Sociological Review, 60,* 928–946.

Liptak, A. (2015, April 12). The case against gay marriage: Top law firms won't touch it. *The New York Times,* p. A1.

Locke, J. (1950). *An essay concerning human understanding* (A.S. Pringle-Pattison, Ed.). New York, NY: Oxford University Press.

Long, A. A. (2005). Law and nature in Greek thought. In M. Gagarin & D. Cohen (Eds.), *The Cambridge companion to ancient Greek law* (pp. 412–430). New York, NY: Cambridge University Press.

Long, A. A., & Sedley, D. (1987). *The Hellenistic philosophers.* New York, NY: Cambridge University Press.

Lorenz, K. (1966). *The naked ape*. London, England: Methuen.

Luhrmann, T. R. (2015, January 18). Redefining mental illness. *The New York Times*, p. SR5.

Madigan, E. (2013). Sticking to a hateful task: Resilience, humour, and British understandings of combatant courage, 1914–1918. *War in History*, *20*, 76–98.

Malinowski, B. (1932). *The sexual life of savages*. London, England: Routledge.

Mandeville, B. (1924). *The fable of the bees*. Oxford, England: Clarendon. (Original work published 1714)

Mann, T. (1989). *Tonio Kroger*. New York, NY: Vintage International. (Original work published 1930)

Markey, C. (2014). *Smart people don't diet*. New York, NY: Da Capo Lifelong Books.

Marks, I. M. (1987). *Fears, phobias, and rituals: Panic, anxiety, and their disorders*. New York, NY: Oxford University Press.

Marks, I. M., & Nesse, R. M. (1994). Fear and fitness: An evolutionary analysis of anxiety disorders. *Ethology and Sociobiology*, *15*, 247–261.

Marshall, S. L. A. (1947). *Men against fire: The problem of battle command*. Norman, OK: University of Oklahoma Press.

Maryanski, A., Sanderson, S. K., & Russell, R. (2012). The Israeli kibbutzim and the Westermarck hypothesis: Does early association dampen sexual passion? *American Journal of Sociology*, *117*, 1503–1518.

Massey, D. (2002). A brief history of human society: The origin and role of emotion in social life. *American Sociological Review*, *67*, 1–29.

Massey, D. (2005). *Strangers in a strange land*. New York, NY: Norton.

May, R. (1977). *The meaning of anxiety*. New York, NY: Pocket Books.

McCabe, J. (1983). FBD marriage: Further support for the Westermarck hypothesis of the incest taboo? *American Anthropologist*, *85*, 50–69.

McFadden, R. (2012, December 17). Daniel Inouye, Hawaii's quite voice of conscience in the Senate, dies at 88. *The New York Times*, p. A33.

McNally, R. (2003). *Remembering trauma*. Cambridge, MA: Harvard University Press.

McPherson, J. W. (1997). *For cause and comrades: Why men fought in the Civil War*. New York, NY: Oxford.

Mead, M. (1948). An anthropologist looks at the report. In *Problems of Sexual Behavior*. New York, NY: American Social Hygiene Association.

Mead, M. (1971). *Coming of age in Samoa*. New York, NY: Harper Perennial. (Original work published 1928)

Mead, M. (2001). *Sex and temperament in three primitive societies*. New York, NY: Harper Perennial. (Original work published 1935)

Meaney, M. J. (2010). Epigenetics and the biological definition of gene × environment interactions. *Child Development*, *81*, 41–79.

Menninger, W. C. (1948). *Psychiatry in a troubled world: Yesterday's war and tomorrow's challenge*. New York, NY: Macmillan.

Menzies, R. G., & Clarke, J. C. (1995). The etiology of phobias: A nonassociative account. *Clinical Psychology Review, 15*, 23–48.

Michael, R. T., Gagnon, J. H., Laumann, E. O., & Kolata, G. (1994). *Sex in America: A definitive survey.* New York, NY: Werner.

Mill, J. S. (1991). *On liberty.* New York, NY: Oxford University Press. (Original work published 1859)

Miller, S. I., & Schoenfeld, L. (1973). Grief in the Navajo: Psychodynamics and culture. *International Journal of Social Psychiatry, 19*, 187–191.

Miller, W. I. (1997). *The anatomy of disgust.* Cambridge, MA: Harvard University Press.

Miller, W. I. (2000). *The mystery of courage.* Cambridge, MA: Harvard University Press.

Mineka, S., Davidson, M., Cook, M., & Keir, R. (1984). Observational conditioning of snake fear in rhesus monkeys. *Journal of Abnormal Psychology, 93*, 355–372.

Mineka, S., & Ohman, A. (2002). Born to fear: Non-associative vs. associative factors in the etiology of phobias. *Behaviour Research and Therapy, 40*, 173–184.

Montagu, M. F. A. (1968). *Man and aggression.* New York, NY: Oxford University Press.

Montaigne, M. (1958). *The complete essays of Montaigne* (D. M. Frame, Trans.). Stanford, CA: Stanford University Press.

Moran, C. (2007). *The anatomy of courage.* New York, NY: Caroll & Graf. (Original work published 1945)

Morris, D. (1967). *The naked ape.* New York, NY: Delta.

Murdock, G. (1949). *Social structure.* New York, NY: Macmillan.

Murphy, D. (2006). *Psychiatry in the scientific image.* Cambridge, MA: MIT Press.

Murphy, G. L., & Medin, D. L. (1985). The role of theories in conceptual coherence. *Psychological Review, 92*, 289–316.

Murray, O. (1986). Greek historians. In J. Boardman, J. Griffin, & O. Murray (Eds.), *The Oxford history of the classical world* (pp. 186–203). New York, NY: Oxford University Press.

Nance, J. (1976). *The gentle Tasaday.* New York, NY: Harcourt, Brace, Jovanovich.

Nature Editorial Group. (2012). Life stresses. *Nature, 490*, 143.

Neel, J. (1962). Diabetes mellitus: A "thrifty" genotype rendered detrimental by "progress." *American Journal of Human Genetics, 14*, 353–362.

Nesse, R. M. (2005). Natural selection and the regulation of defenses: A signal detection analysis of the smoke detector principle. *Evolution and Human Behavior, 26*, 88–105.

Oaten, M., Stevenson, R. J., & Case, T. I. (2009). Disgust as a disease avoidance mechanism. *Psychological Bulletin, 135*, 303–321.

Oates, J. C. (2011). *A widow's story: A memoir.* New York, NY: Ecco.

Ofshe, R., & Watters, E. (1994). *Making monsters: False memories, psychotherapy, and sexual hysteria.* Berkeley, CA: University of California Press.

Ogden, C. L., Fryar, C. D., Carroll, M. D., & Flegal, K. M. (2004). Mean body weight, height, and body mass index, United States 1960–2002. *Advance Data from Vital and Health Statistics, 347*, 1–17.

Ohman, A., & Mineka, S. (2001). Fears, phobias, and preparedness: Toward an evolved module of fear and fear learning. *Psychological Review, 108,* 483–522.

Oparil, S. (2014, August 14). Low sodium intake: Cardiovascular health benefit or risk? *New England Journal of Medicine,* 677–679.

Opler, M. (1941). *An Apache life way.* Chicago, IL: University of Chicago Press.

Oppenheim, J. (1991). *Shattered nerves: Doctors, patients, and depression in Victorian England.* New York, NY: Oxford University Press.

Oppenheimer, M. (2013, August 17). In God's name, or baby "Messiah," competing claims to religious freedom. *The New York Times,* p. A13.

Orenstein, P. (2003, July 6). Where have all the Lisas gone? *The New York Times Magazine.*

Parker-Pope, T. (2014, August 26). The decisive marriage. *The New York Times,* p. D1.

Parry, M. (2013). Study casts skeptical light on campus "hookup culture." *The Chronicle of Higher Education.* Retrieved from http://chronicle.com/blogs/percolator/study-casts-skeptical-light-on-campus-hookup-culture/33389

Parsons, T. (1954). The incest taboo in relation to social structure and the socialization of the child. *British Journal of Sociology, 5,* 101–117.

Penn, D. ,& Potts, W. (1998). MHC-disassortative mating preferences reversed by cross-fostering. *Proceedings of the Royal Society B, 265,* 1299–1306.

Pescosolido, B. P., Perry, B. L., Long, J. S., Martin, J. K., Nurnberger, J. I., & Hesselbrock, V. (2008). Under the influence of genetics: How transdisciplinarity leads us to rethink social pathways to illness. *American Journal of Sociology, 114*(Suppl.), S171–S201.

Pinker, S. (2002). *The blank slate: The modern denial of human nature.* New York, NY: Penguin.

Pinker, S. (1997). *How the mind works.* New York, NY: Norton.

Pinker, S. (2011). *The better angels of our nature: Why violence has declined.* New York, NY: Penguin.

Plato. (1980). *Laws* (T. Pangle, Trans.). New York, NY: Basic Books.

Pollak, A. (2013, July 2). Few signs of a taste for diet pills. *The New York Times,* p. B2.

Pomeroy, W. B. (1972). *Dr. Kinsey and the Institute for Sex Research.* New Haven, CT: Yale University Press.

Poovey, M. (1998). Sex in America. *Critical Inquiry, 24,* 366–392.

Power, M. L., & Schulkin, J. (2009). *The evolution of obesity.* Baltimore, MD: Johns Hopkins University Press.

Pratt, L. A., & Brody, D. J. (2014). *Depression and obesity in the U.S. adult household population, 2005–2010,* National Center for Health Statistics Data Brief No. 167. Washington, DC: US Department of Health and Human Services.

Pusey, A. (2005). Inbreeding avoidance in primates. In A. P. Wolf & W. H. Durham (Eds.), *Inbreeding, incest, and the incest taboo* (pp. 61–75). Stanford, CT: Stanford University Press.

Pusey, A., & Wolf, M. (1996). Inbreeding avoidance in animals. *Trends in Ecology and Evolution, 11,* 201–206.

Quetelet, A. (2015). *A treatise on man and the development of his faculties*. Berkeley, CA: University of California Libraries. (Original work published 1842)

Radloff, L. (1977). The CES-D scale: A self-report depression scale for research in the general population. *Applied Psychological Measurement, 3*, 249–265.

Ransom, J. (2015). *So you've been publically shamed*. New York, NY: Riverhead.

Read, P. P. (1974). *Alive*. New York, NY: Lippincott.

Reardon, S. (2014, January 16). Drug helps to clear traumatic memories. *Nature News*.

Regnerus, M., & Uecker, J. (2011). *Premarital sex in America*. New York, NY: Oxford University Press.

Remarque, E. M. (1961). *All quiet on the western front*. Greenwich, CT: Fawcett Crest. (Original work published 1929)

Robinson, P. (1989). *The modernization of sex*. Ithaca, NY: Cornell University Press.

Roos, J. P. (2008). Emile Durkheim versus Edward Westermarck. In H.-J. Niedenzu, T. Melghy, & P. Meyer (Eds.), *The new evolutionary science: Human nature, social behavior, and social change* (pp. 135–146). New York, NY: Paradigm.

Rose, N. (2007). *The politics of life itself: Biomedicine, power, and subjectivity in the twenty-first century*. Princeton, NJ: Princeton University Press.

Rossi, A. S. (1965). Naming children in middle-class families. *American Sociological Review, 30*, 499–513.

Roth, J., Qiang, X., Marban, S. L., Redelt, H., & Lowell, B. C. (2004). The obesity pandemic: Where have we been and where are we going? *Obesity Research, 12*, 88S–101S.

Rottenberg, J. (2014). *The depths: The evolutionary origins of the depression epidemic*. New York, NY: Basic Books.

Rozin, P., Millman, L., & Nemeroff, C. (1986). Sympathetic magic in disgust and other domains. *Journal of Personality and Social Psychology, 50*, 703–712.

Rozin, P., Nemeroff, C., Horowitz, M., Gordon, B., & Voet, W. (1995). The borders of the self: Contamination sensitivity and potency of the body apertures and other body parts. *Journal of Research in Personality, 29*, 318–340.

Ruprecht, T. (2010, April 4). High school redux. *The New York Times Magazine*, p. 50.

Ruscio, A. M., Brown, T. A., Chiu, W. T., Sareen, J., Stein, M. B., & Kessler, R. C. (2008). Social fears and social phobia in the USA: Results from the National Comorbidity Survey Replication. *Psychological Medicine, 38*, 15–28.

Russell, D. E. H. (1984). *Sexual exploitation: Rape, child sexual abuse and workplace harassment*. Beverly Hills, CA: Sage.

Russell, D. E. H. (1999). *The secret trauma: Incest in the lives of girls and women* (Rev. ed.). New York, NY: Basic Books.

Saguy, A. (2013). *What's wrong with fat?* New York, NY: Oxford University Press.

Salter, J. (2014, November 6). The most wonderful sport. *London Review of Books*, p. 6.

Salway, B. (1994). What's in a name? A survey of Roman onomastic practice from c. 700 B.C. to A.D. 700. *Journal of Roman Studies*, 124–145.

Santelli, J. S., Lindberg, L. D., Abma, L., McNeely, C. S., & Resnick, M. (2000). Adolescent sexual behavior: Estimates and trends from four nationally representative surveys. *Family Planning Perspectives, 32,* 156–165.

Sapolsky, R. M. (2004). *Why zebras don't get ulcers* (3rd ed.). New York, NY: Holt.

Sartorius, N., Jablensky, A., & Shapiro, R. (1978). Cross-cultural differences in the short-term prognosis of schizophrenic psychoses. *Schizophrenia Bulletin, 4,* 102–113.

Saul, H. (2001). *Phobias: Fighting the fear.* New York, NY: Arcade.

Savin-Williams, R. C., & Joyner, K. (2014). The dubious assessment of gay, lesbian, and bisexual adolescents of Add Health. *Archives of Sexual Behavior, 43,* 413–422.

Sax, L. (2002). How common is intersex? A response to Anne Fausto-Sterling. *Journal of Sex Research, 39,* 174–178.

Scheidel, W. (2004). Ancient Egyptian sibling marriage and the Westermarck effect. In A. P. Wolf & W. H. Durham (Eds.), *Inbreeding, incest, and the incest taboo* (pp. 93–108). Stanford, CA: Stanford University Press.

Schieffelin, E. J. (1985). The cultural analysis of depressive affect: An example from New Guinea. In A. Kleinman & B. Good (Eds.), *Culture and depression* (pp. 101–133). Berkeley, CA: University of California Press.

Schiff, S. (2010). *Cleopatra: A life.* New York, NY: Back Bay Books.

Schildkraut, J. J. (1965). The catecholamine hypothesis of affective disorders: A review of supporting evidence. *American Journal of Psychiatry, 122,* 502–522.

Schnurr, P. P., Spiro, A., Vielhaer, M. J., Findler, M. N., & Hamblen, J. L. (2002). Trauma in the lives of older men: Findings from the normative aging study. *Journal of Clinical Geropsychology, 8,* 175–187.

Schooler, C. (2007). The changing role(s) of sociology (and psychology) in the National Institute of Mental Health Intramural Research Program. In W. R. Avison, J. D. McLeod, & B. A. Pescosolido (Eds.), *Mental health, social mirror* (pp. 55–66). New York, NY: Springer.

Schutt, R. K., Seidman, L. J., & Keshavan, M. S. (Eds.). (2015). *Social neuroscience: Brain, mind, and society.* Cambridge, MA: Harvard University Press.

Scott, J. C. (1998). *Seeing like a state.* New Haven, CT: Yale University Press.

Scott, S. (2007). *Shyness and society: The illusion of competence.* New York, NY: Palgrave Macmillan.

Seemanova, E. (1971). A study of children of incestuous matings. *Human Heredity, 21,* 108–128.

Segerstrale, U. (2000). *Defenders of the truth: The sociobiology debate.* New York, NY: Oxford University Press.

Seligman, M. (1970). On the generality of the laws of learning. *Psychological Review, 77,* 406–418.

Seligman, M. (1971). Phobias and preparedness. *Behavior Therapy, 2,* 307–320.

Seligman, M., & Hager, J. L. (1972). Biological boundaries of learning: The sauce-bearnaise syndrome. *Psychology Today, 6,* 59–61, 84–87.

Shatz, A. (2015, October 19). Drawing blood: A French graphic novelist's shocking memoir of the Middle East. *The New Yorker*, pp. 58–67.

Shephard, B. (2000). *A war of nerves: Soldiers and psychiatrists in the twentieth century.* Cambridge, MA: Harvard University Press.

Shephard, B. (2004). Risk factors and PTSD: A historian's perspective. In G. M. Rosen (Ed.), *Posttraumatic stress disorder: Issues and controversies* (pp. 39–62). Hoboken, NJ: Wiley.

Shepher, J. (1971). Mate selection among second generation kibbutz adolescents and adults: Incest avoidance and negative imprinting. *Archives of Sexual Behavior, 1,* 293–306.

Shepher, J. (1983). *Incest: A biosocial view.* New York, NY: Academic Press.

Shor, E., & Simchai, D. (2009). Incest avoidance, the incent taboo, and social cohesion: Revisiting Westermarch and the case of the Israeli kibbutzim. *American Journal of Sociology, 114*(6), 1803–1842.

Shorter, E. (1994). *From the mind into the body.* New York, NY: Free Press.

Shrestha, N. M., Sharma, B., Van Ommeren, M., Regmi, S., Makaju, R., Komproe, I., et al. (1998). Impact of torture on refugees displaced within the developing world. *JAMA, 280,* 443–448.

Silver, N., & McCann, A. (2014). *How to tell someone's age when all you know is her name.* Retrieved June 14, 2014, from http://fivethirtyeight.com/features/how-to-tell-someones-age-when-all-you-know-is-her-name

Siri-Tarino, P. W., Sun, Q., Hu, F. B., & Krauss, R. M. (2010). Meta-analysis of prospective cohort studies evaluating the association of saturated fat with cardiovascular disease. *American Journal of Clinical Nutrition, 91,* 535–546.

Skinner, B. F. (1971). *Beyond freedom and dignity.* New York, NY: Knopf.

Slim, W. (2004). *Courage and other broadcasts.* London, England: Little, Brown.

Sloman, L., Gilbert, P., & Hasey, G. (2003). Evolved mechanisms in depression: The role and interaction of attachment and social rank in depression. *Journal of Affective Disorders, 74,* 107–121.

Smith, G. E., & Pear, T. H. (1918). *Shell-shock and its lessons* (2nd ed.). Manchester, England: Manchester University Press.

Smith-Bannister, S. (1997). *Names and naming patterns in England 1538–1700.* New York, NY: Oxford University Press.

Solomon, A. (2012). *Far from the tree: Parents, children, and the search for identity.* New York, NY: Simon & Schuster.

Sophocles. (1958). *Oedipus the king.* New York, NY: Mentor Books.

Specter, M. (2014, August 25). Seeds of doubt: An activist's controversial crusade against genetically modified crops. *The New Yorker*, pp. 46–57.

Specter, M. (2015, November 2). Freedom from fries. *The New Yorker*, pp. 56–65.

Spiro, M. E. (1958). *Children of the kibbutz.* Cambridge, MA: Harvard University Press.

Spitzer, R. L., & Wakefield, J. C. (2002). Why pedophilia is a disorder of sexual attraction—At least sometimes. *Archives of Sexual Behavior, 31,* 499–500.

Stigler, S. M. (1986). *The history of statistics: The measurement of uncertainty before 1900.* Cambridge, MA: Harvard University Press.

Stone, L. (1977). *The family, sex, and marriage in England 1500–1800.* New York, NY: Harper & Row.

Stone, L., & Stone, J. F. C. (1984). *An open elite?* New York, NY: Oxford University Press.

Stossel, S. (2014). *My age of anxiety: Fear, hope, dread, and the search for peace of mind.* New York, NY: Knopf.

Sullivan, A. (1996). *Virtually normal.* New York: Vintage.

Suomi, S. J. (1991). Adolescent depression and depressive symptoms: Insights from longitudinal studies with rhesus monkeys. *Journal of Youth and Adolescence, 20,* 273–287.

Super, C. M., & Harkness, S. (2010). Culture and infancy. In G. Bremner & T. D. Wachs (Eds.), *Blackwell handbook of infant development: Vol. 1. Basic research* (2nd ed., pp. 623–649). Oxford, England: Blackwell.

Swank, R. L., & Marchand, W. E. (1946). Combat neuroses: Development of combat exhaustion. *Archives of Neurology and Psychiatry, 55,* 236–247.

Tannahill, R. (1982). *Sex in history.* New York, NY: Stein & Day.

Tannahill, R. (1988). *Food in history.* New York, NY: Crown.

Tavernise, S. (2015a, June 8). Global diabetes rates are rising as obesity spreads. *The New York Times,* p. A3.

Tavernise, S. (2015b December 1). In major shift, diabetes cases start to decline. *The New York Times,* p. A1.

Taylor, R. (1984). John Doe, Jr.: A study of his distribution in space, time, and the social structure. *Social Forces, 53,* 11–21.

Terance. (2010). *Heauton Timorumenos* (F. W. Nicolson & J. C. Rolfe, Eds.). Charleston, SC: Nabu Press. (Original work published 163 BC)

Terry, J. (1999). *An American obsession: Science, medicine and homosexuality in modern society.* Chicago, IL: University of Chicago Press.

Tien, Y.-F. (1979). *Landscapes of fear.* New York, NY: Pantheon.

Tierney, J. (2008, March 11). A boy named Sue, a theory of names. *The New York Times,* p. E1.

Tingley, K. (2014, June 29). One child, three parents. *The New York Times Magazine,* p. MM26.

Tooby, J., & Cosmides, L. (1990). The past explains the present: Emotional adaptations and the structure of ancestral environments. *Ethology and Sociobiology, 11,* 375–424.

Toohey, P. (2014). *Jealousy.* New Haven, CT: Yale University Press.

Treffers, P. D. A., & Silverman, W. K. (2001). Anxiety and its disorders in children and adolescents before the twentieth century. In P. D. A. Treffers & W. K. Silverman (Eds.), *Anxiety disorders in children and adolescents: Research, assessment, and intervention* (pp. 1–22). New York, NY: Cambridge University Press.

Trilling, L. (1948). The Kinsey report. *Partisan Review, 40,* 460–476.

Trivers, R. L. (1971). The evolution of reciprocal altruism. *Quarterly Review of Biology, 46,* 35–57.

Trivers, R. L. (1972). Parental investment and sexual selection. In B. Campbell (Ed.), *Sexual selection and the descent of man* (pp. 136–179). Chicago, IL: Aldine–Atherton.

Turner, J. (2000). *On the origins of human emotions: A sociological inquiry into the evolution of human affect.* Palo Alto, CA: Stanford University Press.

Turner, J., & Maryanski, A. (2005). *Incest: Origins of the taboo.* Boulder, CO: Paradigm.

Umberson, D., Wortman, C. B., & Kessler, R. C. (1992). Widowhood and depression: Explaining long-term gender differences in vulnerability. *Journal of Health and Social Behavior, 33,* 10–24.

US Department of Agriculture. (2002). *Agriculture fact book.* Washington, DC: Author.

Valentine, C. W. (1930). The innate bases of fear. *Journal of Genetic Psychology, 37,* 394–420.

van den Berghe, P. L. (1983). Human inbreeding avoidance: Culture in nature. *Behavioral and Brain Sciences, 6,* 91–102.

Vigarello, G. (2013). *The metamorphoses of fat: A history of obesity.* New York, NY: Columbia University Press.

Wadsworth, T., & Pendergast, P. M. (2014). Obesity (sometimes) matters: The importance of context in the relationship between obesity and life satisfaction. *Journal of Health and Social Behavior, 55,* 196–214.

Wakefield, J. C. (1992). The concept of mental disorder: On the boundary between biological facts and social values. *American Psychologist, 47,* 373–388.

Wakefield, J. C. (1999). Evolutionary versus prototype analyses of the concept of disorder. *Journal of Abnormal Psychology, 108,* 374–399.

Wakefield, J. C. (2013). The DSM-5 debate over the bereavement exclusion: Psychiatric diagnosis and the future of empirically supported practice. *Clinical Psychology Review, 33,* 825–845.

Wakefield, J. C., & First, M. (2012). Validity of the bereavement exclusion to major depression: Does the evidence support the proposed elimination of the exclusion in DSM-5? *World Psychiatry, 11,* 3–11.

Wakefield, J. C., Pottick, K., & Kirk, S. (2002). Should the DSM-IV diagnostic criteria for conduct disorder consider social context. *American Journal of Psychiatry, 159,* 380–386.

Walk, R. D., & Gibson, E. J. (1961). A comparative and analytical study of visual depth perception. *Psychological Monographs, 75*(519).

Walsh, C. (2014). *Cowardice: A brief history.* Princeton, NJ: Princeton University Press.

Ward, B. W., Dahlhamer, J. M., Galinsky, A. M., & Joestl, S. S. (2014, July 15). Sexual orientation and health among U.S. adults: National Health Interview Survey, 2013. *National Health Statistics Reports, 77.*

Warner, M. (1999). *The trouble with normal: Sex, politics, and the ethics of queer life.* New York, NY: Free Press.

Watson, J. B. (1924). *Behaviorism.* Chicago, IL: The People's Institute.

Watson, J. B. (1925). What the nursery has to say about instincts. *Journal of Genetic Psychology, 32*(2), 293–326.

Watson, J. B., & Rayner, R. (1920). Conditioned emotional reactions. *Journal of Experimental Psychology, 3,* 1–14.

Wayne, T. (2013, March 3). By any other name. *New York Times Book Review.*

Weller, S. (2013, June 24). Putting down the parents of North West? That is so May 2013. *The Washington Post.* Retrieved from http://www.washingtonpost.com/blogs/she-the-people/wp/2013/06/24/putting-down-the-parents-of-north-west-that-is-so-may-2013

Westermarck, E. (1891). *The history of human marriage.* London, England: Macmillan.

Westermarck, E. (1926). *The history of human marriage* (5th ed.). London, England: Macmillan.

Wikann, U. (1990). *Managing turbulent hearts: A Balinese formula for living.* Chicago, IL: University of Chicago Press.

Wilford, J. N. (2013, October 18). Fossil may rewrite human evolutionary history. *The New York Times,* p. A8.

Wilkinson, A. (2015, October 5). Something borrowed. *The New Yorker,* p. 29.

Williams, G. C. (1996). *Adaptation and natural selection.* Princeton, NJ: Princeton University Press.

Wilson, E. (1994). *Patriotic gore.* New York, NY: Norton. (Original work published 1962)

Wilson, E. O. (1998). *Consilience: The unity of knowledge.* New York, NY: Knopf.

Wise, J. (2009). *Extreme fear: The science of your mind in danger.* New York, NY: Palgrave Macmillan.

Wolf, A. P. (1995). *Sexual attraction and childhood association: A Chinese brief for Edward Westermarck.* Stanford, CA: Stanford University Press.

Wolf, A. P. (2005). Introduction. In A. P. Wolf & W. H. Durham (Eds.), *Inbreeding, incest, and the incest taboo* (pp. 1–23). Stanford, CA: Stanford University Press.

Wolf, N. (2002). *The beauty myth: How images of beauty are used against women.* New York, NY: Harper Perennial.

Worden, J. W. (2009). *Grief counseling and grief therapy.* New York, NY: Springer.

Wortman, C. B., & Silver, R. C. (1989). The myths of coping with loss. *Journal of Consulting and Clinical Psychology, 57,* 349–357.

Young, A. (1995). *The harmony of illusions: Inventing post-traumatic stress disorder.* Princeton, NJ: Princeton University Press.

Zarembo, A. (2014, August 3). As disability awards grow, so do concerns with the veracity of PTSD claims. *Los Angeles Times.* Retrieved from http://www.latimes.com/local/la-me-ptsd-disability-20140804-story.html#page=1

Zerubavel, E. (1985). *The seven day circle: The history and meaning of the week.* New York, NY: Free Press.

Zhang, T.-Y., & Meaney, M. J. (2010). Epigenetics and the environmental regulation of the genome and its function. *Annual Review of Psychology, 61,* 429–466.

Zweigenhaft, R. L. (1977). The other side of unusual first names. *Journal of Social Psychology, 103,* 291–302.

Zweigenhaft, R. L. (1981). Unusual names and uniqueness. *Journal of Social Psychology, 114,* 297–298.

INDEX

Fatness
   mortality and morbidity risks,
      116–117, 227n41
   stigma of, 115–116, 204–205, 227n36
Fats, in food consumption, 104, 105,
      225–226n16
Fear, 123–145, 146–147, 197
   amygdala in, 131
   of animals, 123, 130, 132–133
   anxiety disorders and, 123–124
   Aristotle on, 81, 125
   of being alone, 124, 130, 134
   biology and, 128–131
   of blood, 124, 130, 133
   in children, 134–135, 139
   of closed spaces, 124, 130, 134
   control of, in World War I, 86–87
   cross-cultural similarities in, 140
   culture and, 126–128, 228n7
   of darkness/night, 134, 138
   Darwin on, 124–125, 137
   developed societies and, modern, 123
   disorders of, 125–126
   environment of evolutionary adaption
      in, 129, 137, 140
   Epictetus on, 131
   evolutionary basis of, 132
   as evolutionary mismatch, 201
   expression of, 128
   of flying, 124, 133–134
   Freud on, 134, 139
   Hall on, 134
   of heights, 123, 130, 133, 138, 139,
      140, 228n21
   Herodotus on, 125
   inability for, 74
   mismatched, 201
   mismatched, irrational aspects of,
      131–132
   mismatched, *vs.* mental disorders,
      140–144
   physiology of, 125

   primeval, 137
   of public speaking, 124, 127, 136
   reasonable and unreasonable,
      124–126, 228n4
   Rush on, 134
   of snakes, 129–130, 131, 132, 134,
      138, 140
   social, 135–137, 228n27
   social anxiety in, 124, 139–140
   social structures and values on,
      127–128
   of spiders, 129, 132
   of storms, 124, 130, 133, 134
   of strangers and meeting new people,
      124, 130, 136, 140, 201
   Svendson on, 123
   types of, 123–124
   universality of, 137–140
   of water, 124, 130, 133
Feminism
   on cowardice and courage, 96, 225n55
   on incest aversion, 44–46, 219n48
Fertility rate, decline of, 171, 231n8
First names, 48–71
   abnormal, 66–70, 205, 222nn47, 52
   androgynous, 64–65
   Biblical, 51, 52
   of blacks *vs.* whites, 61
   boys with girls' names in, 67–68
   Carnegie on, 50
   of celebrities, 54
   Christian, six, 50–51
   collective behavior patterns in,
      49, 220n3
   of cultural figures, 53–54
   culture and values in, 49–50, 68
   of ethnic groups, marginalized/
      bullied, 66–67, 222n47
   ethnic identity in,
      African-American, 60–61
   ethnic identity in, Hispanic, 60
   ethnicity on, 58–61

CPSIA information can be obtained
at www.ICGtesting.com
Printed in the USA
BVHW042005100423
662077BV00004B/110